A Walk In My Shoes

Angel Tucker-Carr

Pen2Pad Ink
Publishing

Library of Congress Cataloging–In– Publication Data

Name: Tucker-Carr, Angel, author.
Title: A Walk In My Shoes / Angel Tucker-Carr

Identifiers:

LCCN:

ISBN: 978-1-970135-73-2 **Paperback**
        978-1-970135-74-9 **Ebook**

Published in the United States by
Pen2Pad Ink Publishing

www.pen2padink.org.

Requests to publish work from this book or to contact the author should be sent to: **mrsatcarr@gmail.com**

Preface

When I was a little girl, my dreams and aspirations were probably different from most little girls. I never wanted to be a princess. I don't know if I didn't allow myself to *dream* of being one or I was too busy thinking about my reality. I wonder when it was that I knew that princesses didn't look like me, or was I born into that truth. I honestly don't remember saying what I *was* going to be when I grew up. Sometimes I'm curious as to why I couldn't think past the moment. Maybe my eyes were clouded with surviving the truth that others had painted for me.

I had a mother, father, and siblings who thought I was God's gift to the family. They thought I was the most beautiful baby girl ever; but of course, they're family, they will always think I'm beautiful. I was a very smart girl. I took my homework time seriously—probably too serious at times. Everywhere my mom and dad would take me, people would say, "She's such a beautiful little girl!" For some strange reason, those compliments never took root inside of me. Either I thought it was normal or I didn't know what the word 'beautiful' really meant. I guess it would be safe to say the seeds (words spoken) that were planted weren't planted in fertile ground or maybe the birds came and plucked them away before they could take root. The birds of television commercials...magazines...people...life.

I've done a lot of things in my life. I've been married for more than thirty years. I am a mother of three amazing children, with one being the father of his own child now. I've written books, founded a non-profit organization, worked with the youth, and served in church for many years. I've coached women to become powerful wives, and I've successfully mentored others in building healthy self-esteems and lasting relationships. I've worked on jobs with all types of people from all walks of life. I've had dinner and tea with the rich and I've had meaningful conversations with the homeless. I have friends in very high places as well as friends battling life and overcoming drug addictions. I've been the only Black in the room many times. Some of those rooms were very warm and inviting and other times I could 'hear eyes' asking who invited me.

One day I was at my mom's house talking with my sisters and my cousin. That scenario was nothing new, but the conversation hit me in a very prolific way. While talking and listening, I was gathering stories of how each of us felt being a Black woman in society.

Each of us had our stories and our experiences were very similar, although there were times when we would even say 'wow' to what we were hearing from the mouth of the other.

Topics from hair and body to motherhood and relationships—it was all in there.

Growing up in the seventies in my little country town, I had issues with the things that I saw. I didn't understand why none of my teachers looked like me. I didn't get it that the people on television didn't look like me either.

I was never taught racism at home, in fact, we never heard anyone talk about issues between the White and Black race, but for some reason at an early age, I knew there were differences between the two races. It was around junior when I experienced unfair treatment due to blatant racism. That was when it really hit me that I was a Black girl in a White world where my race could actually determine what I could have in life. These things caused scars early on in my life that I can still see as an adult.

Remember, *scars represent a wound that has been healed.*

Something You Should Know

I chose to write this book in a format that resembles a blog. It was healing for me as I recalled certain events, yet some things were painful, as I blogged and journaled my way through. I wanted this 'blook' (blog-book) to be easy to read but hard to put down.

There are a few things you should know before you start reading.

First, this book has been in progress for many years, and although many things I discuss have changed for the better, much of it has remained the same or gotten worse. There are times when I will speak in past tense as well as the present, but it is all relevant.

Second, in order to protect and preserve the trust of friends and those I have worked with, I've changed the names and identifying moments whenever necessary. If you think you recognize someone from any of the stories, it's probably not the one you think; however, this book is about me and my observations and experiences. When permission was necessary, I was blessed to have individuals in my life who were willing to share their stories with me so that I could be the voice for them.

Last, though this book is intended to serve as insight into the lives of the people (and for the people) who have been underserved, oppressed, overlooked, and stereotyped for hundreds of years, it should not be seen as an "us against them" book. I could never speak for everyone and I won't pretend to do so; but through many conversations, observations, and experiences, I will be able to speak for the masses.

I am hopeful that the content will encourage each of us to see ourselves more positively and be more mindful of others to make this world a better place for all—especially our future generations.

INTRODUCTION

This has been one of the hardest projects I've done. Besides the obvious, which is the content, I've come up against obstacles that literally paralyzed my flow. In addition to the mental chatter going back and forth in my head, there were physical limitations that reared its ugly head. If that weren't enough I had the chatter of those who believed the book was too much for the times that we live in, while others believed the timing was perfect. This book has been in the making far longer than any of the issues that we are seeing and experiencing in the world today.

I experienced anxiety and high levels of fear towards the end of the project simply because of the personal struggles I was facing in my own life—especially at work. I knew then that it needed to be completed, no matter what.

I'm not writing this book to start a movement that is exclusive to any single race, I believe the world is starving for unity and I won't contribute to hate or segregation of any kind. Enough people are doing a pretty darn good job of that already. What we are in need of is communication and honest dialogue; and I am here to start the conversation. I have experienced many mental roadblocks while writing. This is confirmation that it must be done. I have been working on this project for years off and on, but the past two years have been more consistent than ever before because of the urgency that I have about the topics at hand. Anything that is this difficult has a purpose. I struggled with the reason I was writing this book in addition to whether or not it would be accepted and understood. Then I thought about what people would think of me. *Then it came to me, if people think any different of you for sharing your stories Angel, then they don't accept you anyway. People will feel the way they already feel within, this will give them an excuse to use for letting it show. If my truth makes them feel differently, then they might need to go deep within themselves and discover their truths.*

In a world of confusion, chaos, and multi-level anger, people are trying to find themselves.

Disclaimer
This Is All Me!

Before you continue to read what this book is and what it is not and how it came to be, allow me to share something with you. It is important that I say that this is all me and no one else. All of my years of growing up, becoming a young woman and still to this date, when people refer to me or my sisters they say, "Those Tuckers" or "Those Tucker Girls." Whether one person had said or did something or they were believed to have said something, we all have had to take the blame for what one would say or do. That's why it is important for me to say that I am not speaking for all people or all Black women.

This is my language, my words, and my feelings coming straight from my heart through my fingertips. I didn't have someone sitting with me interviewing me for hours upon hours to learn how I talk, think, and feel, and then put it on paper. I didn't have a ghostwriter composing it and sending it to the best editors in the country. This is me – authentic and raw.

I wanted to state that so that you can hear my voice and not necessarily lower the expectations, but know the difference. I have been a part of book projects and have written a book on my own, but this one is different. It was birthed strictly to promote change and to be the voice of the voiceless. I am hoping it will begin the *change* that many people talk about but have done nothing, until recently. This book is not for the judgmental or the fault finder. Not everyone will agree, and I am okay with that. Just because a person doesn't agree doesn't mean that I don't feel what I feel or haven't experienced what I've experienced that led me to write this book. Everything in this book is based on personal knowledge, observations, and experiences in my forty-something years of living, as well as the experience of others. It would be impossible to say all that I need to say in one publication, but this is a good start. Sit back, buckle up, and get ready for the journey. This is my blog gone wild!

I started writing and blogging several years ago (approximately 2008) when I had my internet talk show. We'd (myself and the other hosts) used the majority of my materials as discussion topics for the show. I then decided to finish what I had started—a book. It has taken years to get to this point. I had notes here and there, sticky pads full of topics, and notepads scattered abroad containing things that will be in the pages of this book. I'll say this upfront for the readers.

Please be aware that this book (as I mentioned before) will not be politically correct and at times will possibly be grammatically challenged, because I want to be so real with you that you can't help but *at least hear* what I am saying through this text. Please don't get what I am saying mixed up with the fact that speaking grammatically correct doesn't hold the same power as slang or incorrect grammar. I am saying for this particular project, I am not worried about the rules as much as I would be if I was interviewing with someone.

My goal is to break the myths and remove the labels that people have placed on us, as well as those that we have placed on ourselves. My Christian belief is that we are all created in the image of God for a specific purpose. The first purpose is to worship Him. The Bible tells us that we are fearfully and wonderfully made, and it is time that we acknowledge that and to live by it. Yes, all of us.

How It All Began

As far back as I can remember I have been what others labeled as different. I don't mean different as in race, but different in how I think and act, what I like, and how I process things. I tend to look at issues with a different twist, and I see people in a broader way. It amazes me how we are able to see things so clearly from hindsight, but now that I'm older and seasoned, I know that I was made for this [project]. Being different paid off.

I've learned that no matter what we say or do at times, something will always be taken the wrong way and out of context; but for myself and my children, and for the generations to come, I must be obedient to this call. I am a game changer, a life changer; and I know this book will change lives.

There were many times that I wondered about the content or something that I said, but then I asked myself the question, "Why should I keep this truth locked up inside?" If I am the voice of the voiceless and a mouthpiece for others, then why would I need someone else to speak for me? I can tell my own stories. After all, no one can tell our stories better than we can.

Chapter One
Tears On My Pillow

Just when I think I've heard the saddest story, another one comes about that is worse than the last. I wondered when it would stop. When? I have gone to bed many nights with the television on with images of mothers and fathers paining for the loss of their children who were gunned down and murdered over some senseless cause or no cause at all. When will it stop?

Lately I've been so in tune with stories of women sweating bullets and holding back tears begging to be seen and heard as a person, and not *just a woman*. I'm awakened to the pain because that pain is familiar to me. I have felt the pain of just wanting to be seen as a woman, and not just a Black woman. I've wanted to be heard and not portrayed as angry. I've felt the pain of being ashamed of who I am and didn't even know it. I know the pain, and I can relate to those who want to be known as more than a Black woman.

I have four sisters. In 2012 we lost our dad; but I can't even say that I know what they are feeling. I can imagine, but I can't say for sure because their pain could be deeper in other areas that I don't have pain; yet we all feel deep pain.

I can't sit here and say that I know what it's like to be shot or stabbed; but I imagine it's a shocker and possibly an out-of-body experience. That's just my imagination. I can't compare real pain with an imaginary pain that I'm conjuring up in my head, so, when someone says they know what I feel or how I feel being a Black woman who grew up as a Black girl in a world that boasts of being controlled by Whites, it is an insult.

One day I was taking notes in my phone and I wrote the following: *Do you know what it takes to be me? Do you know what it's like to walk in my shoes?* I'm not talking about glamorous stilettos graced with bling and a famous name attached to them, or simple sneakers I'd wear to my daughter's track meet. I'm not referring to my beautifully-crafted western boots that I wear with boldness and grace. I'm talking about something much deeper. You don't know what it's like, and I can't expect you to know because it's impossible to feel exactly what someone else is feeling. We can only imagine what something would feel or be like, but in reality, we don't know.

Until you walk in my shoes, you will never know how bad they hurt. Angel Tucker-Carr

It would be really difficult for them if they were in my shoes, because being the *only one* has been much of my life's story.

Imagine (If you can)

What do you consider when you are looking for a family doctor? Do you search his or her credentials? What about what he or she specializes in? I'm not talking about searching the area for proximity from your home or work place. Do you search the *area* (neighborhood) the doctor is located? I'm not talking for literal geographical purposes. I'm talking about searching in which neighborhood it's located for acceptance.

You might be thinking I'm referring to whether or not the doctor is accepting new patients, or your particular insurance, but I'm not. Maybe you have searched for a physician of a particular race or their location placement because you don't want a Black doctor; but have you ever had a fear of the doctor not liking you because of your race? Take a moment… read it well. I am not asking you whether or not you trusted the knowledge of the doctor because of his race, (that's not good either), but whether or not he or she would welcome you to his or her practice. What about the front desk personnel? Have you wondered about how they would treat you? Probably not; but if you're Black you probably have.

Many times during open enrollment I have had to change primary care doctors because of various reasons. Sometimes the doctor changed their network and the insurance company no longer includes the doctor. I could keep my doctor if I wanted to pay nearly double or more for out of network fees, if not then I have to go on the hunt to find a new doctor. I have stressed so much before because of that, and to someone who has no clue of what I am talking about it might sound petty. I am a deep thinker. I'm the 'whole picture' person. I don't know if I am the way that I am because of the health issues I've had in the past or what; but when I think of physicians (in addition to what I mentioned earlier), I am thinking about whether or not this person might have to perform surgery on me. If the doctor is a racist, I don't want to be 'put under' trusting them to work on me. What if something goes wrong during surgery? I wonder if they would do CPR on my Black mouth. I wonder if the doctor would think it's necessary to get rid of one worthless Black life. I'm not saying that my life is worthless, I'm saying what many have shown us about our lives. Now that I've brought this situation to your attention, what do you think?

He Likes Me...He Likes Me Not

It's easy to belittle ourselves and not even realize it. I started feeling that I was belittling myself when I would say, "She was so nice to me" or "He treated me good." I'd say it as if that should be commended. That should be a norm and it shouldn't be something that we give people kudos for doing. There are some people that deserve kudos for going above and beyond or just being plain awesome. I commend those people and I write about them. I even send special thank you notes to the supervisors of those individuals or to the individual themselves. (By the way, people appreciate the notes). It's so normal to be treated poorly that we praise the ones that aren't mean. One day my coworker and I were talking about something similar. We found ourselves talking about the kind of day we were having because people weren't being mean to us. It felt so good! Imagine that being your story in life (noticeable when people are nice) because of who you are on the outside.

Much of what I'm talking about goes beyond the treatment alone. It's also the way that people think or the things they say without thinking. "He was a large African American man with a very mild temper." Would that same description be given when describing a White man with the same large build? No. Absolutely not! It's the norm! People point out things like that because to them it stands out as unusual. Sometimes they'd say that about an African American (I say Black) woman who happens to be soft spoken. People say it as if it's rare to find a Black woman who is soft spoken. That bothers me and I don't like it.

I cannot tell you how many times young Black men and young Black women have been described to me as, 'articulate, well-spoken, respectful...' I don't say anything because I realize the person speaking just doesn't know what they are doing when they do it. I have yet to hear those same people describe a young White male or female in the same manner. Think about it. Have you witnessed that, or have you said it yourself? Maybe the people who find these things to be rare need to come out of their neighborhoods and into real society more often, and turn off the television sets where they only see one type of Black person that their news stations show. That would be a very good start.

Last week, I was scheduled for a professional photo shoot with a photographer, and honestly, I didn't know if the photographer was a male or female. Unfortunately, that wasn't what I was concerned about anyway. I wasn't uncomfortable with going to the studio, but whether or not I would be welcomed did cross my mind. He was phenomenal. He went above and beyond to take care of me, and I really appreciated that. Don't get me wrong, I have dealt with racist people who didn't like Black people, but they were professional enough to provide the services anyway. I can tolerate that. I have also seen people who didn't want to serve people of color and didn't care who knew it. I can't tolerate that!

I Didn't Choose This Skin I'm in

Although I didn't get to choose the skin that I have that brings about so much negativity, I still wouldn't change it if I could. I make no apologies for my beautiful, golden caramel coat that I wear called skin. I don't apologize for being a unique individual that God created in His image. I don't apologize for the frame that he gave me—even if there are times that I want to shape it up or lose a little or make simple adjustments. That's life; but it doesn't mean that I dislike the person that I am. I used to struggle to make such bold statements, but now I can make them now with confidence and courage because I know who and whose I am in Christ. I coach others to do the same in their own lives. Self-love is for everyone. I don't care what race or color they are sporting. (Sporting is an old school term that means wearing).

Section Two
Overwhelmed With
Microaggressions

I have lived an entire life so far filled with microaggressions. It's hard enough to live life, but to battle unnecessary daily evils is emotionally draining. It's hell when you have to constantly tell someone that you work with or work for how to respect you as a human being. I had a person that I reported to that would sit and look at me or be in a conversation with me and would say ugly things to me as if I would be too naïve to know he was belittling me. He would say things to me such as, "Why build stores in that neighborhood, when they're not going to do anything but rob and tear them up?" He would sit and tell me what a 'hot' woman looked like, as he went on to describe a White woman who was a size two with blond hair and blue eyes and big boobs. I'm not being shallow to think that a Black woman couldn't fit that description, but let's be real. I know what he meant because he never hesitated to point it out whenever he saw one who fit that description. Everything else to him was unattractive. I didn't care what he was attracted to, but to say those things to a Black woman was rude and belittling.

I understand not everyone will be friends just because they work together, but to treat someone like they don't matter is irresponsible and reckless for the workplace. It has been acceptable for far too long. I have been a product of that treatment many times.

A friend of mine was telling me about a conversation she was having with a coworker of hers. The guy she was talking to was sharing an experience he had recently. He said there was a moving truck in his neighborhood with two Black guys in the truck. He told her he was concerned about the *real* reason they were in the neighborhood, and he felt uncomfortable being they were Black. He went on talking about how Black people were, and they couldn't be trusted. He felt the guys had to be up to no good. My friend said she kept listening to him, and then he said, "Not you Sarah. You're a good one!"

Come to find out, he was concerned for no reason. The truck was a moving truck looking for an address to unload a family's furniture. The one thing that irritates me is the fact that his neighbors will probably never know how racist he really is. Unfortunately, he holds a position that serves and protects. These are the individuals that we are encountering every single day. With that mindset, nothing fair and just could come out of a mind and heart like his.

This has been the story of my life, and this is why I am writing about it.

If you would have asked me what microaggressions were about ten days ago, I would have had to Google it. It sounded familiar when I was asked if I knew what it was, but I know I can't learn if I pretend to know something that I don't know.

My therapist asked me during my first session if I knew what a microaggression was and I told her I didn't. She went on to share with me that she picked up on things when I was talking that showed her I have been exposed to and experienced microaggressions all of my life; but having to accept it (at work) without being able to fully stand up for myself is what sent me to therapy from start.

Microaggressions have a more in depth meaning than what I will give, but it's basically a term used for things that we say and do daily whether it's intentional or unintentional that communicates negative, hostile, insulting, prejudiced slights towards a group or a person. This is my way of explaining what was told to me and backing it up with Google and Wikipedia. Hopefully you get the gist of the meaning. For example, someone can say, "I know that Asian know how to do Math." Another example would be, "You don't sound Black." I used to get that one all the time. Now I get, "It didn't sound like you when you answered the phone." Really? What was I supposed to sound like?

Your Size Is At The Back!

Me: "Excuse me ma'am. Could you tell me where I can find the Levi's?"

Salesperson: "Sure! Go around the escalator to the other side, and keep walking and turn left. You will see them there."

Me thinking: (Hmmm....last I checked, that was plus size! I don't wear plus size!)

Me: "Ma'am, you sent me to another area to buy my jeans, could you please tell me where the junior size Levi's are?"

Salesperson: "Oh, over there."

Maybe I should have asked for the juniors sections from the start, but maybe she should have asked what size I was looking for instead of assuming that with my curvy body, in my mid-thirties, I automatically wore plus size.

Assumptions at its best! It wasn't the first time and it won't be the last.

Uh, that's Not Your Shade!

Salesperson: "Hi! Good afternoon! What can I help you with?"

Me: "I need to get a new compact of powder. I'm out again!" (Speaking in my familiar, bubbly friendly tone).

Salesperson: "What color?"

Me: "Stay Golden."

Salesperson: "That's too light for you! Have you seen that one?"

Me: "I beg your pardon?"

Salesperson: "Try this one! I think this one is more of your shade."

Me: "I'm sorry ma'am. I have been wearing make-up for ONLY thirty plus years. I think I know what color I wear. I have been wearing **this** shade (Stay Golden) for the past several years. I switch between two colors – one for summer and one for the fall like most Black women do, now if you don't mind, please give me the color that I requested. Please!"

Hello? Why would I spend thirty-eight bucks on something that wasn't going to enhance me, just to say, "My color is *Stay Golden? Darnit!*"

Total silence fills the area, and everybody around doesn't know which expression to show. *Does this woman really know what color she should be buying, or is the salesperson assuming that she needs this shade because this woman happens to be a woman of color?*

I can't count the number of times this has happened to me and quite frankly – it's downright exhausting!

One of my friends that I used to work with still gets a 'kick out of' the two of us wear the same shade of make-up. She was a tanning, sun-loving woman which caused her to get pretty golden – well, my shade! We wore the same make-up—and she's Caucasian. Who would have thought? I mention all of these things to set the premise of how we can misjudge and assume things that we don't know. It's okay to assume some things, but it's not good when we won't accept the fact that our assumptions could be wrong.

Here We Go Again!

One day my daughter and I were out shopping for prom make-up. I have a ton of make-up at home, but this was a special day and I wanted everything she had to be as close to personal and perfect as possible. We went to one of my favorite make-up counters in the mall but I didn't find the color I was looking for, so my make-up consultant told me about another brand that she uses. She mentioned Anastasia. I'm thinking, I've heard of that! In fact, my brow pomade is that brand. I went over to that section, and I can't tell you how long I looked around in the area before someone would help me. The girls weren't helping anyone, they were sitting in a circle laughing and talking and at times would glance at me. They're makeup sits out in the opening, but there were only samples on the shelves. The one I wanted was sold out. I waited and waited and while waiting I pointed out their behavior to my daughter. I try to use anything I can as a teaching time so that she could be better equipped for life and this sometimes unkind world that we live in.

After waiting for a while, I went back to the sales counter that I had started at and told the first salesperson no one would acknowledge me to help me. She said, "I can get it for you." I said, "Can you also ring it up?" It might sound petty, but I didn't want those girls at the other counter to have the pleasure of using their ID number to get credit for a sale they didn't make. I wouldn't have bought the items if she had not been able to ring me up herself.

While she was trying to show me more shades, one of the girls decided she'd try to either save face that another person from a different department was helping me, or to get the sale. I told her I didn't need her and I was finally being helped.

While being helped, my salesperson said, "These are really pretty shades, these two on the end would work, but this one on the right could probably be used for eyeshadow or something. It's a little light." I'm looking at all three shades that are listed as blushes, and I know makeup, so I'm thinking why should she open her mouth and say anything at all! The crazy thing is, she didn't mean any harm whatsoever. It came out naturally. I wasn't *looking* for her comment, so I didn't misinterpret anything. They just don't get it.

Normally I would school a person who did what she did, but honestly, I didn't even have the energy to do it that time. I was enjoying time with my daughter and didn't dare want to allow anything or anyone to change the energy we had.

I thanked her for her help and told her I'd see her next time. Maybe then I will advise her not to do what she did anymore.

Ahh....finally, somebody gets it!

Another store that I frequent happened to have a Hispanic woman working at the counter. I had switched lines of makeup and went to another store altogether.

I told the salesperson what color I needed and she said, "Okay. Be right back." She took my word for what color I needed. She said, "That's the color that I wear!" She went on to get a foundation brush, the make-up color that I asked for, and proceeded to stroke my face with the foundation. She was trying to see if I actually wore that color. Most times when you ask to see a color, the salesperson would try the makeup on your skin to make sure that's what you want. Sure, I could have just asked for it and paid for it, but I didn't; so her action was expected.

Her response was, "Wow! Isn't that crazy! We wear the same color!" I said, "I know!"

She was in awe that we actually wore the same shade. I probably would have been surprised too, had I not already gotten over that shock when my Caucasian friend discovered that earlier.

Invaluable

One thing I have come to embrace is my value. I say that with boldness, but there are times when I still have to fight to be bold. Although we have to pick our battles, we must remember to fight the battles that are important and can't be looked away from anymore.

I demand to be treated a certain way when I am shopping somewhere. When I enter into a place to shop, eat or patronize in any way I will demand treatment that is suitable for me; or I will take my service somewhere else. This is a new day. We don't live in the time when people could finally eat in a restaurant, but had to stand to eat the food. No way. Recently I shared a post on Facebook asking Black women to stop going to nail shops where they are tolerated and not appreciated. I won't fall into the mindset of just being glad to have the services done. Back in the day Blacks would perform services for White people, and the White people would talk about them like they weren't even there. Black people were invisible or less than human to them. When we finally got a chance to go into restaurants and other stores, we were just glad to be in there. That's not acceptable to me in 2020 or any year of my life.

My husband used to think I was too extreme and would tell me to ignore the maltreatment; but I would tell him I will not minimize myself for anyone. Constantly telling people how to treat me can be very tiring, but it's necessary. We must teach people how to treat us.

Part I
How Many White Women
Will Be There?

If I could sound out the Scooby-Doo voice that he makes when he thinks something is stupid or scary, I sure would do it right now. I probably made that noise in my head when I was asked the question of how many White women would be attending an event that I was having.

I am the founder of Dare to Bare Your Beauty, and as organizer, I would create various events for women to attend. The events were uplifting, esteem-building as well as networking.

Once a year I would hold an elegant gala where the women would come dressed beautifully, feeling good and ready to be empowered. It was amazing. During the events I would open up spots for vendors to sell and advertise their products.

A particular make-up vendor that I had believed would be a great fit for the event was invited to showcase their products. I had a good rapport with the two young ladies that ran the kiosk that I frequented. They were sweet to me. I would buy from them and oftentimes talk with them for quite a while. If I wasn't buying something that day, I'd still stop and say hello because if I didn't stop, they'd call my name as I pass by trying to do a run in and out of the mall. One day I presented the opportunity to them. They were excited about the chance to be a vendor and were looking forward to it. We would text back and forth leading up to the event, so everything was kosher—so I thought. We were supposedly on the same accord because they agreed the platform would be great for business and being involved would get their product name out there. Their brand wasn't brand new, but it was a mineral make-up, and Bare Minerals had sown up the 'make-up mineral' industry during those days. I liked the way their make-up felt on my skin and the way it made me look, so I thought I would introduce them to my circle. My skin was flawless and I paid a lot less for the look.

Leading up to the event, maybe a couple of days before, one of the girls that I had talked to more than the other one texted me. She said, "Angel, how many White women will be at the event?" At first I didn't know how to answer that question. I was wondering why it mattered, then I tried to give them the benefit of the doubt. How was I supposed to know how many White women would be there? I didn't have a race box to check on the registration form. I was disappointed that I had misjudged them. I really liked them. Before I further jumped into conclusion about why I would be asked that question, I gathered my head and thought maybe they were checking for inventory purposes. I wanted to believe that they were trying to pack lightly and not have to bring all of their products; so maybe they were checking to see how much product they needed or if they already had what they needed in stock. I don't know. I was grabbing at straws. Then it came to me that even if all of the women were White, any make-up artist knows that one color doesn't fit all in any race. My thoughts were right all along. They didn't want to come because Black women were going to be there. I can safely say that because they never asked how many Black women would be there. Through our conversation it was discovered that they felt more comfortable with an event that would be predominately White. I am guessing because they knew I was Black, there would be Black women there, but they never asked the overall ratio of women.

After confirming my thoughts, I politely told them they would never have to worry about me inviting them anywhere again, and neither would they have the pleasure of collecting my money at their kiosk. I was surprised as well as disappointed. I don't think the surprise was about the race issue, it was more about me totally missing whatever I had missed about them. That was rare for me because I can read people well. I missed that one! It is my privilege to say their kiosk and brand wasn't seen anymore.

In today's times people are using social media and the company's pages to share their comments and make an impact. I didn't have the tool of social media, neither do I think I would have used it, but I learned the greatest impact I can have is the use of my dollars.

Networking - Contact or Connection?

Keep Your Business Card! We don't want it because we won't be doing business with you! Okay, so they didn't come out and say it, but actions shout louder than words.

I've noticed during my years of pursuing the dream of being an entrepreneur that networking has different meanings, depending upon what group you're in or which event you're attending.

At conferences and networking events, the White women don't exchange business cards with us Black women unless one of the women happens to be a speaker for the day or a well-known person that they can 'get something from' to benefit themselves.

That's it! I have seen this more times that I even want my mind to recall due to the emotions that I experience when I think about it. The emotions arise from the disappointments of being fooled that I was really making a connection that would help my business or catapult me into the next level. After all, that is what networking is about.

When *we* attend networking events, it's about becoming a contact. What's a networking event if you're not going to network? What they are saying is they don't want to network with us, but our dollars can become part of their net worth.

The Only Black in the Room

You've heard of the elephant in the room phrase. How about the only black in the room? Well, that's not just a metaphorical idiom – it's real. I have never understood why people of other races are so uncomfortable when invited to an event that is believed to be mostly black attendees.

Do you know how many times I have been the only Black person in the room? Do you know how many times I have been the only Black woman at the table in a conference room of thousands of people? I don't know either! Too many times to count. How does that happen? Easily! It happens because oftentimes we are one to every five hundred in a crowd of thousands in some areas and regions.

Through my experiences I have learned that is one of the true purposes of networking. It's like buying a product. After I'd buy something online, sometimes I'd get advertisements or coupons for similar items or from their sister companies. That's the way networking should work. It does for some, and for others it doesn't happen. At networking events, I'd find out about another event or connect with someone there who invites me to something else. If we're not in the place, how do we increase our visibility? We don't. If we do, it is very gradual – by the one or two Blacks in the place. That's if they are not afraid to lose the one spot they think they hold.

I've gone to church conferences that were the same way. Church conferences where everyone is believed to love Jesus, but I end up feeling like an extra at times. Don't get me wrong, I've had some people who would go out of their way to make me feel comfortable and welcomed. I appreciate that, but that's the way it should be anyway. It's the elephant in the room that not many people want to talk about because they want to act as if it doesn't exist; or they feel they would be rejected by their peers if they said something.

I believe the Black women that won't speak up are afraid of losing that one or two White women that they think are backing them in their business endeavors, and they don't want to change that. What they fail to realize is if they were backing their business, why aren't more of their friends and family members showing up to their events? I know we can't make people do anything, but something is wrong if the same one or two is in your corner, but they're not helping you fill your room. I believe some of them keep their mouths closed because they are desperate to get to where they are trying to go; and they think they can only get there on the backs or wings of the ones that they fear losing. They'd rather sell out and pretend that truth tellers are problems. What they fail to realize is that behavior is already a problem anyway to others and themselves. Anytime a person can keep their mouth shut and turn their back on the disparities of others and pretend to be what they are not, they are already a problem to society.

I have sat in rooms with small groups of women in mastermind classes, and I have been the only Black face at the table. Whenever another Black person comes into the room, it seems that the room just got warmer. I have been there. I have been the one walking in and I have been the one who was already there when another Black woman walked in the room. The insecure Black woman reacts as if the bulb just blew out of her spotlight. That hasn't happened many times though. Thank God! I used to say that when another Black woman walks in the room, the first Black acts like Santa Claus just showed up at Christmas when we were little girls.

Some people would probably say that it's not the fault of the Whites there, and I would say I agree. It's only their fault if they have contributed to making the Black person feel they are not welcomed in the first place. I've experienced that too.

It would be really difficult for them if they were in my shoes, because being the *only one* in the room has been much of my life's story.

Speaking of being the only one in the room, I am reminded of a networking event that I took my friend to.

About ten years ago, I invited my best friend to an event that an organization I was a part of was having. It was held at a classy, upscale hotel in the middle of downtown in the city of Fort Worth. The ballroom was beautiful and the dinner was delectable! We had hosts service our every beck and call during dinner

Each month at the event the organizer would give away door prizes that were donated by women in the business. The donations were a way for the vendor to advertise her items and services, and it also helped the women look forward to the chance of winning cool gifts!

It happened! My guest's ticket number was called. She had won the photography package deal. It was an awesome deal, and it was right on time because she was wanting to get her daughter's senior pictures taken; so this was a perfect win. When my friend went to the front to claim her prize, the vendor's face lost all color. She became paper white and didn't have not one hint of a grin on her face. She was so engulfed with anger and disgust that she didn't feel the nudges of the excited ladies at her table. You know how women get, we scream with anyone who wins right after we get past our disappointment of not winning; therefore, the table was having a celebration without her. I asked my friend if she saw her face. She said, "No. I didn't." I said, "She's the same one we came into the building with and met again in the bathroom." She said, "It is, isn't it?" We had already been treated like trash by this individual a couple of times before even entering the room. I honestly don't know if she knew we were headed to the same event, but then again, maybe she did and didn't care that we'd meet again.

When the organizer who was calling out the winners called the photographer's name as a way of pre-introducing her to the winner, she wouldn't get up. I told my friend to give it back and make it known in public why she was giving back the winning ticket. That's just how I operate. I would have told her thanks for drawing my name, but it doesn't seem that the photographer wanted me to win her services. My friend didn't give it back and said that she was going to follow through because she was going to use the package for her daughter's senior pictures. I said, "Okay. That's you."

A couple days later, my friend called and called leaving message after message trying to set up an appointment. She (the photographer) wouldn't answer the calls or return messages. My friend's feelings were hurt, but I asked her why her feelings would be hurt when that woman had already shown her who she was.

That's the exact behavior that I am talking about that is discouraging and it happens way too often. People don't want to serve us as if there is something wrong with us. She didn't know anything about my friend. She knew she was at the event so she definitely had to be connected to the group, but she didn't care. She didn't want a Black person to win her services, and lo and behold, she didn't give her services either. Of course I turned her in to some of my friends who were in charge, but nothing was done at the moment, and probably not later either. I mean, what can be done other than not allow her to be a vendor or give a door prize? We have always been forced to just 'take it' or deal with it, because no one seems to care.

My life has been filled with microaggressions and disproportionate disparities, but they've only made me stronger and wiser – not bitter.

Part Two

Black people are automatically seen as trouble. They have been labeled as someone to fear. We live with those implicit biases every single day of our lives. We have to pick and choose where we go. Not that we don't want to go to certain places, it's the fact that we want to enjoy our visit without problems from people who believe we shouldn't be there. This goes for vacation spots to places as simple as a restaurant. A freaking bed and breakfast is even on the list. We don't know whose bed we're in and who's cooking our breakfast!

The Black Man vs The Black Woman

I don't know who has it worse, the Black woman or the Black man. In my opinion, we all have it pretty tough most times, but I think the Black man can escape the treatment a little easier—especially when he makes a name for himself and becomes rich and famous. Other than that, well...I don't think it would be fair or necessary to say who has it worse. Let me just talk about Black women for now.

Black women have suffered disproportionate disparities and mental abuse on so many levels. We are always talked about and criticized and minimized in everything we do! From our hair to our attitudes, to our bodies to education, to the way we think, to our entire being...it has all been on display for any and every one to discuss, judge and analyze; and honestly it's downright tiring.

There is so much to say, so follow me here.

Section One

I wouldn't be able to share everything that is on my mind in one book, but this book would be in vain and a total waste of time if I didn't talk about some of the myths that I, as a Black woman have been labeled. A true healing of who we are is imperative. It's a matter of life and death – spiritually, emotionally and physically.

Who I Am

I feel it's important to lay a thin layer of foundation for understanding some things that will help guide us past the back cover of the book that says who I am overall.

I never knew much about my history until not long ago. I knew of bits and pieces, but that was about it. I still don't know much, but I know more than I did. I was aware of my dad's mother and her Indian roots, and I knew my grandfather (dad's dad) had Caucasian (I'll use White and Caucasian interchangeably) in him. Come to find out, I knew very little about my grandmother and her full-blood White grandparents one one side. I'm still looking for roots to piece together.

When I was younger my family would visit my grandfather in Plainview, Texas. I will never forget the picture on the wall in his house that stood out to me as if it was the only picture hanging. In fact, I don't remember any other picture on his wall no matter how hard I try. There was a picture of an extremely fair-skinned man with grayish green colored eyes, high cheekbones and a long thin nose. His hair was light colored, but obviously textured. When we'd ask who the man was, Granddaddy would respond with a quick, "That's my daddy." Interesting...we thought. He spoke with an unspoken encouragement of 'let it go and carry on.' We'd say, "He's handsome, Granddaddy." Granddaddy would just talk right on over us as if he didn't want to address anything else, so we'd let it go for that particular visit. I think every time we would visit we'd address the same picture. I think subconsciously we wanted to hear about the man on the wall.

It wasn't until around 1993 that I found out a little more about the mystery man on the picture on the wall in my grandfather's house. Granddaddy had become gravely ill and was dying from cancer. He had come from Plainview, Texas to stay with my aunt and uncle and I would watch him while they worked. I only worked part-time, so it was easy for me and it was a privilege to sit with my grandfather anytime—especially during his dying days. I'd pick him up and ride him around and then take him to see my mother and father. We had many talks. I learned so much; but I wish I had known the importance of using interview techniques that I now have to get everything I could get from him about his history. There was so much to know that I didn't know that I didn't know. There are so many questions I needed to ask, but didn't know to ask.

Illegal Love

At the time I did more listening than questioning. He told me things about his mom and he shared how he felt about his dad. He talked to me about so many things--even his finances. What I am most appreciative of is that he allowed me to feel what it must have been like to be given his mother's name because he couldn't take his father's name. His father wasn't Black, so he couldn't dare take that last name. I learned a small amount about how my family came to be, but what I learned most is as far back as we have been privy of knowing, my foundation was built on who *they* said I was.

If my grandfather had to take his mother's maiden name because his dad couldn't give him his last name, then I wonder what effect that had on my grandfather. Knowing who you are, but not being able to confirm it is something a person could carry for life. I'm one of those people. I'm a product of an identity being given to me.

My Why

I grew up with so many false ideologies about who I am and who I am supposed to be and what I can and can't do, because of my race. I had my mother and father saying one thing, which was I can be anything and do anything, but nothing around me confirmed that. Unfortunately back then I didn't have the knowledge about the Word of God that I have now that tells me who I am. It tells me that I am fearfully and wonderfully made because I was created in His image. I didn't know about the promise that I can do all things through Christ which strengthens me. I had heard it, but I didn't know it for myself.

Growing up in my small hometown of only 1396 people at the time, the majority of the people who looked like me weren't seen the way I wanted to be seen. You could say that the 'playing field' was uneven.

My town was separated by color overall. I never understood why the majority of the Blacks lived across the tracks. I didn't understand it nor did I like it. I didn't understand why the Blacks and Whites were even separated in the cemetery. I grew up believing that you had to be a certain race to do some things such as be a cheerleader or a twirler. That's all that I saw, so if anyone said it wasn't true then I needed proof. A person of color could be in the Pep Squad (cheerleaders without the skirts and title). The Pep Squad crew sat together in the bleachers at the games and yelled for the team. They wore matching t-shirts and the same color pants. I remember the brief time I was in the squad we bore black pants with a gold t-shirt.

The Pep Squad was actually pretty cool though. Granted I was also a cheerleader and so was my middle sister, but it was never without discrepancies or 'recounting the votes.' (As if it was impossible for a Black girl to win fair and square). That's an old school term, but it still works.

My next to the oldest sister didn't make the cut to become a cheerleader, because she was a part of the unfair judging at the worst time. I wasn't going to talk about the fair and square situation, but it wouldn't do this section or this book justice if I didn't.

When I was in the seventh grade I tried out for the cheerleading team and I made it. I was so excited and yet surprised. I wasn't surprised because of an inability to cheer, I was surprised because of the track record that my school had regarding Black cheerleaders. I was also surprised because of the cheerleading sponsor/teacher who was in charge of counting the votes was so unfair. It seemed that each year that any Black girl who tried out would barely miss the mark. Interesting. I know. It was the story that we had become accustomed to hearing.

My seventh grade year was different from the past years others had experienced. It was different because we had gained (yes, it was a gain), a new teacher from Houston, Texas. She ended up being the new cheerleader sponsor; therefore, she counted the votes. She was so sweet and down to earth, but most of all she was fair. In fact, I have tried looking for her on social media, but I've had no luck. I just wanted to tell her how much I appreciate her for being a fair person, and one that made a major difference in my life. She began the change for Crowell Junior High School cheerleaders. She didn't care what color the girl was, and she didn't have any roots in Crowell, so she didn't care what had been the norm for the town. If the girl was good enough to make the squad, then the top girls made it. She believed in diversity and empowerment - even back then. It was our year that changed the rest of the years at that school. Many that came after me see me as someone troubling their calm waters in that school, but what they don't realize is that they were able to put on cheerleading and twirling uniforms because of us. They were able to be voted as class presidents because of us.

That year we had Black, White and Hispanic girls on the squad. We were great! The former teacher was middle aged, but back then I thought she was old. She reluctantly surrendered her position of choosing the team and counting votes. It didn't stop her from her old no-good tricks though. She tried to create an alternate that would actually be 'on the squad.' An alternate was supposed to be just that—an alternate. She was supposed to fill in if someone left. She was the one with the least votes, and technically she wasn't a cheerleader. That teacher didn't like that. She wanted the 'alternate' to make it because after all, she was popular and came from a prominent, well-to-do family. She had family members who had been cheerleaders throughout their years of school and they were popular girls. Nothing against the other girl at all. I liked her and her whole family. It wasn't about her. It was all about the cheating old woman that had cheated so many girls out of cheerleading in the past. She had stripped many of them of their self-esteem. There's no telling what else she had her hands in, because I was too young to know for sure.

The new cheer sponsor wasn't having it. It wasn't that she was being unfair, and that's what the older lady didn't like. She thought for sure the popular alternate should have beat me out of cheerleading. I was the one at stake because in my hometown the squad was mixed with different junior high grades. I was the only Black in our grade that could be removed. She lied and said that the other girl (alternate) beat me, but too many witnesses said it wasn't even close. Strangely enough, that was the same scenario when my sister who was several grades ahead of me went out for cheerleader. The high school girls counted the votes, then 'ole lady' (I'll call her Mrs. V.) tried to cheat my sister, but the high school cheerleaders who counted the votes said that it wasn't even a question. .

Once again, a barely miss scenario kept my sister from making the twirling team. She was great! Unfortunately, as I stated earlier, that was a few years too early for her to have been treated fairly.

Our new sponsor made it the best season ever. I will never forget her allowing us to decorate our own megaphone. She used stencils to draw a little girl in a cheer uniform with a high ponytail. It was the same stencil for each of us. She had skin-toned paint for us to use to paint our little girl's skin. The little girl reflected our image of who we were and how we looked. That alone instilled something inside of us that had been taken away or deflected on purpose in years past. They didn't want us to feel as good as the next girl. They didn't want us to think that we had the same privileges as the White girls. I probably shouldn't say they, because it wasn't everybody. A few people made the difference, and I want to make sure that I single them out for their ability and desire to stand up for right. There have been a few of those kinds of people in my life that I will never forget; and I appreciate them so much.

Unfortunately I had to move away in the middle of my seventh grade year, and the alternate ended up taking my place. Mrs. V. wanted to take my cheerleading clothes and equipment from me, but I was smart enough to say no. Even as a seventh grader I knew better. Those were my things and I am keeping them forever. My suit and shoes are still in my possession. I believe my pom poms and megaphone was lost or still in my mom's storage shed, or in the place that I found my middle school jacket that was stolen. Wherever they are, they are still mine. I earned them and Old Lady V. couldn't take it away from me.

Anyway...

A few days ago I had a complete meltdown. A friend from back home had sent some old yearbook photos that had been printed in the county newspaper and I was all excited seeing my old school mates. I recognized pretty much everybody in the pictures, and if I didn't remember faces of students that were older than me, I recognized their names. I couldn't find any pictures of me. I thought surely I would be in one of the photos of the cheerleaders! I knew them all. I wasn't on them. The girl who had taken my place was now in the photos, and there was no memory of Angel Tucker ever being a cheerleader in Crowell, Texas, seventh grade 1982-1983 school year. That broke my heart! No wonder I am caught in the middle. No wonder I am not connected to hardly anyone in my class that I would have graduated with! I get it now! It was the most painful aha moment ever, but it was necessary. They don't dislike me. They went on with their lives and I became a childhood memory of the past. Mrs. V. contributed to no one having a record that I was anything back home.

Add insult to injury, when I moved to Fort Worth, Texas (the city), it was the middle of the school year. Being the new girl in the middle of the school year is brutal. I didn't connect with people, there were too many people in the school and I didn't fit in. I had come from an almost all White populated town of about 1300 people to an almost all Black school that had more kids in the school than I had in my entire town. I attended four middle/junior high schools. I transferred to one school too late, so I missed playing basketball, which was my favorite sport at the time. I was kind of thrown into a place that had no *place* for me. Now I was the new girl that had no prior memories with the students in my schools down here, but was taken from the only school (people) that I did know.

That night, after all of the reminiscing was over, I lost it. I realized that I had been struggling with an identity crisis that started really young, but had been deepened by life's events and society. I had not fit in anywhere and had not been welcomed in many places.

Trading Places
Being Black Is No Fairytale

You know Black girls aren't princesses! (My mind tells me). The pretty dolls with the long hair and long beautiful gowns weren't black. Princess dolls and Barbies weren't black!

As far back as I can remember I have never been a fan of Sleeping Beauty, Snow White, and Rapunzel, Cinderella or Belle and any of the other female characters who were supposed to be the symbol of beauty and every little girl's dream to become. I didn't know why or what I was feeling back then, I just knew I wasn't a fan. What I did know was that I didn't look like any of those female characters, nor would I ever look like them. I guess the one plus for me was that I never desired to look like any of them, so I didn't grow up with that particular problem. None of that made me angry; I just didn't get why there weren't any Black princesses. I should have known back then that I was different by the way that I thought.

I was never told that I couldn't be a princess, but I wasn't told that I could be either. It's not about what is said in some cases, it's what we're shown.

All of the childhood princesses that I grew up knowing about were White. They didn't have anything in common with me. Their hair was different and their skin color was not like mine. When I was growing up there were the princesses that I've listed, and later came a little darker hue with Pocahontas, and the girls from Aladdin and Mulan. There might be others, but I can't think of all of the names because I didn't watch them and there is no need for me to try to research more just to make a point.

When Cinderella the movie was recreated, starring actor and recording artist Brandy was Disney came out with their Collector's Edition of Cinderella. Then there was a remake of Annie. The remake was fantastic! After the remake of Annie (the movie), starring actors Jamie Foxx and Quvenzhané Wallis debuted, the original Annie came back to the big screen and the theater stage once more. It's almost like people want to make sure that we don't forget the originals, or making sure the younger kids don't get mixed up with who was first. How could we forget?

You can count on a Collector's Edition or the original to come out again for every fairytale princess, if a new one comes out starring a person of color. I am a very observing individual, and I can't help that.

Had I known back then what I know now, I would have known what I was called to do and probably would have wanted to start this change or movement a long time ago; but if we had a way of knowing what we would grow up to be, life wouldn't be such a mystery.

They Don't Look Like Me

Growing up as a young girl in the seventies, in a predominately-White town, I experienced things that my sisters didn't go through. I don't think anyone knew what I felt until I wrote about my experiences in my late thirties—early forties about not being interested in any of the fairytale princesses. None of them [princesses] ever did anything for me as a little girl because early on, I knew they did not look anything like me. I didn't feel jealousy or feel inferior to them, I just didn't feel anything at all.

It was a little confusing to me in another sense because although I felt some kind of way about dolls and princesses, I never wanted a Black doll. It was years later when I realized why I didn't like black dolls. They didn't look like me either! They were dark (not dark with a pretty color, but black as in 'crayon'). Their hair wasn't *'combable'* because most times the hair was curly and the curls were sown down or glued and I couldn't comb their hair.

I liked to comb my dolls' hair. Go figure. I grew up to be a licensed barber and stylist. I didn't like the princesses because they were different from me and so were the baby dolls, but I opted for a White doll because I could do more than look at her. I could comb her hair any way I wanted to and dress her up however I wanted. What good was a doll that I couldn't do those things with? Absolutely nothing!

No Black princesses, no Black teachers... What is a girl to do? Who am I and who can I relate to?

The only Black people I saw on TV or in books were slaves. Little Rascals' Buckwheat sure didn't look like me. The maids on TV didn't look like me or anyone in my family, so finding placement was a hard thing to do (if it were possible at all). Not a teacher in the school resembled me. Not a magazine on the shelf had a Black woman on the cover nor did the face of a Black woman grace any page in the books.

Makeup for us wasn't advertised because none of the major companies formulated makeup in the shades of Black women. All of my growing up years, I didn't see shades of makeup for women of color on the shelves in the stores nor on TV. I lucked out! I was able to use Cover Girl clean makeup by Noxzema (I'm singing the commercial in my head), because I was much lighter skinned in my younger days.

They (the Black girls) weren't afforded the opportunity to spruce up throughout the day, remove the shine from their foreheads and noses to look and feel beautiful. Unfortunately make-up palettes didn't exist (that I know of) for a while, but that ice blue eyeshadow surely did. Ice blue didn't match every woman's skin tone. I also remember an ice green color. The proper word would probably be frost. Foundations, blushes and powders weren't created for melanin skin, and that was so ugly and unfair!

A woman that I know and respect who grew up in the Baby Boomer time has told me stories about when she was in high school. She shared stories of how the girls would go into the bathroom during passing periods or at lunch time to comb their hair and freshen up their make-up, but the Black girls couldn't. Even she (an older White woman) said it hurt her to see the Black girls not having make-up to put on their faces like the White girls had, but no one said anything. None of them discussed it, so it was noticed by not addressed. For far too long, people have noticed but not addressed anything.

Although that seems like a long time ago, it wasn't. Even if it was a long time ago for the youngsters, it doesn't negate the fact that several decades of Black females went through those times of feeling like they weren't attractive and they didn't matter.

Everything was created to make White women look and feel better than us.

What We See Is What We Believe

The only times we saw beautiful Black women on TV was on Saturdays, if we were able to sneak a peek at Soul Train. We weren't allowed to watch Soul Train because of the women "twisting", as mom would say, and the music she didn't like either. She didn't know that we probably needed that, or at least I might have needed that. Then again, maybe not. God had a plan and He didn't need Soul Train to fulfill it.

Commercials advertising soaps, lotions, shampoos, etc. only showed White women using the products. I can't explain exactly what I felt when I saw the commercials, but I recall thinking I can see why only a certain group of women are thought to be beautiful and sexy and bears soft skin because that is what was advertised. Commercials are created to sell a product. Product developers and marketers wanted their products to look appealing and desirable. I guess they didn't think that Black women could draw the necessary attention; or maybe companies thought it would be too much of a risk to have a Black woman advertising their product. Whether it was an advertisement for satin sheets or razors – Black women weren't advertising anything. Oh, my goodness! We sure didn't see Black women advertising panties and bras because once again, full butts and a curvy build weren't *in style*, so I guess they were afraid no one would be interested in the actual product itself. I do remember a Nair commercial having a Black girl. The jingle went something like this, *If you dare wear short shorts, Nair wears short shorts.*

I didn't see Black women modeling lingerie. It sure wasn't because Black women didn't wear it. I used to buy all sorts of lingerie. When I was a little girl, I remember my aunt used to have Fredericks of Hollywood magazines. She wore beautiful slips, bras and panties. Again, maybe the casting crew and producers of commercials didn't think people wanted to see a Black woman in lingerie showing off her body and her beautiful skin. I believe to my heart that no one wanted to create an appetite (if I could use that word here) for the Black woman.

Remember what I said earlier - companies design commercials to make people want to buy, get, and use or want something. In my opinion they didn't want anyone to feel that way about Black women. If they did that, then they might have felt that they were opening doors for their audience to feel there is nothing wrong with us after all.

I don't recall seeing a Black woman spraying cologne on her neck or spreading lotion over her body while her husband looks on with fire and desire in his eyes. We didn't see Black women in the shower washing their hair. We learn from what we see. If you don't see it, you won't want it! If you don't see us washing our hair and bathing, shallow minds might believe that we don't do it. They showed us that no one wanted us, and if they did want us they'd better not let anyone know they did.

I never got so tired of hearing people describing the perfect woman that they find attractive. The first thing they would start out with is, "She was tall, blonde and had blue eyes." I think that description should be *a slap in any woman's face* because that is not what the majority of women look like..

Writers never portrayed us as sexy or beautiful. Ad creators and marketers never portrayed us as someone anyone would want. I said we were not portrayed that way – not that the picture they painted was true.

I remember having a conversation with an amazing guy who happens to be White, and I'd tease him at times and say, "It's sad that you never got a chance to date a Black girl—especially since you are so attracted to them." Don't get me wrong. He didn't discriminate when it came to women. He just didn't know how much he was really attracted to women of all colors until we would talk. He liked everything that we had been given such a bad rap about. He loved curvy women, women with darker skin and fuller lips. It was sexy to him, but he never realized that he was not attracted to only one look, but settled for one look. He was groomed to like only one look.

Whew! We bought the products but couldn't sell them by advertising them. I know; kind of sad and still disgusting. I could go on and on naming products that we purchased and used, but weren't good enough to advertise them. I don't care if things have so-called gotten better (some would say), but I grew up in the times when things weren't better, and those times will always be a part of the fabric of my life. My times were a heck of a lot better for me than it was in my mother's days; so I guess you could call it *better*. I can only imagine living in her times. I don't want better, I want good!

As my mom would say about a soap commercial, *"Heck! I guess **we** don't bathe!"*

The Black Woman

I've always wondered why our greatness is contingent upon what someone else thinks or says about us--especially people who think and see us as a nobody or *less than*.

For hundreds of years, Black women have had to defend themselves about their weight, their hair, their features, and the size of their lips, hips and thighs. I am one of those Black women. Black women have defended the various shades of their skin, the way they speak, their sassiness and swag, and their choices of how they choose to live their lives. The shape of our bodies have blocked us from opportunities, but have opened doors for those who mimic our shapes.

We have been stereotyped about not being educated, being on welfare and government assistance, and being undesirable. There are so many myths and untruths that have been spoken about us. We have always been told that we weren't good enough. If it wasn't said to us aloud it was shown.

Some have said that nobody wants a Black woman and that they are the least sought after of all races of women. I don't believe that, and I don't need a poll to see if that's true. Those (like my friend) who aren't afraid to own up to their attraction will prove that statement is not true. I wonder if it could be *that* particular lie that has made people feel that they can't allow themselves to be attracted to Black women publicly because of the stigma that is attached to it. Maybe years of brainwashing by that which was shown on television and inside magazines have made our features seem unattractive. I don't know for sure, but I have a sneaky suspicion. Brainwashing is capable of doing that. I'm just saying.

In my generation (age group), some of the things that have been said about us are downright disgusting.

The toughest part, if there is a part that is tougher than another, is that people believe these things.

Black women have been denied certain positions and professions because of our race and the stigmas that came with it. Flight attendant is one of those professions. When I was younger, all I knew about flight attendants was that you had to fit a certain category that pretty much said you had to be White in order to be one.

I've seen a documentary of White flight attendants sharing their stories about Black women and flight attending (or the lack thereof). They knew about it. The stipulations and criteria for size, weight and shape was the industry's way of saying (but not saying) they didn't want Black women in the field. I remember taking flight attendants off of the dream jobs list completely! No one that I knew was a flight attendant. It was easier to say that you didn't want to do something than to want to do it and be told that you couldn't.

Modeling? Oh girlfriend, you could hang that up! We had too many curves and the wrong color to be a model. My hat is still off to the couple that they allowed in the industry, but even with them, they urged them to compete against each other because there was no room for more than one or two most times.

The pageants actually gave the criteria for becoming a Miss, Mrs. anything. In or around 1930, the criteria for becoming Miss America was that she must be in good health and White.

May I proudly say that for the first time in history, in 2019 Black women held the crowns in five major pageants: Miss Teen USA, Miss America, Miss USA, Miss Universe and Miss World. Wow! I got chills listing them.

My daughter lives in a time where she has seen a Black president, and now she gets to see all Black pageant winners. She can now feel things are possible for her to achieve; but that wasn't my story. That alone is another reason we must tell our stories because they are very relevant. Many say that we should leave history in the past, and let bygones be bygones. I agree about letting bygones be bygones, but I believe in sharing the true history so that we won't allow history to repeat the ugliness. Also, I believe it's easier to get past something if it's still not happening.

Watch What You Say

I began choosing to change my language and wording when speaking about me as a Black woman. I started correcting people when they would make a statement saying, "She's a strong Black woman" or "She's a beautiful Black woman." The reason I started disliking those comments and other statements like that is because what I was *really* hearing each time a statement like that was made was: "You're beautiful and strong **to be** a Black woman." Insinuating that it's rare! I'm sure that wasn't the intention, but it can be seen as derogatory or degrading. If it's said too often, then it's easy to start thinking about it. Not only will she think that about herself, but others will start thinking about it as well and it becomes stinking thinking - something that we pass on from generation to generation.

Trust me, I understand why Black women started making those statements about themselves. Those statements were made to say that we are proud to be who we are, and we are beautiful just the way we are - since society seems to think we shouldn't be proud or feel beautiful.

Our Bodies

Our bodies! Now that's a topic that could take all day.

Until being thick and having curves came *in style*, being curvy was a no-no! Even though now it's accepted and sought after by the majority of women, we are still deprived of the compliments of having those things naturally.

Curves and being a little thicker have been credited to the women in the industry who have paid for them or decided to stop watching their weight and then they call it curvy!

Baby Got Back

In 1992 Sir Mix-A-Lot came out with the song entitled *Baby Got Back*. Oh my goodness! Some people were offended, while some applauded the song. I can see why it could have been offensive, but hey, he was on to something. It was my anthem and I didn't even know it until many years later!

At first I had mixed feelings about how people might have felt about the song because I felt some kind of way myself. Sometimes I might seem contradictory in what I say because it is my natural character to care how others think and feel; therefore, it can sometimes seem that I'm riding the fence (so to speak).

When my sisters and I would go out to predominantly White clubs, the dance floor would fill up at the first beat. The beginning sounds sort of like the beginning of the theme song for *Jaws* the movie.

"Oh, my, God Becky, look at her butt! It is so big! She looks like one of those rap guys' girlfriends...Who understands those rap guys? They only talk to her because she looks like a total prostitute. Okay? I can't believe it's just so round, it's like out there! I mean gross, look! She's just so, Black!"

Uh, yes, those are actually the lyrics to the song that I got from online. I'm totally laughing out loud right now. Oh my word! Is that not crazy! The lyrics are so in your face and might be degrading to some people, but Sir Mix A-Lot only said publicly what some people were saying privately. He said what we were being shown in magazines, runways and on mainstream television.

By the end of the intro the floor is full! I wanted to say, "Do you like the song or not?" The actions were contradictory to the controversy about the song.

When I said the song was like my anthem it was because the song made me feel like somebody was finally letting the world know that not all men wanted a woman with a flat butt, and some men actually liked women with protruding butts. To each his own! We are all different, and that's why I'm glad he came out with the song. The song made those of us with a butt feel desired—not just a select few who shared a build that the world had told us was the only desired shape. Notice I didn't say Black women, because there are some Black women that I know personally who are flat behind as a chair! They know it and they are okay with it, as they should be. I finally *started* somewhat embracing my butt more when I heard that song. Maybe I shouldn't say embracing my butt, but appreciating my size, shape and all that I possessed.

The lyrics of the song's intro is really degrading about Black women, but it was meant to be in order for us to realize what some people really think and have said about Black women. It's unfortunate that the intro of that song could very well be the conversation between the ones who believe so strongly about a curvy woman's shape – namely a Black woman. I hate to say it, but I can relate to someone feeling that disgust towards me about my butt. It wasn't always spoken aloud except for a time or two, but I definitely felt the stares more often than I can count.

Curvy Isn't a Trend. It's a Shape!

Until it became a trend to be curvy and thick, most designers didn't make clothes that fit women with curves (full hips and thighs). Later on, I became aware of a few full-figured clothing stores, but the clothes didn't fit the average curvy woman like me. They were too big! They were just big and not curvy! Not only were they too big (in cut), they used to be unattractive and super expensive compared to other stores. I'm only using the term full-figured because it's a familiar term to more people these days. There was a time when a size 12 was considered full figured.

Later on designers began making jeans with a little more curve (just a little). Some of the pants were just curved out, but not necessarily bigger in the butt - just a wider hip. Then padded jeans entered the stores. Pads? Are you kidding? Me in pads? I'd look like something is wrong with me in padded jeans! Padded jeans (in my opinion) was a way of helping women have an illusion of a protruding butt without feeling bad for not *really* having one. It was also a way to keep women who didn't need pads from being proud of it—in my opinion. I feel the pads were marketed in a way that it was considered as an accessory instead of a desire; therefore, women could feel good about putting on and taking off - like eyelashes and nails. It wasn't until buttock implants became popular that women wanted to keep those butts that they had come to covet and love.

It bothered me at first because women with a butt were talked about negatively for so long, yet secretly women were buying what they talked about Black women for already having. We were talked about and made fun of for having larger butts until music videos started showing there was a love for curvy bodies and bigger butts. No, they weren't what some would call 'video girls' either.

Lingerie Looks Good On Curves

Let's talk about lingerie. Oh my goodness! Lingerie was always my favorite thing to buy.

I remember when a popular lingerie store only carried a limited number of larger panties and clothing in their brick and mortar stores, and if you wanted to buy their brand in a XL, you had to shop online. I guess being an X-Large didn't seem to be sexy, so they didn't carry them.

I guess they fell into the societal norm of thinking that strip of material down the middle of the butt cheeks to create an illusion of curves sufficed for showing women with actual curves and a butt. All varieties of shapes should have been shown.

All of our lives we have been conditioned by what we have seen and what we have been told constitutes sexy. Black women and their body shapes were not openly considered sexy. The conditioning has been an unfair attack on the beauty and sexiness of women everywhere--especially Black women.

It was the same trickery used throughout the years that caused millions of women not to embrace what they have been blessed with, because of how they looked did not line up with what was 'said' to be perfect. That's why I couldn't understand why people have the nerve to wonder why Blacks came up with ways of embracing and highlighting *Black this and curvy that!* Almost every division that has been created is because of the lack of acceptance of every(body) literally.

One group says that only one way is right and one type of woman is beautiful and sexy. The other group came from the people saying, "We are beautiful and sexy too!" Majority of the people just wanted to be seen fairly. For far too many decades, generations of Black women were affected by this nonsense. It is past time for it to stop! Not just get better, but to stop.

Ain't I A Woman

Sojourner Truth wrote a speech titled, *Ain't I a Woman,* which I recited in my Composition II class in college many years ago. When I first read the poem, I had a hard time getting through it because my brain wanted to read it the grammatically correct way; but it was when I thought about the poem being written in a slavery-day tone, it made more sense. I was able to speak the poem with heart and clarity. When I finally put myself in her (the author's) shoes, and in the places of the other women who experienced the same feelings that this poem was representing, my heart sank. All she was asking for (in the poem) was to be treated like a woman and to see her as a woman. That seemed to be very important to her. I can understand that feeling. I have asked the same thing many times before.

In the poem she speaks of having a desire to be helped over puddles and helped out of carriages like other women. "Ain't I a Woman" she said. She continued talking about how she was strong and had borne thirteen children and watched most of them sold off to slavery. I will never forget the effect the poem had on me because I could relate to being a Black woman wanting to be treated like a woman; but I couldn't even fathom my children being sold off to slavery. The question is, why couldn't she be treated as a woman? Why are we (Black women) still asking that same question today? In many instances I am reminded that much of the world believes there are women, and then there's Black women.

I sincerely believe the strength that the writer was referring to might be the same strength that many of us possess today that a vast majority see as a flaw. Many Blacks are still seeing their loved ones ripped away from them by murder and too often prison.

For many generations, people *placed* Black women in to unfair categories. Angry, too this or too that, or don't like this or that... We hardly ever hear positive things that didn't have some kind of backlash. There were times that I would hear men say they like the strength of a Black woman (a sista), or a sista won't let you get away with that; but that statement was always met with a counterclaim such as, that's why Black men wanted White women – they want someone who they could tell what to do. I always wondered why they just couldn't leave it as a compliment that some Black women are naturally strong mentally. We don't fall apart and commit suicide because a man decides to leave for another woman. We might not handle things the best way all the time, but we are not likely to commit suicide and leave our kids alone. Does it hurt when a divorce happens? Heck yeah! Would it be hard to take care of the kids alone? For sure! Somehow we know that 'this too shall pass.' One thing I can say is that I believe many Black people have either encountered so much pain and distress or have seen their mothers, grandmothers, fathers, etc. go through pain, that we really believe that we can get through anything.

If we are strong we're not submissive. If we have an opinion, we're dominant. If we get upset, we're *angry* Black women. Now I do know some angry women who happen to be Black, but truth be told, White, Hispanic, Asian, Indian and other races of women can be angry too. I've seen some really angry White women on videos that are coming to surface these days in the wake of racism in America. The White women captured on video are using racial slurs, tearing up vehicles of neighbors, throwing items from their shopping cart, and calling police on innocent Black people. We tend to not think they are angry because they have been called the model citizens that we are supposed to be like in the eyes of most of America.

Carry On...
Liar, Liar, Pants on Fire

I have come to learn that some Black women have an honesty problem. They will say they are alright even when they are not. It's not that they are trying to lie, maybe they don't see it as a lie because they really feel they are okay. They smile when they want to cry. They say they're good even if they're not. They laugh when they are feeling sorrow. Many of them do these things because they know the expectations that are on them is to be strong no matter what—even if it means that she will be degraded for the strengths that she displays.

If you don't believe me, ask the women in the inner city areas that are numb to burying their children, their neighbors' children and other loved ones. We are well aware that tears don't get us anywhere, and we have learned that voicing our opinion has fed into the stigma of being angry or unhappy. If you're still having problems believing me, then ask the women who were nannies all of their adult lives who took care of other people's children, washed clothes for families, cooked big meals and issued snacks to kids that were not their own. She fed and nurtured other people's kids while hers were left at home finning for themselves, as the oldest child would play the part of the mother for his or her siblings. That Black woman did all of those things for White women families while the White woman sat at home or went out with her friends for spa days and lunches, then returned home to be displayed as a trophy for her husband when he came home.

Our strength has been our kryptonite
Before you speak, think.

Before we expose some myths that I can't wait to address, let's talk more about the ***strong*** Black woman that everyone seems to have an opinion about, but know very few facts.

Let's talk about the *strong* Black woman

Sometimes I wonder if her strength was given to her because God knew the pain she would endure her entire life that would be inflicted upon her by so many people—even those whom she loves. I wonder if He strengthened her and gave her a strong exterior because she would need tough skin (figuratively speaking - don't get it twisted), to go through this life, being the most negatively talked about female of all races. (Seemingly). I don't need statistics to say this, I've lived it.

Think about our ancestors for a moment. It takes a strong woman to be able to work all day (before sunrise and past sunset), be a wife to her own husband and yet please the White men that came into the huts at night to have their way with her. It took a strong woman to be able to work in the fields all day pregnant (God only knows who the baby's father was), and give birth to the baby only for the baby to be sold to the owner of the next plantation or a far-away land. If the baby was indeed the child of the rapist, the fate of the child was definitely unknown. I know we never refer to the man entering the huts at night as the rapist because it was normal, accepted and expected; but by definition, that is what he was – a rapist. The conceived child could very well become the 'child of the house' (formerly called a derogatory name – "House Nigga"), or left in the huts to be raised by the woman and her husband who was forced to raise a child that he didn't father. Only the massa of the plantation could make that call of where that child would dwell and whether or not he would go or stay. It took a strong woman to handle that.

It took a strong woman to watch her babies be taken out of her hands and thrown on the back of a horse-driven wagon and given away to someone else. To me, that's worse than an abortion that America has fought so hard to abolish.

It took a strong woman to see her husband hung on a tree beat to death for no reason at all. That strength is what I believe we have been able to draw from, just knowing that this too shall pass.

Black women defaulted to being the head of the house because their heads of the house (husbands) were taken to become field hands for the master who sometimes came from far-away places to purchase them--leaving a single parent to take care of the children. Sound familiar? Sounds like what we know as today's dead-beat dads. Let me clarify something. I am not saying that men of today leave their homes because they were ripped away to work on plantations of the massa's choice; but what I am saying is that the deep-rooted seeds of the Black man leaving his family didn't start in today's times.

The Black woman had to be strong. If she was lucky or *unlucky* enough to be the house "worker" she still didn't get a chance to mother her own children unless they were the children of the massa of the plantation. (Let's call it what it is here, in case a young person is unfamiliar with the term, a person who worked in the house on the plantation was called a House Nigga).

She had to give more attention to the massa and his wife's children than her own. She even nursed them when they were hungry. She woke up with them and cared for them when they were sick as she would do for her own children. That's a strong woman. That's a woman that can't be reckoned with. That's a woman that any woman would want to be like and would envy. Too bad many Black women today can't see that their strength is indeed a gift. They have fallen into the holes of seeing themselves through the eyes of the White world. Whether they add up or fall short, the measurement comes from what they have been told is the standard.

Many of the slave women had to leave their own husbands behind while working in the house for the rest of their lives. What do you think happened to the homes of the Black families?

Let us not forget she had to take care of the massa's wants and sexual desires too. That wasn't a good position to be in because from what we have been told by our ancestors and have seen in movies, that behavior only made the massa's wife hate that slave woman even more. The wife knew that she couldn't give to him what he was willing to take from that Black woman. That was unfair of him—especially knowing that he wasn't leaving his wife for a slave woman. He couldn't! (I am not saying that he should have left, so don't get that twisted.) It was to satisfy his curiosity and greed – no matter who it hurt; but he also did it out of the desire for the slave woman. I know that it is hard to accept, but it was the truth. It was possible and it happened. Period. I am a product of that behavior. Cheating with a Black woman! That is so degrading! (Yes. I'm being sarcastic here).

Her (the Black woman) dignity, respect and self-esteem were constantly challenged – never being or feeling good enough. Black women didn't have proper clothing, soaps and perfumes unless they made them. They sowed the dresses that the White women stepped around in all day long, but they weren't good enough to wear the dresses that their hands created. They cleaned the commodes that they weren't allowed to use. They washed the dishes that their Black lips couldn't touch. They washed the windows that their eyes couldn't look out of to gaze at their families working in the fields. They couldn't even use their eyes to look up at a White person in passing, just to say hello.

I am so glad that new information from slaves and children of slaves have been brought up to share about the innocent, sweet, submissive, loving, beautiful, docile wife of the plantation owners that we don't hear much talk about from back in the day. New information has revealed that the White women were heartless and evil towards Black women, and it has been revealed that they too had their share of sexual acts with them. Some of these stories from the times of slavery have also provided information about the White women ordering heinous acts on the Black people. Now that I think about it, it doesn't seem too far-fetched. I mean, they had to have known what was going on.

I can't imagine not being able to go to my master bathroom and choose which fragrance of oils and creams I would like to use whether it be morning or night. Those women, my ancestors, my people didn't have beautiful vanities with the matching brush and comb sets sitting on the dressers to be used at their discretion for beautification. They didn't get a chance to enjoy the finer things in life, but they made what they had work for them! Black women only had their hands that they used to braid their hair or leave it in its natural state. They made products for their hair and body, but then they were taken from them and sold for the White families to benefit. Many are still benefiting from some products today.

The Black men back in those days admired their women for such strength and beauty. The men knew that their wives would stand by their side, stand by her children and be a mother *and* father to the kids in the husband's absence.

Even in the early years of the fifties and sixties, Black men and women admired one another. I am not familiar with earlier times, so I'll stick with what I know. I enjoy watching footage of men dressed in their suits with their wives in their pencil skirts or nice fitting dresses with gloves and matching hats, showcasing their flawless locks. I am inspired by the women of that time. They knew how to mother their children and be wives to their husbands. What happened? Some of the Black men of today are intimated and embarrassed by Black women, but thank God, there are many who love and appreciate them the same. I believe the embarrassment of Black women that some have portrayed comes from the false information and lies they have been fed about the Black woman.

As a matter of fact, I believe that many Black men have an expectation (good and the bad) of who a Black woman is and what she could and should be. I also believe that some of the views Black men have of Black women have come from the derogatory remarks and thoughts of others.

I believe the preconceived ideas of some expectations come from their personal knowledge and experiences of watching their own mothers, grandmothers and aunts that sometimes have had to raise them. They see a strength in Black women that they love and admire, but yet many have allowed their minds to be tainted to believe that the strength of a Black woman is something bad and intimidating.

If only 'that' Black man would become educated or stop reminiscing on what they do know about their ancestors as well as their mothers and grandmothers, they would appreciate what they see in the Black woman. I'm not saying that all Black women are strong, neither am I saying that all Black men don't value or appreciate the ones that are.

If only the few would realize that sometimes the female family members didn't always choose to be the head of the household and stand strong alone. It was oftentimes because of the men being taken away. The taking away is still happening through our prison systems of today that hand down sentences for petty offenses that cause the man of the house to be locked away from his family for years upon years sometimes for life.

Today, It's A Choice

The Black men of yesteryear respected Black women for who they were. Many of the Black men of today have been conditioned to think the Black woman is hard and tough as if it's always a bad thing. Maybe she is that way because she is often left to be the mother and the father in the home – only this time it is by a decision that was made by choice and not by force. Some Black men team up with others and help taint the name and character of the Black woman instead of upholding her – she is always being judged by everyone.

Maybe it's the Black man's ancestral demons of feeling inadequate coming to haunt them when [ancestors] were forced to watch White men come into the huts and rape their wives, and knowing they would be killed if they even *thought* to have looked at a White woman. I believe it is a *mind thing* to show the world that they have *arrived* because they are able to pick one of the White man's trophies now; but in the past, they were murdered for the act.

Division and supremacy started way before our time (today), but yet we are still fighting the demons of our ancestors when it comes to respect and beauty. We are still being held to a higher standard than any other woman on the planet. Can't be too much of this or too little of that – or we are considered a "no go!" It is time for that to change.

For Us By Us

I wanted to leave you hanging there for a minute with that title.

Take Fubu For Example...
For Us By Us

FUBU was a popular clothing line that was thought to have racist intent. It simply stands for, *For Us, By Us*. The creators from Queens, NY were reportedly proud to be able to produce urban clothing wear for inner city kids, and weren't necessarily trying to be racist and keeping anyone else from wearing their clothes. They (the creators) said that it was a positive statement – one of empowerment. I personally believe anything we do is a problem to the majority. If you don't want us in your clothes, then what is wrong with someone making clothes that represent the people that are underserved?

I remember when FUBU came out. I was already out of high school and wasn't much of an urban wear girl, but I did purchase shirts and a few pairs of shorts for my then twenty some odd year old husband.

Damned if you do, Damned if you don't. That's how I feel about anything Black people do. All of my life clothing was made strictly for other races when it came to women, but they just didn't own up to it. If you can't find what you like, then what's wrong with creating your own? If Blacks did not do anything, they are said to be lazy and are waiting on White people to do it for them. When they do create and become business owners, entrepreneurs and investors, it's a problem. Many Black business owners and creators are no longer relying on the 'dollar' that someone else told them how many they could make.

Speaking of not relying on the dollars of others. As soon as Blacks come up with a product or system that includes Black people it's a problem.

I was reading about the Tulsa Riot. That grueling story enlightened me on so much. I wanted my children to know about the story so that they can paint a different picture in their minds other than what the media and history has taught. History never taught me about the wealth of the folks in Tulsa in 1921.

Let me share...

The Tulsa riot was said to have been one of the worst incidents of racial violence in history. It occurred May 31 and June 1, 1921. Black businesses and homes were destroyed in the Greenwood District (often referred to as Black Wall Street) of Tulsa, Oklahoma by mobs of Whites. There was no real reason for it other than meanness and evilness to rob Black people of their wealth. It was said that Whites were given weapons by city officials to use on the Black people. Wait! Weapons given by city officials? Wow! They went into the neighborhoods and looted and burned down businesses that Black people owned. It is mind boggling to hear people talk about Black people looting and rioting in cities, but we don't hear complaints about White people doing those things. It's like they never talk about anything other than the good things they are known for doing. Listen, I know the looting of one's own neighborhood is stupid when trying to make a point, so I'm not referring to those cases. I personally don't think committing acts of such kinds is smart or justifiable. I'm talking about how incidents have been hidden that we feel aren't becoming of White people.

Although numerous individuals were killed in the Tulsa riot and others left homeless, news reports kept it quiet. I had never heard about the race riots in Tulsa. I wonder why.

In November 2018, the 1921 Race Riot Commission was officially renamed the 1921 Race Massacre Commission. I wish I had known more about this event and many more long before now.

It seems most White people have never wanted to see Black people on the same level as they are (or feel that they are), whether it's money, beauty or fame. Many of them are always wanting to be a step or two above Blacks no matter what.

Tulsa isn't the only place something happened this tragic, but I believe it was the worst we know of so far.

What they did to those people affected their kids, their grandkids, their great grandkids, etc. Look at how many generations and families had to start over building wealth.

Part Two
It's A Root Issue

When I was about eight or nine years old I remember my best friend at the time patted me on my butt and said, *"Fat butt."* I don't remember responding, but I remember feeling 'some type of way.' I was a kid, but the strange thing was the fact that I was slimmer than most girls in my class, and my friend was thicker than me. I wore a size 10S in the sixth grade while my other friends wore 12 and 14R. The R stood for Regular, and the S stood for slim. A couple of us wore our Lil Taters pants that we thought were too cute! I was always slender, and some would even call me skinny, but her comments made me start paying attention to my size and build at an early age. Conditioned...perception... beginning of the roots.

Although I knew that I was smaller, I still became quite insecure and started paying attention to my body at that point. I didn't know whether to like it or cover it. I tried to walk so that I could pull my butt in so that it wouldn't get much attention. One person made me feel that way, but sometimes that's all it takes. If you haven't read my children's book *Little Betsy Mae*, then please do. This particular excerpt is mentioned in the book intertwined with the storyline of Betsy and her insecurities. It's a really good book that I delve deep into how the roots of low self-esteem is developed and take root but most of all the book talks about how to overcome it. It's a perfect book for young girls as well as their mothers.

There are a number of things a person can experience throughout life that can and oftentimes than not, will destroy self-esteem if it's never addressed or known to address. Those things will end up taking root and will start to grow. Growth isn't seen right away, sometimes it will take a while to show blooms. I took the root of insecurity with me everywhere I went through all stages of my life for most of my life. I just started unpacking that insecurity nearly three decades later. The seeds that lie dormant are the ones that I personally feel we need to be made aware of because they have a way of springing up when you least expect it, catching us off guard and unaware of the 'why' in our lives. We have to identify roots and dig them up. The good thing is that it's possible to do so.

Speaking of seeds...we never know what minds they fell on and took root.

A Message to the Black Men

Black men, I have a message for you specifically regarding Black women. When I first started writing I didn't know how to address this topic without being passive aggressive. I was more concerned about how it would be perceived or received, than telling the truth.

Black men, many of you have hurt the Black woman like you'd never imagine. Many Black women won't admit it because of pride, and it's okay. I understand. I have felt the same way. Many won't agree or admit because they might feel it makes them look weak in some kind of way. I understand that as well. I have found my strength in this message. I now know that your choices have nothing to do with all Black women; and many cases it has nothing to do with the women that you grew up around. Some of you have amazing Black mothers. You have strong, beautiful sisters, aunts and grandmothers. I used to believe that many of you came from areas that you didn't see a healthy role model of a Black woman, but I found that to be untrue in most cases.

The way you have turned your backs (intentional and unintentional) on us have screamed messages that everybody heard except you. Your choices have contributed to other races feeling that we were less than all other races of women. You helped write the stories that people tell that we are not worthy of love. People enjoyed believing that something was wrong with a Black woman, because after all, many of you guys started dating and marrying White women as soon as you felt that you could. You might have felt that you were following your heart, but to the minds of the racists, bigots and supremacists, the message that was sent to them was so much bigger. It spoke to them that you don't even like us, and you don't like yourselves.

I watch men on television that are strong in character, stature and voices on Black issues, but only to learn that you didn't speak up for Black women, and you go home to White women. We don't get it! I have so many ideas of why you have chosen your paths, and I have taken a stab at the reasons in other areas of this book; but I could not pass the opportunity to tell you that you have been a part of the problem when it came to the Black woman.

The media and any force behind it also contributes to the images of the Black woman. They painted for us a picture of an absent father, unless the Black man was fathering a bi-racial child. The media also delivered messages that the Black man could stay with his White wife, but not a Black wife.

During sporting events and after professional championship games the cameras always zoomed in on Black professional athletes with their White wives, further digging daggers into the backs of Black women. Why don't they show the men who are married to Black women? They don't want the message of Black women being desired to be the message that goes out. I have come to realize what those messages were all about now. They were created to send a message to the young Black women the same message women my age received. That message is, "Young Black girl, teen, woman... no one wants you.

Is that the message you want to send to your daughters? Is that the message that you want to send to your sisters? I didn't think so. You can choose whomever you want to be with, but please understand your role in building and uplifting and not tearing down Black women.

Come On Man! You Too?

One of my pet peeves that I have is when a Black guy talks about a Black woman in a derogatory way. It is especially bothersome when they think it's cool to say, "She's built like a sister" when referring to a White woman that they find 'fine.' What? I've even heard Black men say that a woman of another race has lips or a butt like a "sister." Really? I don't know about you, but I think that's so twisted. Although I haven't heard that statement as much as I did in the past, that is what we as Black women used to hear often. It was nasty and ugly. It was basically saying that we like your look, body, lips, hips and butt, but we would rather find someone else with those features.

When I asked about the stupidity, I received an answer that went something like this: "You get the best of both worlds. You get a sister's body and lips without the attitude." So you DO like a Black woman's looks and build? I still laugh when I replay that comment in my head. What do you define as attitude? Oh, I remember! An attitude is a misconstrued opinion. I'm fair. I get what they are saying about a 'sister's body' but that alone could be considered stereotypical; but before women started evolving (I like to call it), most Black women were curvy and had protruding butts. I think it's safe to say that is what the men were referring to when they say, 'built like a sister.'

I feel the need to break right here and make this disclaimer. I said that I would be real with you in this book and tell it like it is so here it is. Sometimes even I have to say amen or ouch! So, I do understand what "attitude" means, but I won't condone that being used as a blanket term for *all* Black women. Like I said, some people misconstrue an opinion for an attitude. Some guys take not being a push-over (i.e. being talked to in a disrespectful tone and being disrespected verbally or accepting a guy staying out all times of night). The attitude that I said I understand I believe comes from the *body language* and the rolling of the eyes, the gesture that was popular when I was growing up. Remember Dee from the sitcom *What's Happening* and Penny on *Good Times*? That kind of attitude was popular in the seventies and eighties. They'd put that hand on their hip and roll that neck and those eyes, but most people don't do that anymore. I believe that behavior is taught and groomed through certain environments. Not every Black woman neck pop or smack their lips when making a point. My mother never did it, and neither do I! I don't feel that I have to yell or roll my neck to get my point across.

Yep! True story here...

Quite a few years ago I was upset about something that had happened at work, and of course, I confronted the issue. I believe anything can be discussed as long as people do it decently and in order. My colleagues knew that I was upset and of course they all agreed that I should have been. When I took the time to confront the person I was unhappy with, I had the talk and I walked away – no foul no harm. My colleagues thought I had decided not to have that talk.

Them: "What did he say?"
Me: "We talked?"

Them: Already?

Me: "Yes."

Them: "We didn't hear anything!"

Me: "I don't confront and discuss the way you have been conditioned to think that I do in order to get my point across." (Walked right on back to my desk)

Them: "Oh!"

"Get to know me before you discuss me."

They were expecting a show and they were going to have a ring-side seat. I'm not that way. Not all of us enjoy making a spectacle of ourselves being ignorant, loud and belligerent.

For real, for real...

On a different note, one time a really good friend of mine was called to deal with a situation at work that involved some Black girls and guys who were in an altercation. I knew what the call was about, but of course I didn't go to the calls. I'm in the office all day. When my [White] friend returned she said, "I wish you were there! You could have gotten ghetto on them." Well, I was taken aback by the comment because first of all, I don't go ghetto on people, and second of all, I wanted to know why I would be a good fit for mess. It was because I was Black that I was expected to be able to handle Black girls and their ignorance during a fight. I was livid!

I asked her when she had ever seen me go 'ghetto' on someone and what made her think I would do such a thing. She meant no harm at all with her comment. I can tell you that from experience and from our friendship, but she did feel that I could get with them because I'm Black. Was that a bad thing? No; but I didn't like her feeling that I was the rough and tough one when I don't carry myself in such a manner and she had never seen me that way. It was a thought that she might have had deep down and it came out. I love this girl. We are great friends and that's why I can say that she meant no harm, it just came natural.

What I respect about her is that she and I can have decent conversations and I can correct her or call her down about saying things that are inappropriate when it comes to race. I finally said, "You are way more ghetto than I can ever be!" She said, "Yeah, you're right."

It's Just a Black Woman! Who Cares?

We all know or should know that Black women aren't equally supported in society. Prime example: a video of a woman being beaten by a White male made news everywhere November of 2019. The incident took place in the Deep Ellum neighborhood of Dallas, Texas, but I am sure anyone anywhere would probably say they've either seen the video or heard about it. That male slugged that woman in her face, on her head and even uppercut her in the face. He assaulted her while holding a weapon (gun) in his hand. The beating was allegedly over her having her car blocking the entrance/exit of a parking lot. According to the report, she tried calling for help but he knocked the phone out of her hands onto the ground. (Could be an assaultive offense). I've seen a guy given a citation for moving a female officer's finger out of his face. The woman swung at him after he knocked her phone from her hand and that's when the slugging took place. I can't stand to watch it because it's truly sickening how he hit that woman. Hate was written all over his face and in his actions. We all know that if a Black man had been caught on video or even reported of doing the same to a White woman the consequences would have been much stiffer.

When all was said and done, the WOMAN was brought up on felony charges for breaking the window of his truck. Most of us would agree that we would want to do more than break out his window. She was charged because 'they' say the damage to his truck was $2,500. I don't know what kind of windows he has, but the truck's body didn't look worth much more than that, from my view of the pictures that I saw on the news.

We have witnessed story after story like that one, and nothing happens to anyone who does something to a Black person—especially a Black woman. Black women and kids go missing more than most would imagine because it's not made known. Many of them are considered runaways so that the authorities don't have to handle their cases the same as a missing person. A Black life is just that…a Black life. Our lives have never mattered to the majority, and it is still the same story. I really hate to believe this, and it doesn't change my views on the subject at all because all lives matter to me; but I do believe (to some people) human trafficking would not be as big of a deal as it is if only Black girls and women of color were the victims.

Black Women and Healthcare

Black women suffer from the lack of healthcare. They don't care about our health or our minds. When I heard about the number of Black women that die from childbirth I couldn't believe it. I didn't know that, but I shouldn't have been surprised since healthcare isn't readily available for everybody. Pregnancy and childbirth is very natural, but it can involve complications that could kill a woman. According to the Centers for Disease Control (CDC) Black women are three to four times more likely to die from pregnancy-related complications than

White women. Why? Because it is believed Black women symptoms are dismissed in addition to the poor care that is available or no care available at all to them in their socioeconomically challenged lives. Even with insurance copays can be more than affordable. I have learned that friends of mine have had to pay thousands upfront before checking in to the hospital for delivery. Many women opt to use county hospitals to avoid the expensive fees. Please understand I am not against county hospitals, I am only making the argument of the difference between private care and county care. Many are not privileged to have the care that will aid in saving their lives and bringing healthy bouncy bundles of joy into the world.

I've had my experience(s) watching individuals get poor care from the county hospital and their branches of clinics. My dad was diagnosed with cancer and given only three months to live when we found out. He had been under the care of doctors and using the county hospital and clinics for care. He was diagnosed with COPD, asthma, and acid reflux, but he had stomach cancer, lung cancer and another type of cancer. In fact, the doctor called me on July 3, 2012 after I had picked him up from the hospital, and he told me that my daddy needed to come back to the hospital ASAP. The doctor was very apologetic and he told me that he and the team of oncologists would be there to meet me with my dad, because they had given him wrong reports. His cancer had grown and it was far gone. It was the total opposite of what he had been told in person. I will never forget his smile on his face when he got in the car and told me that his cancer had not grown and he was doing fine. How could I tell him that the doctor had called and he needed to go back right away?

It was the day before the 4th of July, and all plans were to have fun with family for the holiday, but that was far from possible after talking with the doctor. I advised the doctor that we would take him in on July 5th because from the way he was talking, one day wouldn't make a difference. Why should we ruin everybody's holiday, especially my dad's, when there was nothing more they could do. We finally went back to the doctor and the rest was downhill history.

Many times I tried to find ways to put my mom and dad on my insurance to make sure they had healthcare better than what they were receiving. Don't get me wrong. I appreciate Medicare, Medicaid or any other assistance, but I felt if I could choose their doctor for them they could live long healthy lives. I couldn't carry them. They weren't my legal dependents.

One other time I tried to make my mom an appointment with one of my doctors so that she could be seen and be taken care of properly, but I was told by the receptionist (I guess that's the title) that the doctor couldn't see her because she didn't have insurance. I told her that I would pay cash. At the time I could have paid for anything she needed done, but at the bare minimum all she needed for that day was an office visit. They said they couldn't see her. I have had an individual try to justify the rejection, but it didn't fly with me. They were too concerned with getting their money and refused to see my mom. They felt that she wouldn't be able to pay for any 'extra' that they might try to get out of her, so they denied her. I was hurt—really hurt. All I wanted was to allow her to have a fair chance at being seen by a doctor in a doctor's office and not a county clinic. I was reminded of how many people in general, but especially those in lower income areas are getting bare minimum health care and there's not a darn thing we can do about it. I believe had my dad had his own personal primary care physician, his life would have been preserved longer.

When it comes to Black people, we are just not treated the same as other people. .

Put That Down! That's Too Heavy for You! (You're a White Girl)

After you read that title, you're probably thinking I'm fishing. I'm not! This really happened.

Back when my sisters were in high school, we had moved back to my hometown that I have talked about several times throughout this book. Needless to say that some of our teachers were from back in the day and unfortunately, many of them didn't realize their bad habits and stinking thinking. They sure didn't see or acknowledge their racist ways.

My sisters were in a play and some of the cast were moving props around on stage. There were guys and girls in the play, so the guys were doing what they did back then – they moved things for the girls that were too heavy. One of the White girls picked up a heavy framed window pane and the teacher ran over to the girl and said, "Lizzy (name change), put that down! You'll hurt yourself! That is too heavy for you. You're a girl! Terry, move that window for Lizzy." My sister was like, "What? Who do I look like? What do I look like?" She-Woman? The teacher spit that off so quickly that she didn't even think about her telling the one girl to put the window down, but told the Black girl to pick it up. That is the type of 'bull' that happened far too frequently all of our lives. So we're supposed to be strong like men because people like that teacher didn't see us as being anything precious or fragile. Like I said before, there are women, and then there's Black women (to some people).

Oh but the window frame didn't get moved by my sister. She wasn't having that. It didn't help that we had lived in the city for a couple of years and then went back to my hometown. We had been given a taste of being treated fairly, so going back allowed racism to show up like germs underneath an ultraviolet light.

I don't know about you, but that kind of thing could make a person angry.

Perception is Powerful

The other day I was watching an infomercial about sex and women over forty. I have seen the title a number of times while passing through channels, but this time I decided to stop and check it out.

Different women were shown talking about their dealings with menopause and hormone imbalance. The stories the women were telling used to scare me, but now pieces of their stories are mine. I can't relate to everything they said, but I'm getting pretty darn close. I then thought about some of the hormone products that I've seen in my urologist's office as well as my OB Gyn. I've done soft inquiries about the products in the past so that I would know more about them so that when I needed them they would at least be familiar to me. Those products are expensive and they're maintenance meds, which means they will have to be purchased for a lifetime (possibly). That particular thought catapulted me to the next thought that I had after listening to the women even longer. Hmm...these women are talking about how angry they could get in a matter of seconds and how their up and down yo-yo emotions got the best of them in their relationships. Maybe that's it! Maybe hormones could be an answer to some of the anger problems that have been attached to Black women.

Products are expensive and oftentimes insurance doesn't cover maintenance products. I'm not saying that Black women aren't able to pay for medications because many of them can afford the meds and some are even describing them because of the positions they hold (doctors). Follow me here... A select few Black women didn't grow up going to counseling and seeing doctors and specialists for issues that women from other cultures and affluent socioeconomic backgrounds had access to. We are branded for being crazy or angry for the same behavior that other women get counseling or meds for, but hardly anyone wants to address that truth.

I am aware of instances where Black women who were going through menopause were monstrous acting--much like any other race of women, but Black women didn't get the same understanding as other women. Many never received the help they needed nor have been able to forgive themselves for needing help. When men go out on a limb and do the unspeakable, it's called mid-life crisis. White women have an excuse (from society) for the same things that we go through. They are considered depressed or stressed, but Black women are angry.

I can't completely blame it on other races because we've done it to our own sisters in our culture as well. We've (some) made jokes about counselors and needing help and have caused the idea of seeing a counselor as something negative. Counseling has become a stigma to much of our race—especially when I was growing up. Thank God I can see some small changes taking place in some areas of emotional and mental health in the Black race. I have a few friends that are counselors and even a couple are actually psychology instructors. The field is growing with Black personnel, so I believe it will bring about a major change in the near future. The healing that is needed will take place, and the next generations will be better for it.

Yes, All.

Allow me to talk about all races of women for a moment. Sometimes I blog about the different cases that I see women dealing with and going through. The blogs are healing and refreshing for many – including myself.

Women have a load of responsibilities. Some of the responsibilities are normal, but many of them have been dropped in our inboxes by society. I am sure you can relate to hearing someone at some point in time saying what a man needs from a woman. It's not enough to stop there, but they will also tell us how to keep the man from shutting down, leaving without physically leaving; how to keep him from ending up in someone else's bed, and how to please him and how to treat him. We're advised on how to nurture him and love him without treating him like a child making sure you don't act like his mother, but some of them act like they want a mother. We are called Mom instead of by our names, but when they want a lover they have no problem calling them by their names. We're supposed to support him without smothering him. We're supposed to let him have his freedom, but watch him enough to see if the signs are there that he might be running away from something. We're supposed to recognize when he needs to talk to a professional. We are tasked with understanding his cheating is probably a sign of his childhood issues. We're not told to stay with him through infidelity, but it's hard to leave someone you love when you're trying to understand them. I don't know about you, but I'm already getting exhausted just listing.

Doesn't this sound like a lot to do? What time does she have for herself and then her children? How can she be who she needs to be trying to be all that the man needs and all that she needs? The children need a mom that can be everything at all times. If we have children that are in different age brackets, now we have to be everything to each one but never skip a beat. We have to mother teenagers and toddlers all in one household sometimes while taking care of the role of 'wifey.' Someone will eventually be drained and stressed, and it looks to me like it would be the woman.

The Angry (or Mislabeled) Black Women

Some people say I have an attitude – maybe I do…but I think you have to. You have to believe in yourself when no one else does – that makes you a winner right there."
~Venus Williams

I know exactly what an angry Black woman looks like, but I can tell you from experience that sometimes their anger is misconstrued.

Disgruntled, Ambitious or Angry?

Years ago I had a conversation with a few friends at work and we were talking about our goals and dreams of being successful. I talked about what my day would look like if I didn't have to work an 8-5 on a daily basis. (I have been an entrepreneur at heart for many years). During our talk, one of the friends said that I was disgruntled. I'm thinking to myself, "Where did that come from?" We were both talking and planning our future businesses with enthusiasm and hope, but for some reason we weren't seen the same! She was called ambitious and aggressive, but I was disgruntled for wanting the same thing for my life.

"What makes her aggressive and ambitious, but me disgruntled?" I asked. He had no answer, so I continued.

"Your immediate response came from a deep-rooted idea that I couldn't be ambitious because of the 'angry Black woman perception. No matter what tone I used, you didn't hear ambition. You heard complaining and disgruntled. Somehow she is ambitious and wanting to better herself and you understood that quite well. Why?"

"I'm sorry. I never saw it that way. I guess you're right." He answered.

I went on to tell him that the mindset of people like him and that is where perception overrules truth and causes division.

I made sure he recognized the patterns he was going by and it's the same one that most people use. I broke it down to him because much of what is done is done out of subconscious normalcy.

He finally got what I was saying. I was appreciative of him listening to me because he had a different mindset and a way of thinking that he didn't even see. He was looking at me through the lenses that had been crafted for him through television, his upbringing and hearsay. I know it wasn't personal knowledge because he had already told me that he had never really been around women of color. He immediately went negative on me, but to him what she was doing was automatically powerful and positive. He thought nothing negative of the sort because she was 'supposed' to want more. Needless to say, an apology was given to me and I gladly accepted it. It was then when I knew he needed to be educated about not only me, but his thinking had to change altogether. He immediately took the stance that I was disgruntled and unhappy with my job. Why? He was like everybody else – go straight to negativity when it comes to a Black woman. I guess since I am Black, I had to be angry.

Wanna Work For Me? *Hell Naw!*

During the same era of time while talking about starting businesses, the 'ambitious' friend asked me a question that reminded me of The Color Purple scene when Miss Sophia was asked to be the White woman's maid. The only difference is I didn't knock anyone out and I wasn't forced to work for her anyway against my will. (You can laugh. It's okay).

We were talking about franchising a store that we both used to love to shop at and out of the blue, she asked me if I wanted to work for her at *her* (speaking in future tense) store. I paused before I spoke and asked her to repeat the question because surely I had heard her wrong. I mean, we both were talking about opening our *own* individual store, but for some reason she thought it would work out better if I worked FOR her. She didn't mean anything by it, but in her eyes it was normal for me to work for her. I asked her if she wanted to work for me! It was crazy for her to go straight to the Black woman working for the White woman. Why couldn't we open a store together? I know some of you are thinking I'm making this stuff up or making something out of nothing, but how about turning these same scenarios around or putting yourself in my place. How about that? Maybe everything that I'm saying won't be so easy to blow off if it was you

I was talking about or if it was happening or had happened to someone you know and love. Think about how you would feel, especially if you and your ancestors have always been thought of as the workers and not the employers.

It's a mindset, I tell ya!

The 'S' Word

The 'S' word is not the one that comes to mind. I remember my oldest son having a problem with saying that word when he was about two or three years old. Well, I guess I shouldn't say he had a problem with saying it, because it came out pretty clear and often. He would say the word at the darndest places – like church! It never failed. When he decided to say it, the church would be quiet or during a time when the congregation was supposed to be quiet, like during announcements. Talk about wanting to slide underneath the church pew. I can't lie. It is very possible that he heard it from me back in my earlier days. I call them my B.C. (before Christ) days.

The 'S' word I'm referring to right now is the word **submissive**. Yikes! Yes, I said it. They say that Black women aren't submissive. That's a bold statement that covers way too much and way too many people. What does that look like to you, and who told you that nonsense?

Lots of women hate the 'S' word – not just Black women. I know that to be true because I happen to have friends of all races.

They say that we are hard to get along with, and we are not submissive in our relationships or to anyone in authority. I keep saying, 'they', so who is they? Good question. I can't identify 'they' because it's really a majority of an entire society.

Some people are self-sufficient. I'm a self-sufficient woman in a number of ways, but I lack some sufficiency in a few areas; or maybe I haven't had to tap into that ability because I have been married for a long time. I've been married all of my adult life, so some things I didn't have to do. When I got married I was barely an adult (by age only). I wasn't even the legal age to drink or go into an adult store.

Negative comments about women having problems with submission comes from women who have been single for a long time and have done it their way, and I believe all women are judged on that merit. I understand the struggle of giving up the lead and making individual choices in a single woman's life isn't just a Black woman's issue. Women who have great jobs and careers and know how to maintain a healthy lifestyle might struggle more in the area of submission than other women.

Some women have no problem giving up their independence and staying at home depending solely on their spouses. In fact, some welcome the time to sit back and be housewives. We don't get a chance to hear things broken down for all women. We only hear about everything being about what a Black woman does or doesn't do. After several years of marriage, my sister gave up her great paying job to be home with her young sons. If a Black woman is single into her forties she is said to be everything but the right thing. She's hard to get along .Nobody wants her. She won't submit and she's this and she's that. How do you know? We get sick of being singled out and talked about for every little thing that we do or don't do..

Ms. / Mrs. Independent

I want my husband to be the leader of our home; but I also have an opinion and a voice of influence in my home. Some would probably say that I have a loud voice in my home, because my husband believes in me and my ability to make decisions about certain subjects. If being submissive is explained properly, women (all) would understand what it means and what it takes to be submissive. Most of the time we just hear that "S" word in a negative sense. When it is said, many Black women have a deleterious connection with the word and they immediately go on a defense, which is misconstrued as being rebellious or 'hard to get along with' for the men who choose to believe that theory.

"White women mind their men." Sounds a bit offensive doesn't it? Well it should because God did not create marriage for us to 'mind' our spouses. When that phrase is said to a Black woman by a White woman or a Black man says it, a Black woman [some] automatically comes back with "Go get one, because I'm not going to *mind* you." That's not what is said verbatim, but you get what I'm saying – I hope. What happens here is that we are now putting the two races of women at odds without even realizing it. The Black woman wants whoever makes that statement or is 'thinking it' to know that they are just as good as the White woman. The statement that I just made is then misconstrued as jealousy. Then the White woman feels that she is wanted more (by Black men) than a Black woman because she is easier to get along with and knows how to be a woman – unlike that non-submissive Black woman. (Yeah, right)!

Sounds crazy? I know; but it's true.

Why Isn't She Submissive (by society's standards)?

Maybe she's not considered submissive for reasons that haven't been talked about. Before we continue to talk about the Black woman who isn't submissive, let's talk about a few more things that might interfere with her being submissive. Now we're talking about submission in the authentic way—not the opinionated submission definition.

Unlike what I said earlier about women and careers, I believe there's another side to the independent woman. The independent woman seems to be able to submit easier when she is secure in her financial status, able to trust and have a healthy self-esteem. I know what the Word of God says about submission, but I'm talking about in the flesh.

A woman who has to get up and hit the floor running to work just like her man wants to be treated with dignity and respect. I'm just saying that when a person works hard for their money that person wants to make sure her money is allocated properly. Nothing is wrong with that and has very little to do with submission. When a woman has been independent for a long period of time and taking care of herself, it will take time for her to be what many describe as 'submissive.'

Women in all classes, ages and backgrounds have been known to help their husbands build companies, get their education while they supported them wholeheartedly, only to be left behind when he becomes successful. That scenario is not a Black woman's issue, it's a multicultural issue. Submission is an equal-opportunity word. Heartbreak and distrust can destroy submission. Only God can rebuild true submission and trust when it has been broken.

The other type of woman who might not be considered as submissive is the one who takes care of her household. She might be frequenting pay-day loans from rinky-dink companies that give her just enough money to cover her bills, but not enough to last her until the next payday. . Maybe it is her experience of wanting to submit, but it would be quite difficult to submit to a man who doesn't treat her like his one and only – because she's not. Maybe it is difficult for her to submit because submission takes trust and it has been broken more times that she can count, and broken pieces don't mend back together very well. No matter what glue you use, there will always be gaps when something has been broken too many times or shattered one good time. There will always be pieces that are out of place and they don't fit back together firmly.

I didn't forget about self-sufficiency. I consider myself to be self-sufficient in almost every area of my life. In my marriage I know how to hold down the house, take care of the needs of my children and my husband as well as make sound decisions. Some of those decisions have to be made at my discretion because of an immediate issue, but I also know how to consult with my husband on things that we need to discuss that involve decision making. Normally, he has the final say. I learned how to do better in that area as I got older. I used to go to a car lot and purchase a car and come home like, 'here it is.' He'd ask what I did, and I'd respond with 'what it looks like?' That was the immature me. I wasn't being headstrong or rebellious, I simply didn't know any better.

I am self-sufficient in my relationship. I am the bill payer with the money that goes in the bank because I am better at getting it done. If I get overwhelmed with something else that I might be dealing with, my husband will take over until I get back to it. So, making statements that Black women aren't submissive is too broad for me NOT to address.

Submission to Authority

I have been totally mislabeled on my job – too many times to count. First and foremost, I have been on my job for a very long time. To be exact, I have been there for twenty years (as of November of 2018). This is my second time around, because I went to another agency and stayed past the time I was able to include the time I put in before I left the company I am at now. I wanted to give you an idea through this timeline to show that I grew up on my job. I started there as a shy young woman in my early twenties, and I am now in my late forties. Many changes have occurred in my life over the course of time that I have been there.

People change, but some people don't want to accept your change. I experienced the same reluctance to *changing* at my own home in my marriage. My husband met me when I was ten years old. We married when I had just turned nineteen (two months prior), so he always saw me as the nineteen-year old girl and that caused problems after I wanted to grow up.

Throughout the years I have had the opportunity to work under many different supervisors. A few of my supervisors were hard to work under because I was already labeled by society because I was a Black woman, well-put together and knew my job. I looked more put together than I was at times, but my natural being can give the impression that I am confident and sometimes bold. That should not be a problem, but it is when you are around someone who isn't confident or has the stigma of what a Black woman is supposed to be. I was always having to fight out my own insecurities, do my job and do life all at one time.

I work better with people who see my self-sufficiency as an asset to them and the company. Sufficient and submission are two different animals, but a self-sufficient person knows how to submit. Their confidence in who they are as an individual allows them to see the necessity of submission. I am so grateful to my last supervisor who embraced the person that I am and fueled it. Another one of my supervisors was confident in my ability to be myself and do my job well, but it was something about the last one. He allowed me to show up as myself every single day. I didn't have to be *his creation* or bow to him to be right. He knew that if he would let me be me, I was good to go! We worked perfectly together because he saw me as a woman, and not just a Black woman that he would 'expect' me to be anything other than what I showed up as. I appreciate that so much. I saw him as a man and not a White man who was power hungry and wanted to throw his weight around and treat me more like a hired hand that someone he happened to supervise.He saw me as who I was, which is a Black woman that he did not pass prejudgment towards. That is what makes the world a better place to be – a better place to work. What I am saying is that we don't have to be like anything that we don't want to be, unless we choose to be that way. Insecure people and people who see you less than what God created you to be are the people who cannot see the best in a person.

Our strength has been a gift to many, but yet seen as a curse. Our strength has been labeled as controlling and headstrong, but before we get deeper into that, let's take a trip down memory lane. Shall we?

Part Three
Myths Of The Unknown

So, let's talk about a few of those myths about *all* Black women.

Instead of individualizing, we're just thrown in one big pile, and only a few of us that meet a certain criteria get to get out of the pile in one piece.

I can't even say, "Let's start with the popular myths" because we have so many! Let's explore some of the things that have been said.

Unfair Labels

There are so many labels that we have walked around with that came from others, that I can't possibly list them all.

They say we don't play golf or like hockey, they never add in the fact that we haven't been welcomed in those areas. Sure, I've heard people say that isn't true, but they know it is.

I know for me it has never been about needing more Black people to be somewhere before I felt comfortable. It's just whenever I'd show up to something where there was no one who looked like me there, it was uncomfortable. I know in my heart that it wasn't that they didn't want to be there. It was either they didn't feel welcome or had never been introduced to a particular sport or event.

Other things that have been said about us and what we don't like to do comes from what I call "surface talk". Several seasons I would go out with my daughter for her golf lessons, and I'd be so tired from trying to get her there on time, that it would have been easier to just not take her. I was running from work, but more times than none, the other mothers there had been home all day waiting for 'something to do' in the evening. It was their girl chat time. Don't get me wrong, when I finally settled at the course, it was freeing and peaceful. No matter how hot it was some days, the breeze from the waterfalls were exhilarating. The shade from the huge trees made me forget how hot it really was out there.

The message I am sharing here is this. Not all people have an opportunity or the time to do some of the things that we have been slammed for not doing.

Let's not forget the expenses of some of these *exclusive* activities and sports. When your pocket isn't lined and the doors are closed to you, it's that much harder to force the doors open. Hats off to those who have been consistent and found ways to get in.

Black Women Don't Work Out

I feel really insulted even talking about this topic, but it's obviously necessary that I do since that seems to be a topic that I have heard about way too much. Black women don't work out. Come on now! That goes right along with the myth that Black women don't watch their weight. In America, obesity is an equal-opportunity issue.

Do you know how many Black female athletes there are in the world? I can't count them all but I have a long list of names that would take me more time than I need to spend naming them. Professional athletes alone are too many to count, but when you add middle school, high school and college athletes, the numbers are astronomical. When a person hears the word athlete, most people think of a Black person. They think of major league basketball players and professional football players. There are great athletes in every race, but I'm sure for most people they associate athleticism with Blacks. If that is the case, then how does a person become an athlete without working out?

I'm not sure of how much you know about being an athlete, but allow me to enlighten you on what I do know. You can't be an athlete without putting in the work. You can play a sport, but to be an athlete is different. I've played recreational and organized sports all of my life, but as I got older, I didn't practice like I should have. I relied on my natural abilities and past athleticism to carry me through. Well, let me be truthful with that statement. I've played since I was eight years old. I started playing softball and basketball in an organized setting; so most of my life I've played some type of sport.

It was only in the past several years that my health made it difficult to do the type of working out I was accustomed to. I was never a gym rat, but I loved taking weight training classes and attending body pumping classes at one of the gyms. I've had memberships, but like many people, the busier life became with the kids, I carried the tag on my keychain as a just in case.

It just wouldn't be fair to say that all Black women don't work out or go to the gym. I have cousins and friends who stay at the gym. They watch what they eat as well as exercise faithfully. My daughter works out every single day!

I really don't know where all of the myths that have Black women attached to them originated, but it ticks me off something fierce! I can't stand to hear people say things about us and joke about what they don't know. Their jokes are what people have used against us as long as I can remember. It's not funny.

Do any of these names ring a bell with you? Allyson Felix, Gabby Douglas, Serena Williams, Venus Williams, Flo Jo (Florence Griffith Joyner), Wilma Rudolph, Sonja Richards Ross, Simone Biles, Simone Manuel, Althea Gibson, Cheryl Miller, Jackie Joyner-Kersey, Lisa Leslie, Laila Ali, Tidye Pickett (whom I recently discovered), LoLo Jones, Marion Jones, and the list goes on and on.

Now there's a new kid on the block, just in time before the book is sealed...Cori Gauff who is a fifteen-year old who defeated one of her idols and role models, Venus Williams. Gauff is the youngest qualifier in Wimbledon's history. You go girl!

How did I forget to mention Misty Copeland? Misty Copeland is the first Black woman to be promoted to principal dancer in the American Ballet Theater history! It's always unsettling to say 'firsts' when I attach a Black name to the word 'first.' Why? Because many of the firsts are for organizations that have been in existence for hundreds of years, but their doors weren't open to Blacks. Sometimes firsts can get misconstrued and people believe that Blacks just started doing a thing, but the truth is, they were doing some of those things the majority of their lives too. Labeled as first is a great accomplishment for her, even if it might have been overdue. We don't know. Misty was just too good to be denied! She was underrated because of her 'thick' (as they described her) unbecoming body as a ballerina. Misty has lots of muscles and curves and her body doesn't fit the stereotypical idea of how a ballerina should look, or at least what we've been programmed to believe about a ballerina.

The women athletes (some deceased) that I named are/were top athletes and Olympians. They are tennis players, boxers, basketball players, track stars, swimmers, dancers and more. I feel bad that I can't name all of the amazing women that I would like to name, but you should have a clear picture of why it is important not to take the negative clichéd information that we're given to heart. Look up any of the above-mentioned women and see for yourself. This is how we become knowledgeable and we can stop assuming or talking about what we don't know. Those women inspire me! They are inspirations for countless women and girls across the globe. They paint pictures that erase the lies and myths that we (Black women) are tired of hearing about us not working out.

It's so sad that many Black people have been convinced of the lies and have been made the butt end of jokes and even joked themselves, not realizing what they are doing.

Black Women Don't Swim

Simone Manuel. Two gold, two silver in the 2016 Olympics. I think she swam!

When I moved to the city, that is when I really started hearing all of the stigma relating to Black women and water. I was confused because growing up, my sisters and I would swim every single day of the summer, unless there was a storm coming. We'd get up and do our chores and put on our bathing suits and walk to the city pool. Shortly after I moved to the city, we frequented the city pool as well, so I didn't know about Black girls 'supposedly' not liking the water.

Soon I realized a lot of Black girls here in the city didn't swim much because many of them went to beauty shops to get their hair done on weekends, and it was quite pricey to get your hair done. (My mom did our hair, so that wasn't my experience). They couldn't get their hair wet and full of chlorine knowing that their momma couldn't fix it or didn't want to fix it. Most Black girls didn't have what I like to call 'wash and wear' hair. Their hair was professionally styled.

Seems like this kind of talk is what has been part of what became the stereotypical talk of all races towards Black females and their dislike for swimming.

What is wrong with Her Hair?

Before I talk about Black hair, its textures and the attention it gets from everybody in the world, I must share this piece of information first. I am pretty sure by now you've heard the story about an eleven-year old girl from Louisiana who was sent home from school because she was wearing extensions in her hair.

She attended a Roman Catholic school, Christ the King Elementary School in Terrytown, Louisiana. I absolutely could not believe what that child must have felt when she was called up to the office and sent home because of her hair. Her hair wasn't in psychedelic colors or an exotic style that could be distracting to others. She wasn't wearing the extensions down to her butt that could be considered a safety hazard to her or others. Even if the extensions were that long, that would be a personal choice, but I could at least understand if that was the case and had led to the argument, but it wasn't.

Think back for a moment. It could take some of us a while to think back to that age, but for me, it doesn't take me very long since those weren't my best years anyway. I had moved from a small country town to a big city. I didn't have the clothes that would have been considered in style; in fact, I didn't have many clothes at all. I had very few pieces that

I wore every single week. I always felt that all eyes were on me no matter what I was doing or where I was. My mind couldn't even rest on the playground or at lunch because I was uncomfortable with myself and my looks. Honestly, I don't even remember what I wore in my hometown (except for my Lil Taters pants), but it became very prevalent to me to start noticing what I had and did not have when I moved to the city. The pain of embarrassment ran so deep that I will never forget it. You are probably wondering how I started talking about the little girl at the private school and then started talking about myself. Easy! That embarrassment has been with me for almost thirty-eight years. That's why! That little girl, whose name none of us will remember, will always remember how she felt that day.

The school had reportedly said they changed the policy during the summer regarding students wearing extensions. What kind of pathetic rule is that, and why was it ever put into a policy? I mean, really! Without talking to anyone from the board that came up with the policy or any officials, I can make a strong speculation of why the rule was put into place. That policy was put into place to affect the Black students at that school. They were elementary students! How much can they get into by wearing extensions? The age shouldn't matter, but I am saying that a child in elementary school is probably wearing extensions because a parent made that decision to add extensions to their child's hair. That alone is a disrespect to the parents that are paying for their child to attend that school. I don't care if it was free! No one has a right to target anyone or a certain group of people; and that was definitely targeting. There is no way that rule would have been put into place if it didn't affect the little Black girls there. I wonder if there would have been a rule if it were all White or Hispanic students attending school there.

In case you don't know what extensions are and trying to create a picture in your mind of what her hair must have looked like, let me help you. Extensions are pieces of hair that are added to a person's natural hair usually in a braided or twisted form, but sometimes weft hair is referred to as extensions. Adding extensions isn't new or rare. The child's hair on the video were in braids a little shorter than shoulder length with curled ends. What could be wrong with the style other than being a so-called Black style? If her hair was distracting to anyone, I think it would be fair to say that the distraction probably didn't come from the other students. Maybe the distraction goes much deeper than a hairstyle. Maybe the teachers and administrators need to be checked out to see why her hair was such a distraction.

I watched that crying child being escorted from her school with all of her belongings. That made me cry, because I felt the pain and embarrassment of what she must have felt. I wonder what was going through her mind. How would she feel about her mom for making the decision to allow or encourage her to wear her hair that way? We're talking about a kid who couldn't defend herself. I also had empathy for her mother and her family. Any good and loving parent hurts when their children hurt. Her mother wasn't called to pick her child up from school because she was fighting, being disruptive or disrespectful or dressed inappropriately, but for her hairstyle! A hairstyle that was clean looking, in great taste (my opinion), and pulled up at the top. The descriptors are important because if only a surface story was told, many of you would say that a private school is a business since they are not funded by the government, and they had a right to refuse her. Every right isn't right.

They (the administration) had a right to dismiss the student; but was it right? We better stop hiding behind our rights and putting a Jesus mask on what we say and do while hurting people. I don't care how many people we fool – it's not right. It was totally unnecessary for the little girl's brother to feel that he had to go to social media and explain why his little sister wore braids. He explained that his mom had it done to save her time in the mornings. I get it, but he shouldn't have had to share anything with anyone. That was no one's business, but felt the need to share it in order for those who sided with the school and thought 'it was their policy' and they had the right to make the rule. He explained that his mother gives her braids so that she (the girl) can style her hair in the mornings in a timely manner. I am a mom. I have had a daughter to get ready in the mornings, as well as sons. It is not easy getting your children to school in the mornings, oftentimes before 8:00 AM, and being at work by the same time. I started taking children to school over twenty years ago, so I know the task. Taking kids to school in the mornings is a job before going to your job! I can write an entire book on my experiences of fighting traffic. No mother needs another issue to worry about with her children.

The story of the little girl being walked out of a private Christian school made headlines all around the country – as it should have. All of this hate and division must be exposed—one story at a time.

Don't Touch a Sista's Hair

Hair shaming has been a sport towards Black women, all of my life, but it became more known to me as I got older. I know that the stupid statement about not touching a sista's hair probably originated from Black people. I think it's so dumb because we get a negative rap already, so an ignorant statement like that one is only fuel to an already blazing fire.

We are also often shamed about how much we spend on our hair, yet not all Black women spend a fortune on their hair. People assume that we do. The more educated we become, the less people are spending on hair. Beauty is a multi-billion dollar industry that many women contribute to, but they only focus on Blacks when it comes to hair. A friend of mine who happens to be White was telling me that her niece was wanting to get her hair done again, but it was going to cost about $250. That's a lot of money! Granted it included a color, cut and style that would last for months. Before braids became something more people could do, that was about the price of getting a braided style by some stylists, which also lasts for months. Some Black women might pay more to get their hair done because it's done more often, but on average, some Black women wear styles that last as long as White women styles last. Remember, I worked around it. It takes longer to create some of our styles, but that comes with the territory, so it's important that we learn how to own the territory that we have been given; embrace it and work it! So if we ask you to not touch it, it's about our personal space and the pride we take in looking presentable.

That's A Lie Too

They'd say, "You know how a sister is about her hair! A sister will hurt you about her hair!" No. I don't know how she is about her hair. How is she? Do you mean, "You know how *some* sisters are about their hair?" Maybe we're referring to the times of styles like freezes, finger waves, French rolls and sister curls. Those were styles that you couldn't agitate. Granted some Black women kept their styles in way too long, and they already knew it; but they are not *all* Black women.

Now, in the same sense of the matter, some women have gotten difficult hairstyles that they had to be gentle with because they are not stylists and they couldn't get their hair back the way the beautician fixed it, and they wanted the style to last. I was never a fan of those styles because they had no flow and they fit the stereotypical thought of not being able to touch our hair-but that was me. I was a little rebellious, but then again, I wasn't attracted to those styles for myself. Many women around my age and a bit older relied solely upon their beauticians. The younger generation is more independent when it comes to hair now.

There's a stylist from Russia that I follow on Instagram who is gifted beyond words. His name is Georgiykot. I am fascinated with his work and his talent. I'm pretty sure his styles are not to be slept on. His styles are so out of this world gorgeous and masterfully crafted, to me they are better suited for hair shows, runways and weddings. They are most likely not expected to last weeks on in. If they were, I'm sure he would tell them how to sleep and how to wrap it up at night for safe keeping. Any exotic style takes special care and attention on any hair type.

As a side note, I have never lost sleep trying to keep my hair in place, nor do I sleep with my hair wrapped. I want to rest at night. I don't hang my head off of the bed to sleep, nor to be intimate with my husband. Personally, I have never shied away from anyone touching my hair. In fact, depending on who you are and your status in my life – I love it! (Wink, wink).

Don't Believe the Hype

We have bought into that craziness about not touching our hair and have acted accordingly. One time my great niece was patting on her head to scratch it. I looked at her and said, "Girl, scratch your head! Nothing is preventing you from scratching your head." She didn't understand. She had seen girls and grown women patting their heads to scratch, so she thought that's how she was supposed to do it too. That's learned behavior.

Many years ago, before it became acceptable for women to wear weave without being degraded and joked about, some Black women didn't allow a guy to go through their hair. It wasn't about not touching it as much of it was about not being the center of a Facebook post, YouTube video, or a comic act if the guy touched a track while stroking it. I've never heard a White guy who didn't do standup around Black people joke about his White wife or girlfriend's extensions and weave. They admired the beauty, wanted us to believe it was real and kept it moving. They didn't care as long as it was a pretty style and they looked good with it.

Inquiring Minds Want to Know

My hair might be intriguing to the curious minds wondering what it feels like, but I am not a museum exhibit, nor am I part of the petting zoo. Oh! I forgot. You can't touch anything at the museum anyway. It bothers me because I don't see anyone asking to touch a White woman's hair out of curiosity.

My best friend and I worked in the same office for nearly fifteen years, where I watched the women in her area ask about her hair on a regular basis. She would tell me about it after it happened, but of course, I told her how to stop them from asking if that was her hair – all the time.

Is that your hair? Really? It's not a stupid question if that question was asked to any woman with a pretty hairstyle, different texture, or hair that *grew a little faster* than the normal person. No matter what, it is none of anyone's business. My friend would often wear different styles, but I don't think that gives anyone a right to ask if she is wearing her real hair. Why does it even matter? Would it look any differently if it were hard or soft? Would it still be pretty? I would always tell her to put them in their places. We all liked each other and most of us were real friends, so that would have been easy to put a stop to. I told her to tell them that it bothered her and it made her feel uncomfortable about changing up hairstyles. I understand because no one wants to change hairstyles and be on display each time.

One of the same individuals walked up to me one day and felt my hair, and said, "Oh! Your hair is soft!" What did she expect? Hay? I really don't comprehend the curiosity about our skin color and our hair. Maybe I can't comprehend because I have never cared whether or not their hair was soft. I have watched reality shows where I know when the women on the shows are wearing extensions. No one says anything! If a White woman wears weave, it is cosmetic. If a Black woman wears weave, it is everything wrong. I have even heard Black men say weave is a deal breaker or saying they want a *real woman.* Oh well! What's a real woman anyway? Good luck finding one that wears no cosmetics at all, because that would be considered real to me.

You see, when we say you can't touch our hair, that's wrong. Other races of people actually thought you couldn't touch it. I've been around people who would ask another Black person, "Can I touch it?" I'd just look and shake my head, thinking to myself, "It's not a pet!"

I feel that Black women are the only women that so many people have something to say about regarding every inch of who they are as a person, and we get tired of it.

Today's Black Woman

Many things have changed according to the way Black women take care of their hair, so I know what they are referring to when they say don't touch our hair; but to make that blanket statement about all of us is false.

Over the years, I have gone to the school to either drop my daughter off or pick her up and I couldn't tell whether the kids were getting out of school for the day or just finished with recess. My daughter would laugh at me because I'd say something like, "School is just now starting, right?" She'd say, "Mom!" Some of the girls' hair were torn up! They didn't care who touched their hair or played with it.

The statement about not being able to touch a Black woman's hair is not as relevant today. Black women and girls have become more educated and versatile when it comes to wearing hairstyles and they realize there is more freedom with their/our hair. Some of the statements that people are making about not being able to touch a Black woman's hair is ancient. It's as old as saying that all White women wear Aqua Net hairspray. I'm not knocking that hold of Aqua Net though. I've used it too!

Women years ago wore certain styles that were designed to last a while. As I mentioned before, Black women spent money on getting their hair done and some styles were impossible for the average person to fix after it messed up. Remember my friend who went to the beauty shop for a shampoo? Granted, some people left their styles in place way too long and took the 'don't touch my hair thing' too far, but that's exactly where it comes from, and it's time to stop saying that; and Black women need to stop feeding into that bull. Young people have inherited the clichés and thoughts that they have no idea of where they originated or how they started in the first place.

Black Women Are On Welfare

Really? Do you really buy that? I don't; because I know better. I'm a Black woman and I'm not on welfare. My sisters are Black and they're not recipients. My mother wasn't. I know it exists, but to feed into the stereotype of all is unfair.

Are there Black women welfare recipients? You bet there are! Welfare recipients come in all races and ethnicities. I have known people from all races that had their times on welfare, waiting on government checks and using food stamps (aka EBT). People who hold prominent positions in our community have shared their experiences of living on welfare, before becoming what they dreamt to be and beyond. There is nothing wrong with getting assistance - that's why it's there. I applaud those who used it for what it was for, and moved on when they were able to do so.

If a poll was taken in an area that was poverty stricken with Whites, then the numbers would be higher for White people receiving welfare. If we take that same poll in a lower income predominantly Black area, you will find more Blacks on welfare in that particular area. What I am getting at is in order to make bold statements about subjects that are so negative, we should do our best to make the statements in truth and not from our biases (preconceived assumptions).

I am confident in saying that I believe the lack of jobs that are available for Blacks have contributed to the problems of the welfare system. If you think that's not true, then ask the folks in California and Chicago whose parents and grandparents lost everything they had when the big companies they were employed at shut down or were moved out of those areas.

I am grateful that welfare was started because of the good it has done when it came to feeding hungry children.

It started out as a way for poor single mothers to be able to stay home and take care of their children. That was a good thing. It was also believed that having mothers at home would help prevent children from being on the streets, and they could see after their own children. Even better!

Black Women Always Have Kids

I get so tired of hearing Black women have kids. Black women don't have kids by themselves! Ugh! In fact, all races have kids! It's such a stupid to make a statement.

The last time I checked, two people conceive kids – whether through intercourse or artificial insemination, it takes two. A plant doesn't just spring up out of nowhere without a seed being planted. The same goes for a problem. It starts somewhere. We have to start at the root; and the root is not Black women having kids! The root is the lack of education and applying the education that is received.

Black women having kids come from Black men leaving the Black women with the kids. The same woman that will talk about the man who isn't with his children will sometimes be the one with the man who has 'Black' children somewhere!

If we're going to address the problem, then address the entire problem and not just bits and pieces of it.

Black Women Aren't Sexy (or Romantic)

Says who? Who said Black women aren't sexy? I'm a sexy woman and I'm Black! I'm a very romantic person and love to be romanced.

I won't sit here and try to speak for all, because not all women are sexy to everybody—some just aren't sexy, and it's not just the Black women who aren't. It all goes back to what we have been conditioned to believe what sexy is.

I'm addressing all of these things that we know hold true for all races, but if these things weren't stated about us as Black women only, I wouldn't even be writing this book.

Sexiness could be about what a person wears, how they smell, how a person carries themselves, how they walk, what they do, etc., it's an appeal that anyone can have. Unfortunately, sexy have always been connected to someone of a race other than Black. (I.e. commercials, movies).

Black Women Aren't Desirable

I know you've heard that Black women aren't desirable or no one wants Black women. If you haven't heard it, maybe you've never heard it put so bluntly.

One day my husband made an innocent comment which was more of a rhetorical question. We were watching basketball, and he said, "I wonder what made Dirk (Nowitzski) marry a Black woman." I said, "Why wouldn't he?" He said, "I didn't mean it like that!" He responded with an attitude, but I told him that's the bullcrap that people ask themselves and others as if there's a problem with marrying a Black woman. I was a little rough with my response, but for a person like me who studies inequalities, that was a triggering moment. We have to stop saying that people didn't mean any harm by what they say or do and let it go. We have to address issues head on. I know he didn't purposely ask that question with malice intent, but I wanted to educate him on what I heard and how I took it. He's my husband so I know that he didn't mean it negatively. He didn't see that what he was doing was a contribution to the pile of poop thoughts America has had about Black women. I asked him if Dirk had married a White woman would that question be asked. I said, "He'd still be marrying out of his race since he's German.

You see what I'm saying? Race seems to matter most when it comes to a Black woman.

No one finds it strange when a biracial person marries either someone other than another biracial person. They are expected to marry whomever. That should be the case with everyone.

We have to get out of this "stinking thinking" that some of us have about Black women that it's a privilege for that Black woman to be chosen by someone other than a Black man. That's absurd!

Black Women Stink

I've heard this BS before, but allow me to share content from a letter that someone wrote and it happened to circulate around social media.

A post 'letter' went around on the internet was from a female named 'Jamie.' Jamie was a self-proclaimed White woman who had a mouthful to say about Black women and their bad relationships or the lack of relationships with Black men. I won't even try to say everything that I remember about the letter, but I remember 'Jamie' talked about why they (White women) were taking all of the Black men from Black women.

Well, she started out with a lie, because they are not all taken, but that's what people like to believe. Anyway, 'Jamie' went on to say that Black women all wear weave, they stink, they are hard to get along with, don't watch their weight, and several more untrue statements. Ever since I read the post, I have been stuck on the Black women 'stink' lie. I am not going to be petty and make any comparisons, but I am a Black woman. I was raised by a Black woman, and I have four Black sisters. I also have Black friends. They don't stink! I have smelled funky women of all races – believe that! From hair to private, I've smelled all races! Funk is an equal event that is shared by many. To say that Black women stink was unnecessary and a sign of 'Jamie's' own insecurity and jealousy. Maybe "Jamie" (I'm sure it's a pseudonym) grew up watching the same commercials, seeing the same shows, and reading the same magazines that I did—never seeing us with soap and shampoo!

Whenever someone puts down others, it's to lift up themselves.

Jamie went on to say things like, Black women are too big, too materialistic, gossipy, and have too much baggage. I wonder where that baggage comes from. I had to stop there to address that because I have heard about baggage, as in children and bitterness or anger of past relationships. The woman alone doesn't make children. Before anyone of any race talks about Black women having children out of wedlock, I encourage you to look at the other parent of the child. I believe that there are too many children born out of wedlock and not just Black children either. There are too many Black children in single household families, but they're not the only ones. I would love to see more men stay with their children as well as women making better choices of having children – timing and with whom. That is definitely something to address, but it wasn't 'Jamie's' place to say it in such a derogatory manner.

I have been admired and approached by White men and Hispanic men regularly – from my twenties to my forties! Unfortunately, many in the past had a fear of crossing the line of color. They were afraid of how they would be treated by their own family, friends, and most of all their own race in general. It was not their lack of attraction that kept them at bay, or it was because I was married. Their fear of what society would think kept them in what they felt was their place. Some people might have convinced themselves that Black women aren't attractive or desirable because they stopped at the color of their skin.

Black Men Don't Want Black Women

Whaaat? Wait! Now I know that's a lie. However, I know that's what is shown in the media, so I can understand how people can take that and run with it. Imagine how a young lady in her teens would feel to hear that she isn't wanted by a man of her race. If you think it doesn't do any damage, then imagine the other way around. Imagine young whitefemales being told that White men don't want them. Instead, they want Black girls. It doesn't sound right because you haven't lived in my world.

Of course there are many Black men married to White women. Many of those men are athletes who were once married or in relationships with Black women. Sometimes their circle changes and they are around circles of people and women that are closed to the average Black person. You are the sum of the five people you hang around.

Some Black guys go off to colleges that are predominately White. If they are an athlete, that puts them in the front line to be 'picked' or they get to pick for themselves. Now they get to choose the popular girl or the cheerleader because he has a status that allows him to go home to meet daddy!

I get so sick at the end of a professional sports' championship game. You see the families run on the field and all of the cameras follow the star of the game. The Black guys have White wives on their arms. There are Black men who have Black wives and Black children. Why are we not seeing these guys? We only see them when they are in trouble or have allegations against them for 'cheating with a White woman.'

There are some Black, Dominican and Hispanic men that seek out White women once they become notable, but to say that 'Black men don't want a Black woman' doesn't sit well with me. Most importantly, it doesn't hold true for all Black men.

We always hear about the Black men who married White women, but we don't talk about the famous Black men who married Black women. Although there are too many to name, let me name a few for you: Denzel Washington, Idris Elba, Will Smith, Boris Kodjoe, Russell Wilson, Deion Sanders, Steve Harvey, D.L. Hughley, Morris Chestnut, Jay-Z, Jesse Williams, Sterling K. Brown, L.L. Cool J, Steph Curry, LeBron James, Chris Paul, Russell Westbrook. At this time, these guys are married to beautiful Black women. The list could go on and on with actors, athletes and other celebs. I had to do this because we are always pointed in the direction of thinking Black women aren't getting married, and no one wants a Black woman.

All Black women are not the lone wolves, no matter how they want us to believe that we are.

True Beauty

We've all heard at one time or another that 'black don't crack.' For what it means, we know that it's true. Scientists have given reasons as to why it doesn't 'crack' (meaning look old), but even with that, I see a problem with the explanations. I have a problem with someone trying to explain our skin pigmentation assuming that dark skin is tougher. If that's the case, then why are they saying that white skin is weaker and it tears easily and looks old quickly? Don't wait for that question to be asked. It might make someone think differently about the natural beauty of White women and they dare not want that to happen.

Everything that is good or positive about us has a backlash or a theory behind it. I remember being compared to dark-colored clothing, saying dark colors keep you cooler. What does that have to do with me? I'm not made of cotton or polyester.

I believe subtle statements that have been made to me and towards me throughout my life have entered my head subconsciously causing the pain and low self-esteem I have carried with me. I wonder if they have the same thing happened to others.

Beauty by Numbers – Do the Math

Several years ago, I saw a segment on television and unfortunately it's also available online (the WORLD WIDE WEB), about *precise* facial proportions of the perfect face that equates to being beautiful. I said unfortunately because the internet is where the world seems to get their answers to life's issues and questions—especially our young people. Precise means correct, accurate and particular! You know what is really precisely crazy about all of this? Someone took time to come up with this chart!

This chart/tool that *someone* came up with basically shows proportions and measurements that are supposed to calculate if a person is beautiful. It measures how far your eyes are apart, how many inches your brows are from your forehead, your hairline, your nose width, etc., and that is supposed to determine your beauty. Is that not ridiculous? They were hoping to make measurements that would omit Black women from being considered beautiful by a science. The broader the nose is, then the further apart one's eyes might sit. The other hope is that it would throw off a measurement somewhere else causing an average Black woman's measurements to be 'off the charts.' That is ludicrous! You can't help how far apart your eyes are, how wide your nose is, how thin or thick your lips are, or what shade your skin is. It's crazy to even think that people have the nerve to say what's beautiful according to proportions and measurements of the face! The question that I have is who set those standards? Who gets to say what is beautiful and what isn't?

For far too long we have allowed people to dictate what they believe is beautiful, but one person's preference does not constitute the truth. One race can't dictate what is beautiful. One person might say that the most beautiful nose to them is one that is very thin, long and pointed on the end. Another person might say they are attracted to a broader-type nose. Someone else might like a rounded nose. Each feature attracts someone, but not everybody. How can someone say what is perfect? It's perfect according to somebody's standards.

What about eyes? Some people have barely opened eyes while some might have bright wide-opened eyes. Some have rounded eyes, some almond shaped, and some might have beady eyes. I know the term "beady" is kind of funky, but that's what I was brought up to say. Don't judge me. (LOL)

Your People Magazine

Each year a certain magazine would name the top 100 beautiful people; and each year I sit and wait to see just how many beautiful Black people would make the list. There have been a couple to make the list here and there, but oftentimes they were the new face(s) on the scene that fit what the majority portrays as beauty to them on a Black person.

Sometimes I believe magazines and movies would choose the least attractive Black woman (their thinking) as a way of influencing society to create an image of our beauty so that they didn't compete with anyone else. Totally my opinion! What do I mean by that? they choose the woman with the features they want to portray and they have already deemed as undesirable. Most times they'd jack up her hair to make everything except her looks be the focal point. They do okay (just okay) with picking the handsome Black men for their list. One of the problems is they don't put enough of them in the magazine. In addition to some of Hollywood's male actors, I wonder if they have seen many of the football guys without their helmets. Have they seen T.I., Idris Elba, Shemar Moore, Morris Chestnut, Common, Omari Hardwick, Denzel Washington? I mean…I am just asking. There are so many more. I know some have made the list, but I'm waiting to see how many or which ones made it shouldn't be the case. I find it strange that only a couple Blacks out of one hundred people can make the list. There are many handsome Black men that are not the 'hot commodity of the year' but it doesn't make them irrelevant. The most popular guy or girl in hit movies at the time seems to be the one they will *allow* on the list.

That's why Blacks started making their own lists.

Your Lips Aren't Black Enough

I can't make this stuff up!

"Your lips don't stick out enough", said the dentist to the patient.

I just had to say it like that, because that's how I felt when my former dentist told me that. He meant no harm whatsoever by that comment. I will always believe that and nothing can change my mind unless someone who works with him tells me something different.

A few years ago, when I was at the dentist office and my dentist told me I needed braces because my profile wasn't like the one of an African American (referring to the area between my lips and my nose). I didn't know how to respond to that. I hope he wasn't looking for a 'thank you' because he didn't get one. I absolutely adore that dentist. His chairside manners are beyond caring. He is the sweetest person you could ever meet. He is one that I enjoy having work done from, so I'm not complaining about him as a person. He's a complete sweetheart in my opinion. He just said either what he thought to be true, or what he had been taught in dental school; or maybe it was self-taught through years of observation. He felt that I needed braces to bring out my top lip more. You think you're puzzled! What about me sitting there listening to that? I never addressed his comment, and that is not like me at all. Anyone who knows me knows that I will address what I have a question about, or something I don't like. I had a moment of when you think of what to say once you leave. Funny thing is, I still don't know what I would say because he really didn't think anything of what he was saying. In other words, he was not being mean or hateful. He just felt that my top lip was too flat to be a Black person. I'm not a dentist. I'm not sure of what he thought or had been taught about my lips and how they should look as an African American (Black) woman, but that wasn't cool. I guess my lips are too flat on the top! Another one of those, 'not good enough or not fitting in moments.'

Who says that I should look a certain way or have certain features because of my race?

This is what we've had to put it all of my life and my mother's life. I don't think the ugliness stood out in many of the ways we see it today, but I would think it was because Blacks had their own thing and didn't and couldn't mix with Whites. Black had their families, their neighborhood stores, and anything else they needed. They were sufficient in what they had and were proud of their families.

Truth Be Told

Now that we've talked about some of the myths and beliefs, let me explore some truths. You see, Black women have been degraded for far too long. We've been discredited or given no credit at all for the gifts that we do have. Allow me to share.

Our Skin

If dark skin was so unattractive, then why is darker skin desired by so many individuals? Why did tanning salons all of a sudden start popping up everywhere? Research reveals that the tanning industry has about ten to thirty million tanners annually. If tanning is used to improve appearance, then I guess darker skin isn't such a bad thing after all. If dark skin is unattractive, then why do stores sell tanning sprays, bronzing makeup and products for darkening the skin? It's called supply and demand! The stores supply because there's a high demand for those items. From using beds to sprays, many are desperate for a darker complexion. Some even risk getting skin cancer from roasting in the sun. We have been degraded all of our lives for our darker skin.

What about full plumped lips? Before lip injections and surgeries became popular with average people who were not part of the Hollywood and the entertainment industry, companies created lip-plumping lipsticks. Also before injections and the popularity of plumping, women used a lighter color lipstick with high gloss in the middle of the bottom lip to give their lips more definition and a pooched, full look. I know because not only do I know makeup, I used to sell for a company who sold lip-plumping products before the products hit all of the markets.

Black women aren't the only women who wear extensions and wigs. In fact, Black women caught on to the trend much later. Although extensions have been accepted more, there's still an underlying thought that some people have--if a Black woman has pretty hair it must not be hers.

Our butts, oh my word! Our butts were never accepted by the majority (at least not openly), but then pants and undergarments were designed with padding added to create an illusion of having a nice, round, fuller, better looking butt. Different exercise programs that promised a bigger, more round and lifted butt became very popular in the early nineties. Exercise machines were created to lift, round and tighten the glutes. Fitness centers were hiring people who could teach classes that focused on building up women's butts. It's okay; but what isn't okay is the fact that the very thing that we as Black women were taunted about was what others were buying. Beauty is a multi-billion dollar industry. If all of those attributes (darker skin, bigger butts and lips) aren't attractive, then why are billions of dollars spent for those changes?

A Class All By Itself
Black Royalty

The world was watching! From the moment the two were spotted together prior to becoming a known item, to the stroll to the royal altar. The world looked on as the handsome Duke took the hands of his beautiful, flawless fiancé and looked into her eyes as the priest said, "Will you Prince Harry take thee Meghan (Markle), to be your lawfully wedded wife...?

Of course the ceremony was nothing like ordinary, but one familiar thing was that the two hearts that were beating for one another playing to the tune of their own beat of love. It was what every woman finds beautiful. The world continued to watch the stunning couple, now known as the Duke and Duchess of Sussex.

The marriage news turned the stomachs of many individuals while others rejoiced at what could be called be the marriage of the century. Much of the world was wowed by the magic of Harry and Meghan's unbiased love for one another. As the news of the expecting Duke and Duchess spread throughout the land more and more individuals became frustrated and even angry that the two were about to bring a half Black child into the royal family. So much negative energy.

Many masked their thoughts and anger with doubts of if it was really love. Crazy thing is that celebrities marry all the time. The question of true love between the couples doesn't warrant the anger Megan and Harry received.

Some questioned how they would make a marriage last coming from two different backgrounds. Was it the backgrounds in question or the color of their skin?

I would hate to have so much negative energy sent my way if I were them. So, I pray for them and ask God to keep them and protect them from their known enemies as well as those covered by sheep's wool.

I explored a bit about interracial dating already, but I want to go deeper into a different direction. Everybody's definitely not in favor of the mixing of races. I know because interracial dating and marriage hits home for me.

Interracial Dating, Yes. No. Maybe?

Some time ago, a White male friend and I were talking and one question that people often ask came up. He said that he had been asked if he would date a Black woman. I replied with, "I absolutely hate that question because it's as if you're asking if a person would date an alien or an animal!" Ugh! He never saw it that way, but he understood what I meant. Now don't get me wrong. I have been asked if I would date a White guy. I didn't take offense to it, but it seems to be a trick question when people ask about dating a Black woman. Maybe it's because the opinion of the White man has been held as the one to go by. So if they say yes they would date a Black woman, a Black woman is supposed to feel they are 'somebody.'

The crazy thing to me is that White people can date or even marry Asians, Italians, Greeks, Irish, and almost any other race. Nothing is hardly ever said. It's as if it's normal. Well, it is normal, but I can't understand why it's not looked at that way when it comes to a Black person.

Interracial Dating (I know he didn't!)

Several years ago a friend (that I worked with) and I used to go to lunch together regularly. We went at least twice a week—sometimes more. Those who didn't know us thought we were in a relationship together, but once they got to know us they knew we were just close friends. Once I was at my neighborhood Walmart, and a cashier there said, "Where is your husband?" I'm thinking to myself, *'She doesn't know my husband.'* When I realized where I knew her from [which was my job - another department], I knew exactly whom she was talking about. I said, "Oh no! He's not my husband! We work together! I have a husband, and it's not him!" I laughed, she laughed, and then she said, "I didn't know." She only saw us on campus, but I guess she was young and didn't put two and two together that we just worked in the same office.

When we'd go to different restaurants for lunch, the ugliness that we experienced each time we were together was normal for me, but he had never had that kind of treatment and *looks* for just being with someone. Remember, he was a friend and coworker, so there was nothing out of the ordinary about us being together—other than race. Had we both been of the same race, we would not have been looked at (like we were) for being together.

Most of our outings for lunch were around noon or shortly before; which was the time most senior citizens would be out for lunch. Well, you know what that means. I can't say that we didn't get a smile or two from a couple of people now and then, but trust me, it wasn't often. I don't know if they were fake smiles or not, but that is something that I choose not to try to dissect.

It wasn't long before he started noticing what we were experiencing each time we were out together weren't isolated events. That was the normal behavior of people when they would see us together. Again, not everybody, but many! This was around the years of 2008-2013 I don't remember the exact timeframe, but I do know that it was too recent for mistreatment of couples in interracial relationships to be happening in our society. Put it this way, it was the [pre] make 'American Great Again' days. Our time together were the days when people didn't show their hate for others the way they are showing it today. When I hear people talk about certain issues referencing race and how things have changed, I think to myself – changed for who? It sure hasn't changed for Blacks. I take that back. It has! It is worse than before. One day he and I went to a restaurant (that is now closed, and I will not name), located on a popular street (Hulen Street) in our city. When we first walked into the restaurant, it was as if we had walked into Alaska with a swimsuit

158

on. Little elderly couples turned around and looked at us with disgust. One little freshly teased-white-haired frail woman nearly fell out of her booth when we passed where her and her husband were seated. No. I wasn't looking for anything.It was right in front of me. I have to make that disclaimer, because I can't tell you how many times people have said, "I didn't see that. I don't be 'looking' for that kind of stuff." They stared so much that I thought I would have to close the mouth of some and help others off of the floor after they fell out of their seats! Some were pointing, and others just gave us looks that would kill us dead if it were possible. It was crazy! I think that was the worst time we experienced in a restaurant. I bet they were thinking, *I'm glad he's not my son!* For that matter, I'm glad he wasn't either!

The host seated us, and told us that our waitress would be with us momentarily. The waitress came over to take our drink order and said she'd be back. You know, the normal routine...

When she came back, I noticed she was catering more to my friend than me, but it was okay. I have had waitresses do that quite a few times even when I go out with my husband. My husband and I would laugh about me getting upset about the female waitresses catering more to him and his needs than mine. I would always say, "She does know that I control the tip, right?" I meant that too. I'm just saying. It wasn't long before I realized the waitress that we (my friend and I) had wasn't just catering for a good tip. She was catering to him because he was White, and she wanted me to know that I was not welcomed to be served by her while I was with him. I couldn't understand that—especially because of her age, and she happened to have a few Black coworkers as well. She never acknowledged me after she took my order. He noticed her behavior, but he didn't want to bring it to my attention any more than it already was [right in my face]. Whenever she'd come back to the table, she would talk directly to him. I think the final straw was when she turned her back to me completely and started flirting with him as if I was a nobody and was totally invisible. She didn't know whether we were together as a couple or not. She had not asked, and he did not give her any indication that he was available by flirting or 'coming on' to her. At this point, I had enough myself. I don't believe in going off on anyone immediately.. Even the couple sitting at the table across from us looked at her with disgust because they too saw what she was doing. They looked at me like they wanted me to know they didn't think it was cool for her to be treating me that way. You know how it is when people give that look like, *I'm not in that!* It wasn't hard to tell what she was doing since the aisles were fairly close and not many conversations were private unless you whispered.

My friend had all that he could take as well. I was so proud of him. He would normally just say, "Let's go" or ask me am I okay. He didn't react that way that time. He said, "Look, I am here with her, and I'd appreciate it if you would respect that." She looked at him as if he had said something wrong to her. She looked like she wanted to say, "Well, I'd never!" She turned with a slight jerk and walked away. I was really proud of him because normally he liked flattery. However, he realized the behavior wasn't about flattery at all. It was pure disrespect towards me because of the shade of my skin.. He apologized for her actions, but I told him he didn't need to apologize for her. She needed to apologize for her own actions. Since that wasn't going to happen, I really didn't care. I don't know what she expected to get or what she has gotten in the past, but that behavior was a no-go for me. If he had not said anything, I would have said something. I believe she was mostly embarrassed and of course angry that he would not allow her to disrespect me - no matter what she thought about us being together. She didn't get one copper cent from us for a tip.

That was one of the most disrespectful times I have had while being with anyone—especially a man. When a person blatantly disrespects someone simply because of race, their ignorance is beneath me. I would understand if I was treating her in an insolent manner, but I am never that way towards anyone for no reason at all. Even if I am having a bad day, I can push through and treat someone the way they should be treated, because it's not their fault that I'm not in a good mood. I might not be as talkative when I'm in a foul mood, but I won't treat them wrong or with disrespect. I don't treat anyone poorly, so I definitely wouldn't treat the cook or the waitress bad and expect to eat the food *they* will be serving me. I mean, come on! How arrogant and stupid would that be? People do that and I look at them like, *"You do know that they are bringing your food, right?"* That's why I never understood why slaves were treated like trash and the people treating them that way ate the food the slaves cooked. I finally concluded why they treated slaves the way they did and ate the food the slaves cooked and served to them. I believe they treated the slaves that way because they knew that the slaves had been cowardly and they had instilled so much fear within the slaves. They controlled their minds through fear tactics. The slaves knew what would happen if they tried anything; so a slave wouldn't dare attempt anything [stupid]. I get confirmation after confirmation why I was born in my time – the seventies. I wasn't made for those times. Slaves were beaten for something as simple as reading, let alone trying to do anything to the food of those that treated them like garbage. They were beat *just because* or for hateful entertainment. They beat the slaves for any little thing they did or didn't do, so tampering with the food would have gotten them killed! Can you imagine how brainwashed they were? That is how powerful a mental stronghold can be. Wow!

I assist victims who have experienced different forms of abuse. I can't number the times that I have been asked by others why the people stay in abusive relationships, or why they never told anyone about the abuse. Abusers use tactics much like slave owners and others who controlled slaves. They used things like fear of where they will go, the lack of money, and having no one to depend on. Slaves had greater things to fear such as being beat and killed, but it's all one in the same. The mind is powerful; but in the same sense, that power can be used negatively causing another person to be weak.

The restaurant fiasco was one of the most disrespectful times I have experienced, but I can't say it was the worst. I have had way too many situations dealing with unfair treatment to share in one book. It's sad, but it's true. I would have to make a documentary if I shared all of my stories as well as the stories of others.

She Can Be Served, but Not You

Imagine how hard it is for a mom to tell her son to be careful constantly because he is in an interracial relationship, and he lives in a city notorious for racial inequality. I don't have to wonder. I am that mom.

Many stories have been shared with me about the unkind treatment they have received in places. My son doesn't share these things because he doesn't want me to worry. I learned about an incident that happened recently in a restaurant they went to visit.. My daughter-in-law was sharing with me the hurt and anger that she felt when a server chose not to serve her and my son. At first she overlooked the treatment. However, when the server flat out refused to serve them, she had had it. The worst part of it all is that they are justified for their actions in places of business. Most people would say, "Just don't go back, or talk to a manager." I would say those things as well, but I also know that sometimes it doesn't do any good because the manager oftentimes condones their employees' behavior and them feeling that way. Out of respect for their position, the manager will say they will talk to the employee about their behavior and never do. If a person presses the issue, (only if they do or take it to the media) then something more will [possibly] be done. I'm grateful for video on cell phones now that allow people to capture bad behavior and share it with the world of social media users. If it's bad enough, then the news will oftentimes acquire the video and air it. I like that they are doing that now because for too long things were going unnoticed and unheard of.

Too bad she didn't think to record the unfair treatment they received from the waiter.

Although not all Black people are supportive of interracial relationships, it is more accepting in the Black race than in the White race. I rarely hear Black people talk negatively about interracial relationships. Most Black people accept interracial relationships and they move on. Even if they don't accept it, they don't try to make the individuals miserable or threaten their lives.

I'm Use to 'Em

One night, (I'll call him John for now) John and I were out looking for items to furnish his new apartment. We were such good friends and I enjoyed helping him at any time – especially during the tough time he was going through. One late evening, we went to a suburban area Walmart store. We went there because it was close to his home. The only reason I thought about going across town to another Walmart was because a store across town would be more comfortable and accepting of us being together. You see, we didn't have the same feelings towards the store closest to him. He thought nothing of it. I'm in my car driving and thinking all at the same time, "He expects me to go out here? Really?" I already knew what was going to happen—so I thought.

I am laughing in my mind already while writing this. The memories do this to me even almost ten years later. When John and I see each other, we still laugh about what I said to him that night. We finally made it to the store, parked next to each other and got out of our cars. He said, "Are you okay? Are you comfortable?" He asked the questions because it was obvious that, while still in the parking lot, we were about to have some major issues. I said, "I'm fine John. I'm used to 'em." He said, "What is 'em?" I said, "Them!" He said, "You sound like what others say when they say 'those people.' I had never thought of it that way. In fact, I didn't mean anything by it; but I understood why he said that.

We laughed so hard about that night – all night and thereafter. He knew I didn't mean what I said in a derogatory manner like the 'those people' statement. He said, "I know you didn't mean anything by it. You were just talking; but it was funny how you said it." I apologized through my laughter each time we talked about it. He didn't try to defend them, and I didn't try to defend myself. That is how we learn from each other on both sides.

We made that incident the highlight of the night and ultimately the foundation of our friendship. If we focused on how people treated us in that store and on what I said, it would have ruined the night and hindered what we set out to do.

That was the beauty of our relationship. We used situations like that to talk about touchy subjects and learn from one another; and we learned a lot from each other over the course of our years together. Instead of sitting back and passing judgment, he was able to see what I experienced firsthand. I am forever grateful because maybe what he gleaned from our friendship will allow him to make better choices and be less judgmental of others because of their skin color and race. Well, hopefully.

Years later he once told me that he never knew what that behavior looked like (until that night), and he sure had never experienced it for himself. As I said before, we had gone through situations like the one in the restaurant on different occasions, but I think deep down John thought women were jealous of us being together. He thought the women had a problem with me 'having him' and they were jealous because they couldn't 'have him.' You'd have to know John to find the humor and truth in those statements. There was so much that I taught him by just being around me for those few years. Oftentimes we would say that people of opposite races should spend time with one another and see things from the other side. Most people go their entire lives assuming instead of knowing. How can someone see racism if they have never been exposed to it? Racism (on the giving end) is oftentimes seen as someone being too emotional, looking too far into things, being sensitive or just flat out complaining. Nearly always, it is none of those things.

I learned that all bad behavior isn't intentional. Some people just don't know—like John. It's their normal. It was 'John's' normal that he knew nothing about Black people, and honestly, I think had he not met me he wouldn't have cared to know anything about us. He didn't have a need to know. His world was all White and he only saw a touch of Black for a few hours a day. They never penetrated his life's patterns. I used to say to him, "You don't know what to think of me, do you?" I'd say, "You have never seen anyone like me because I don't act Black or White. I just act Angel." I meant that. I always told him that I didn't fit what he had seen or expected of me. I didn't do the rolling of the neck, popping the shoulders, shifting the weight from one hip to the next, talking loud, going off a person. You know... the "stereotypical" black woman.

When we (he and I) were growing up, that is how people showed Black women on television and unfortunately still do. He didn't know how to answer that question at first, and finally he realized it was a rhetorical question anyway. I didn't need an answer. It's obvious that my skin is brown, but for most people it would be hard to say that Angel acts Black or White – if they are honestly speaking. I am a person first, and I demand to be seen as such by anyone that I am in communication with, no matter what. I can't make people change or treat me a certain way; but I can teach them how I expect to be treated (through my response) to how they treat me.

The crazy thing is that we both discovered that John had no problem dating a Black woman, but he never knew he was attracted to a Black person because his father was a racist and would forbid him dating a Black girl. I would mess with him now and then about being attracted to Black women, and one day he admitted that he doesn't have a preference and some Black women are as attractive to him as any other race of women. He went through his teen and adult years omitting the feelings that he could have possibly felt for someone one day. Many adults (White males) I have had close contact with have volunteered information (to me) that they had at least one racist parent if not both. It's not that they didn't know it was wrong, it was *how it was* in their households. Luckily for some, they later found out it was wrong. For others, they use the excuse that 'that's just the way that it was back then.' How could we expect much out of someone who grew up either never seeing a Black person come around or having a foundation of racism? It becomes a cycle. They grow up and have children and their children will believe there is something wrong with Black people, and so on and so on. Most people will never admit they actually feel that way because they haven't had to face the reality of being a racist.

Drawn by Attraction, Separated by Color

When I was in high school, I think it was my senior year I ended up going out with a guy who happened to be White. I'll call him Josh. It was pure attraction. We had played softball on the same team for several seasons, and we later found out that we had been attracted to each other from day one. I knew he liked me, but back then I was extremely shy. I wasn't about to say anything to him about my feelings. After all, my mom didn't teach us to approach a guy, so that was never going to happen. He and I were like magnets anytime we were around each other. Wherever I was, there he was. Whenever we were in the dugout, we would stand together towards the end of the exit door and talk until it was time for us to take the field one of us had to go bat. I made it to every practice that we had, and so did he. It's important that I say that because practice wasn't always my favorite part of playing sports, but he made it fun.

We didn't have cell phones back then, so if you set up a date, you had to do it over the house phone, with a letter or in person. Then, you had to stick with the plan.

Our softball team consisted of different races, but the majority of the team were White. I would hear comments about me in the dugout that were geared towards Josh whenever I went up to bat. The comments weren't negative, they would be teasing him about liking me. Josh didn't know how to approach me. So one night after a few seasons had passed, we were all invited to one of the player's houses in a small backwoods town. He didn't see anything wrong with all of us Blacks coming out to his house, but we mentioned the danger of driving out there at night. He agreed that it was a little dangerous, but we all went anyway. We figured we might as well go and if anything should happen, we were all together. It was that night of the get together when the guy who invited all of us over decided to talk to another teammate on the team about Josh's feelings towards me. They were playing matchmakers. They both approached me to tell me that Josh had major feelings for me, and he wanted to know how I felt about him. I told them how I felt and of course, they couldn't wait to take the news to Josh. Thinking back on that night, it was funny because Josh was in the house as well, but he was talking through them. When he found out the feeling was mutual, he came up to me for himself.

At that moment, we didn't need anyone else to speak for us from that point on. I was a little disappointed at first. Josh actually had someone with him, but it wasn't official and he still wanted me. Although I didn't like that he was there with someone else, I couldn't let the moment get by me by worrying about her!

We decided to go out, but that night I also found out Josh was going to the military very soon. I was so taken aback that we had finally connected and he was going to be leaving. We fantasized about each other (not just sexual either). We wanted to be with each other so badly and never even knew the other person felt that way.

We made the best of the time that he had left before leaving, and started going out. My mom wasn't exactly the happiest camper about the situation, but it was only for a moment. The first date he picked me up from Billingsley Field House, where I told him I would be. Billingsly was a public school gym in Fort Worth, Texas where most schools played basketball games.

Josh told me what time he would be there, and he came to pick me up. He came inside the gym. I spotted him and went to the lobby to meet him. No one would have said anything to me about dating a White guy. I didn't want any of the guys from our team to see me with someone from another school. I don't think I would have lived that down.

I will never forget that night. It was so cold outside! Josh was wearing a light-colored denim jacket and blue jeans with a dark-colored shirt. He was dressed similar to me, since he knew I would be leaving from a basketball game.

Josh was driving his dad's car that night, and it wasn't long before his dad became the subject of conversation. I think he needed to get what he was about to say off of his chest . We sat in the car for quite a while before leaving the gym parking lot. We regretfully talked about how long we had wanted to go out together, but neither of us had the guts to say anything. We laughed and also talked about how much time we had wasted by being quiet about our feelings, and now he was about to leave soon. I could tell Josh wanted to tell me something more. He finally said, "My dad would go crazy if he knew we were together, but I don't care." I said, "He's prejudiced?" Prejudice was before the word racist was being used. Back then, everything was prejudiced when dealing with race relations. He said, "Yes! Very! It's bad because no one at the corporation he works at knows how racist he is." He went on to say how much his dad [stepdad] hated Black people, but he was over the area of the company where the majority of Blacks and Mexicans worked. No one knew his true feelings. (That reminds me of a vast majority of people today). My heart started pounding when Josh told me that. I started thinking about what my mom had said. Mom didn't want me hurt. She had told me that his parents could follow us, or his dad could have someone follow us. She said this before she knew anything about his dad being a racist. In fact, she didn't know that about him and I wasn't about to tell her she was right when I got home. She was speaking in general. I guess she was thinking about what would happen back in her time. That stuck with me. It didn't stop me from seeing him though; but I must admit that the fear was always there. I feared what mom feared... being somewhere with Josh and his dad pulling up. It was so sad that I was barely seventeen years old and feared what would happen to me if Josh's dad saw us together.

Josh and I went out again. This time we went to a mall in North Richland Hills, Texas. Let's talk about North Richland Hills back in the day! North Richland Hills is a small town I guess I would say it is within the city of Fort Worth not far from the Hurst/Euless/Bedford area. Most people knew that area for their dislike of Black people. I'm not quite sure of the demographics, but it had its own culture for sure. It was one of those towns that the people made sure you knew that you didn't belong out there. Blacks knew the town for its racism. I had been to the mall out there before with my sister for business, and what I remember is how people went out of their way to make us feel like we didn't belong. They succeeded in their efforts. I never allowed anyone to know they intimated me – even as a kid in high school I knew not to let anyone 'see my sweat.'

I can't tell you why, but one night Josh and I went to that particular mall to the movies. I think we were trying to stay far enough away from the areas I was familiar with so that we wouldn't run into anyone. I don't know. I'm just guessing because I don't remember exactly why we chose that location. I don't know; maybe it was the only location the movie was showing.

I still remember the movie we went to see. The movie was *A Good Mother*. We were young and vibrant and were having a great time together. As young as Josh was, he was protective of me. He felt the stares and he didn't like it. He tried to protect me from the behavior of the people - constantly asking was I okay, and if I was comfortable. (Much like John did – nearly thirty years later than Josh). I told Josh I was okay – even though I wasn't completely, but for some reason I felt safe with him. He made me feel like he was protecting me.

We sat in the movies. No matter how hard I try to remember, I can't remember anyone of color in that theater. It might have been others, but I can't recall anyone else at this moment. Josh had no problem putting his arms around me in the movies, and then early into the movie, he turned my chin around and started kissing me. At first, I wondered if he was rebelling or did he just want to kiss me right then and there. It was a little bit of both. I believe he wanted me to know that he didn't care about who was around and he was happy to be with me wherever we were. As far back as I can remember, I was always a romantic! He fulfilled that desire with no problem. We left the movies and spent more quality time together before he dropped me off at home. We both were on cloud nine, but it was bittersweet since he would be leaving for the military in a few days. I guess I didn't think about keeping in touch because I felt he would find someone of his own race and I would be a thing of the past—especially since his dad didn't approve anyway. He drove me home and we pulled up in front of my house. We kissed goodnight and I got out of the car.

I will never forget how he made me feel. He was the nicest person ever, and we had so much in common. The one thing I think about most is what could have happened had he not had a racist father. I think about the number of people we walk around every day who actually hate us for the color of our skin – like Josh's dad.

It was roughly four or five years later when I saw Josh again. We met at the same softball practice field where it all got started. I didn't know who he was, but it didn't stop me from speaking to him. He was a grown man now! He was much bigger and muscular than what I remembered. Plus, I didn't expect to see him there. I had thought about him over the years, and wondered how he was doing. You know how it is when you see someone outside of where you would normally see them and you can't quite place who they are and how you know them? They look familiar, but that's about it. That is what happened when I saw Josh, only this time, he didn't look that familiar.

I heard someone call my name, and I didn't know anyone there, so I looked around to see who knew me. Most people were on the field practicing, so I could narrow down where the voice was coming from – a few feet from me in the bleachers.

"Angel?" He asked.

"Uh, yes?" I answered.

"You don't know me, do you?"

"Uh, not really. Should I?"

"I'm Josh."

I nearly fell without tripping over anything other than my emotions.

"Josh? Oh my, gosh, Josh! What are you doing here?"

"I was about to ask you the same thing? You're looking great!"

"So are you! Wow!"

Needless to say the woman he was with was probably wondering when all of the excitement was going to end. Finally, he introduced me to the person he was with, but he didn't say wife or fiancé. He didn't even say girlfriend, so I wasn't sure what the relationship was, but I knew it was something because as soon as he went out to the field to join the other players, she lit into me.

"How long did y'all date? Did you know he was back? Did y'all ever go together?" She started firing question after question after question. I'm thinking, 'you already asked that when you asked how long we dated.' I finally got tired of playing a game of trivia and asked her if she asked him all of those questions, and if not, she probably should since I didn't know her. I knew him. She stopped long enough to try to make a decent conversation with me, but I wasn't interested then. She volunteered information such as what school she graduated from and how much he had talked about me – *the girl he played softball with named Angel (before he went to the military).* I won't lie. It made me feel good that he had talked about me. Not because he was so handsome, but because I wondered for a long time if he was just doing something to try someone different or he really cared. It didn't help that I was about to get married; so we didn't pursue anything further.

I love my husband and am very happy, but I often wonder what could have happened had things been different and we had our freedom without racial tension and inequalities amongst us.

Not Much Has Changed

We are living in the year of 2020, and some things have changed a lot over the years; but when it comes to interracial dating (Black and White) and marriage, the feelings towards it haven't changed much for most people—especially the elderly White and Mexicans. Some people tolerate it while others despise it. If a person is against dating someone of another race, then don't do it. Love who you want to love, but leave others alone. I have never understood why there is so much anger when it comes to individuals choosing to date or marry outside their race. If they are trying to get with someone of another race just because of race, then that's another problem altogether. Sometimes people have married another race because they feel they've 'arrived' when they do; but we have already talked about that. I hate to say 'outside their race' because there is only one true race—the human race.

We must change our language and the way we speak, since words are powerful. What we speak we will begin to believe. I am guilty of having spoken words into my life throughout the years, and I can attest to the fact that I ended up growing gardens of the seeds that I had planted. In some instances, my crops had a lot of dead harvest.

Our words have conditioned our thoughts. Our thoughts have become our beliefs - thinking that there is something wrong with the outer covering of our skeletons--especially if the covering is darker.

I have heard all kinds of excuses given about being against interracial marriages and dating. Many older individuals will use the reason for how it affects the children because the world is cruel. What does that mean? The world is cruel, but we should not accept that statement and allow it to be our means of determining effective relationships. When they say that, what they really mean is the world will see them [children] the way they see them – unacceptable. That belief is embedded in the heart. These particular individuals believe in love, they believe in marriage, they believe in family, but they believe it should be within one race of people – your own race. It bothers me to know that some of these people would not see themselves as racist or wrong. It is who they are and who their family is. They don't mean any harm. When they say they are "concerned about how the children will be treated", they honestly believe that story they have told themselves. They know how they feel or how their friends and family feel about interracial couple children. Some will go as far as dating individuals of other races (ethnicities), because anything that is not Black or African American is acceptable. In fact, they don't even look at other races differently. True racists will see all races outside of their own as unacceptable. Maybe that's why they don't see themselves as prejudiced or racist. They don't hate other races. They just feel people (Blacks) should stick with their own and stay out of their families. Whenever a Black guy marries into a family that isn't known for mixing races, sometimes I'd hear, "He treats her so well" or "He's a smart, hard-working man." I take it as if they are saying it's unusual, and that was the reason they were okay with him in their family. Hell, I'd say that about any man coming into my family, no matter what race or background.

Please don't get it twisted or flatter yourself thinking that White people are the only people who are against interracial dating and marriages. Although I would feel safe saying more of them are against it than Blacks, but they are not the only people who feel that way. I believe many Blacks that are against interracial dating feel people who seek and choose to date or marry someone other than Blacks are "turning their backs on their own people". Some aren't attracted to White people either, or they choose to stick with their own race (color) of people. Blacks already receive the least respect of almost all races (it seems).

Blurred Lines

Over the years, I have heard many people ask the age-old question about Black men. Yep! You got it! "Why do Black men or men of color marry White women or women of other races when they become famous or self-sufficient?" Honestly, I think that's a question that should be answered by a **competent**, truthful Black man or found out through neurological testing. Of course, I have my thoughts that I refer back to slavery days as I mentioned earlier in the book, when I spoke of how Black men were tortured by White men over White women. It's almost like some Black men feel like they are shaking their fist in the faces of other races, including their own, when they get a chance to date or marry a White woman. It's not just black men either. Dominican, Indian, and other ethnic descents see marrying Caucasians as a way of coming up in society.

Honestly, I have no problem with interracial dating/marrying, but a *problem* does exist. Some get angry about Black men marrying women of other races. Some see Black men who are with a woman of another race treat Black women with such disrespect. They walk by a Black woman, who is the race of their mothers, aunts, sisters, nieces, ancestors...and act as if that woman is a disgrace. Some people have problems with the people who set out to date a certain race because of their insecurities or shallow reasons such as satisfying their demons of the past. Love is love and it shouldn't matter who you fall in love with. Some people are childhood sweethearts, or high school crushes, or college lovers. They didn't look for a race, they found love. I think that's beautiful! I appreciate the MEN who can be true to themselves no matter what race of woman they have chosen to be with in a relationship.

This is what I'm talking about...

One evening after work, I was walking out of a pizza place with my pizza boxes in my hands trying to hold the door open with my back, and a Black BOY (not a man due to his actions), around the age of my oldest son, who was with a White young woman his age let the door fall on me. All I could think about was scolding him as I would do one of my sons. I was his elder, but he was so fixated on showing his date that he didn't care about me. They both were dressed in workout gear, and he treated me with disgust. I was equally disgusted with him, but for a totally different reason.

During the shutdown for COVID-19, I drove my daughter to the same pizza place. We had driven up and already been made aware that only one person was allowed in the restaurant at a time to pick up orders. She was standing by the door waiting for another customer to come out, when I noticed a big, white, nice truck pulls up. A Black guy and his biracial son pull up and they get out. I watched their interaction at the door where my daughter was standing. I could tell the kid was young, but he was a big guy like his dad. I'd say he was about twelve years old—old enough to be taught how to treat a female. I guess they thought my daughter was just standing at the door for no reason, so he and his son attempted to go inside, and I guess my daughter told them that only one person could go in at a time. When it was her turn to go in, they both stood and watched her open the door. Then on her way out, she too had to use her back and juggle two pizza boxes and wings on top of the boxes. Neither the male (he's not a man) nor his protégé helped her. I was shocked. His behavior showed his son how to treat a woman. I don't think he would have ever done a woman who looks like his son's mother that way. The behavior that he exhibited in front of his son is what causes ignorance and division later.

Those are the ones that I have zero respect for, and I never will. Behavior like the previous examples is what so many people 'take and run with' when they say Black men treat White women better. It's those individuals who make that statement seem true, but it's not true for every guy in an interracial relationship. I know that because I know many men in interracial relationships, and I happened to have raised a son in one.

I also believe some of the reasons stem from stereotypical thinking and listening to one-sided stories that others taught them about Black women, White women or Asian women. When a young man grows up in a predominantly White area and that is all he knows, it is no excuse for him to act like a Black female is nothing to him.

"Marry Up And Enjoy The Benefits" Says The Professor.

A few years ago, I went to an event for Latino students, faculty and staff. I didn't feel out of place. I knew a few people in there anyway, but even if I didn't, it still wouldn't have bothered me. Initially I was there to support a friend of mine who was doing a presentation on a topic of grave importance to the Hispanic community. The topic was domestic violence and abuse. I didn't assume that it was important in the Hispanic community, that is what we were told by the organizers of the event, who were Hispanic men.

We went to the presentation and I was taken aback (to say the least) by what I heard the leaders sharing with those in attendance. One of the organizers started out talking about how his daughter had married a White man. He bragged about golfing and privileges that she has been afforded by marrying that man and how well she is doing. He went on and on talking about his daughter through the man. I started wondering if he was proud of who his daughter had become, or the fact that he was proud that she was accepted by a White man.

Again, I'm okay with the bragging, and it's also fine if he is shallow enough to feel that marrying a White man is moving up or marrying up. He was telling the students that they too can 'marry up' and achieve things like his daughter had if they stayed in school. I'm like, WTW! They didn't spend much time on talking about the topic that was supposed to be the keynote. They were supposed to be talking about strengthening the Hispanic race and how to get away from the machismo culture in the Mexican race. That would have been good, but the one who was talking about his daughter marrying up, as if she had married Jesus, took all of the time and focused elsewhere.

To me, it was like his entire agenda was to encourage students to think that marrying someone White should be the ultimate goal that measures success. I thought that was sickening.

There's Black and Then the Rest

Working in law enforcement as a dispatcher, I could never understand why subjects would be run through the system as White unless they were Black. I wondered how we could possibly know a description if everyone was White male or White female. Black was just Black! I guess that's part of that one drop of Black blood rule that was put into place centuries ago. If a person was Hispanic, we would check Caucasian then check the box in the next column labeled Hispanic ethnicity. (Still don't understand that one either, but it is what it is.) Seems to me that everything and everybody wanted to be set as far apart from Black as possible.

I was reading an article about a man in New York who was arrested for killing a Black man that he didn't really intend to kill. Well, let me rephrase that...it wasn't an accident. He meant to kill him, but he originally intended to kill interracial couples. He allegedly told the NYPD that he was looking for an interracial couple to murder and he didn't care who it was. He just knew that he wanted to kill any couple—especially a Black man with a White woman. He reportedly said that he "was sick of Black men being with White women and he was angry about it." He boasted about how his plan was to see a couple and just start stabbing them without warning. That is evil.The worst part about it is that he is not the only person who feels that way. The difference is that he is a murderer. He probably didn't start out that way, but he allowed his hate to overtake him. Yes. That is possible. Since the guy wasn't able to kill an interracial couple, he was so angry that he killed a homeless Black man. When he was interviewed (according to what I read), he had no remorse for killing the homeless man, but he was upset that he didn't get a chance to kill an interracial couple. Towards the end of the article, he said, "He was just a homeless guy that no one cared about." Reports state that he was more than just a homeless guy to the community and many celebrities stopped and took pictures with the man over the years. Even if that wasn't the case, he was a life that mattered to God.

When I read the story, my son and daughter-in-law came to mind. They happened to be in New York around that time the incident took place. I didn't hear about the story until after they left New York. News like that is what bothers me and makes me worry as a mother about my child. Imagine the evil that the murderer carried within his heart.What is even worse is the fact that a couple could have been attacked and killed while walking down the streets of Manhattan, New York for no other reason than being a mixed couple. They wouldn't have known what hit them. That could have been my son and his wife.

Part Three
Ooh, The Black Curse

Black cat. Black magic. Black list. Black sheep [of the family]. Black! Black! Black! Why can't the sheep be blue?

The color black has always been associated with something bad or ugly; while the color white is associated with good things. White represents *gentle, angelic, untouched, pure, harmless and clean and fresh.*

Black is associated with bad, dark things like funeral wear, death, curses and evil. *"Ooh, he came back to her in all black!"* We automatically think that person came back from something evil or from hell.

He was blackballed. She was on the blacklist. Think about it!

"She appeared to me in all white. She looked like an angel."

We assume that person went to heaven. I received an email from someone who was in marketing, and that person said, "Make sure and add me to the whitelist so that my emails will go through." He didn't mean any harm. That's what it's called. If a person is blacklisted that means it's a no-go. If they are whitelisted it means they are all cleared.

I can hear it now. You're probably wondering what all of this has to do with race. I don't think the 'black this' or 'black that' is intentional, but it doesn't mean it doesn't do damage. Although there might be an innocence to it all, we have to be careful of what we say about the color black when we're talking to children and young people. They might associate the Black race with the color black. We wouldn't want that to happen. Now would we?

Black this and Black that. What is that all about?

Black people might have flaunted the Black power symbol, but have you ever wondered why? The black fist could have very well been raised to say, 'No more. You can't make us feel weak, disgraced, like garbage or any other way that we had been encouraged to think about ourselves.'

The mantra "I'm Black and I'm proud didn't start out as something to be ugly towards other races. Blacks wanted the people naysayers and racists to know they are proud of who God created them to be. It has been seen as something negative and looked down upon when others hear it, but it had nothing to do with White people being less than Blacks. We

(Black people) didn't spend energy trying to degrade White people, we just wanted to be left alone; but that was too much to ask.

Please don't ever think that this White supremacy crap just started. The ones that are on fire right now have been tucking their sheets away since their ancestors passed them down, just waiting on the right time to get them out and cut fresh eyelets in them. These bad actors are taught very early in life how to hate, while newbies allowed a seed to be watered. The only reason they kept their sheets under wraps is because they were afraid. They knew that Black people were no longer totally under their thumbs and outwardly controlled by their power. Noticed I said totally and outwardly. I strategically chose those words as a way of pointing out that there are still some ways that White people are in control and hold power. That is what the skinheads, nationalists and racists are afraid of losing. They can no longer have every company controlled by one race of people who only hire one race. They can no longer openly beat and hang Black people as a sport and get away with it. They might be doing the hangings and beatings still today, but it's not in their sheets—they are using other legal attire. Is that the power they are marching to keep? Do they want to be able to throw Black people off of buses and burn down their houses while they watch the

Black families run out? I'm just trying to figure out what they really want.

They are out of the backwoods now. They feel empowered again because of the unleashing of the beast allowed this ugliness to happen. If a person doesn't stand against something, then they stand for it—especially when they have the power to halt the hate crimes, the hate talk, and the malicious activity. I understand that no one but God can remove the hate from their hearts, but if there were harsher penalties for the known hatred, maybe it would stop. Some people are glad that they are coming out in the opening with their hatred. Whenever beasts openly walk down the streets like Nazi murderers and it is condoned, the killing will increase. When they had to hide and kill Black people, they had a harder time doing so. Now all they have to say is that they "ear for their life" or throw an amendment out there and call it a 'right.' Now they are using the term 'citizen arrest'. It's just another nice way of saying they killed a Black man who was trying to get away from them.

Section Two

"Everybody has asked the question, and they learned to ask it early of the abolitionists, 'What shall we do with the Negro?' I have had but one answer from the beginning. Do nothing with us! Your doing with us has already played mischief with us."

Frederick Douglass

They Don't Get "Us"

What does that mean? Why do we say it? What is there to get? Oh, I am asking because I have caught myself saying things like that only to finally stop and say, "Get what?" For what reason does anyone of a particular race have to be 'gotten' and understood? There's nothing to get! Let us be! We are people and we want to be seen and treated that way. We are all imperfect. It is so normal for people to think and to communicate to others that we are some *'thing'* that needs to be understood. No other race (that I know of) continuously says, "We just want to be understood." Do you want to know why they don't say it? They don't say it because they don't feel that anything is wrong with them. Quite frankly, they don't care if anyone thinks something is wrong with them or not. Society has made White people be the standard. If someone talks correctly, then stupid people will say they 'talk white'. If someone of another race says they are dating or married to a White person, it's like they've reached a goal. That is crazy to me, but we've done it as a society. Those of us who didn't do it allowed it.

White people have programmed Black people to automatically think that we need to be understood on every level. It will take generations to change that way of thinking. That stinking thinking did not start yesterday, last year, or even in the last one hundred years.It started with our ancestors. Our ancestors had no choice but to possibly believe that deep down something was wrong with them since they were treated like a plague. Therefore, the mindset has to be reset even in our own race. It will take time to deprogram human beings, but deprogramming will allow future generations to begin with a clean slate on a level playing field.

We are all different from each other. We are different culturally and unique individuals—all of us. To believe that different is wrong is what we must get away from in our society.

The amount of hate and belittlement in the world has pushed Black people to come up with ways to uplift themselves and others through shows, magazines, taglines, mantras, etc.

In a world that believes Blacks are unbearably different (and at times hated), there have platforms created where we can be celebrated. They have been created to make sure that Black people know they matter, and they have somewhere they can go to see people who look like them.

Here are some of the platforms that were created for Black people to be heard, seen and included: Black Entertainment Television (BET), TV One, Aspire, Black Girls Rock, Black Girl Magic, Black Lives Matter, Essence Magazine (Where Black Women Come First), the Black Collegian, Black Girls Run, Black Love, NAACP, Historically Black Colleges and Universities (HBCUs), and the Negro League Baseball.

It's raining, so y'all can go to school today!

Maybe you chuckled some when you read that, but it's not funny. It's true. My mother and her siblings used to pull cotton when they were kids on nice weather days. They weren't allowed to go to school if they had to work. My mom would tell us how embarrassed they would be whenever the school bus would pass them loaded with children going where she and her siblings wanted to go so badly. She said she would just put her head down hoping they wouldn't recognize her. They recognized her since she would be absent that day, and it didn't help that there were probably a couple hundred people in the town as a whole. She and my dad talked about how the kids on the bus would be taunting them and throwing stuff out of the windows at them. The only time they were able to attend school was on rainy days since they couldn't pull cotton in the rain. What kind of life is that for a child? Not a very good one I'd say. No wonder Blacks were looked at as dumb and illiterate. Thank God that my mother turned out to be a very smart woman. She is domestic, artistic and also intelligent. My mom would read the newspaper from cover to cover, and get mad if someone read the paper before her and got the pages out of order. I guess that's where I get it from. My dad actually taught history in school, so that should speak for his intellect itself.

I used to get tired of hearing the old folks say, "Back when I was growing up..." I get it now. I understand what they mean because I say the same thing to my children. I can speak for them at the age that I am now. It was their way of telling us that going to school is a privilege since they were denied the honor. I look at so many young Black men and women/girls and boys and think to myself, "How dare you let the pain and tears of our parents, grandparents and ancestors go to waste? How dare you not take up on the privileges afforded to you?

One Saturday, a couple of years ago we were watching college football. At the time, my husband was in that mode of being positive and making sure he didn't say anything that seemed negative which really got on my nerves. He deals with more Whites than Blacks, and he really didn't see racism as much because he turned a blind eye to it (in my opinion). For a long time I think he didn't see that he was good as long as he was doing something for the people he was dealing with at the time. Then again, I don't think he 'noticed' much outright racism because he was in the business for helping them. He was needed! He has a track record of helping young men get into college through baseball scholarships. He was tolerable.

When my husband finally started seeing what I had been talking about, he didn't think I was negative about everything regarding race relations anymore. Prior to his revelation, we were watching the college football game when they showed the first graduate of the college and I made this statement: "Isn't it sad that they were graduating from college when Blacks weren't even allowed to attend school?" That particular alumnus graduated in the late 1800's when Black people weren't even considered human beings according to some people.

Listen, I am not saying that our ancestors in the Black race didn't graduate and attend college because they did! My uncle graduated from college in the sixties., However, we also know that education was one of the main deprivations of the Black race. That is why I share and shout from the rooftop about the people that I learn about who broke barriers, leaped over walls, and jumped through hoops to get their degrees. Thank God for the internet because we can actually learn about these people that teachers and professors never told us about. Then again, maybe they were teaching only what they were taught.

Many of us have learned that those individuals made major grooves in the roads they traveled. Remember knowledge is power. Therefore, if the ability to gain knowledge is snatched, then what do we have? So many times, I hear people say that their great grandmother, grandfather, mother and father went to certain colleges, and they are following suit. Must be nice. That is not the story of many Blacks.

I wasn't a fan of HBCUs because I was influenced to believe that an HBCU was just another way of Black people separating themselves. I was ignorant (lacked knowledge) of why they existed in the first place. As I mentioned earlier, Blacks had to create things in order to be a part of them or to gain access. Many colleges didn't allow Black people to get an education where Whites did. In 1954, *Brown v. Board of Education* ruled that segregation was unconstitutional. So, if a race of people aren't allowed to go to school with another race, what else are they supposed to do? You build and organize your own. I get it now. I understand how and why HBCUs exist.

On Saturday mornings, I search for "Bama Style" TV show on Aspire Television Network. I read that the show first aired on Lifetime, but it was stated that they (Lifetime) wanted a more concise version of the story—whatever that means.

I am surprised at how much I enjoy watching that show. It's based on Alabama State, an HBCU, and I love it. It's a reality show that is a combination of the movie *Drumline* and a bit of *Stomp the Yard*. I know there are thousands of students at the school, and I'm only seeing the band and dance teams. Still, I like the culture of the show. The realness of issues. It's all about the band, the drill team, and the Honeybees. The Honeybees are the heavier curvier dancers. I like that. I like to see all people included. Why should something that is an extracurricular activity be limited to a certain size young lady? Far too long that has been the bar set by others who didn't see a curvy body as beautiful or desirable.

Sports and Entertainment

I like almost all sports, but I will watch fewer than I like to play. Football is my favorite sport to watch, but track is right behind it if not in a neck n' neck race. I have always liked volleyball, tennis, basketball, and I forgot about gymnastics! My sister

Diana and I loved watching gymnastics and figure skating when we were growing up. I still watch it when I can catch it on television. Figure skating was so elegant and graceful to me, but I saw something that stood out even more than the gracefulness: That something is their strength. Especially the guys. The way they can keep their posture while lifting a person above their heads and never miss a beat amazes me.

Sports has changed so much through the years that I'm not a hardcore fan anymore. I just like the games. The reason I'm not a true fan, as some would say, is because there's so much money involved in it, and I don't think many of them play for the game anymore. It's a business and about how much money can be made. I say that because I see fans lose it over a player being traded or choose to leave a team. Why should I be upset about someone leaving their 'job' and going somewhere else? Some people get so worked up about a player leaving a team, and most of them don't even care. They'll throw that new jersey on their shoulder, hold that press conference and keep it moving! Yeah, some have a hard time leaving teams because they have been planted in a place as with anyone leaving a job they've enjoyed working. Others are like, *"Show me the money!"* I now watch and root for the team of choice, and that's about it.

Sports (especially the NFL) have become such a controversial sport. The players are loved when they are out there playing, but, just as quickly as they love them, they hate them the same or harder.

Look at what happened to LeBron James when he left Cleveland. People were dogging him out, burning jerseys, and booing him when he returned with an opposing team. I feel that anger goes way deeper than disappointment and anger for switching teams. It's almost like the player escaped the plantation. Players are free to make their own decisions. I know that's a hard pill to swallow, but it's the truth. I haven't seen White players get that kind of outrage when they trade teams.

Sometimes the way I see it is that they are owned, and I don't like it. If you think they are not owned, see how they get told what to do. Listen, I know every job has requirements and procedures, but I'm talking about something different here. It reminds me of how the slaves were commanded when they would have to jump around and entertain company on the plantation for as long as the owners wanted them to. Then, once they've entertained enough, they would send them on their way. The slaves were free entertainment, but whenever they were finished with them, they were nothing. Many athletes make millions of dollars, so by no means are they entertaining for free, but there is still a parallel to the past.

The NFL players have been threatened with losing their jobs as players if they did not stand during the National Anthem. They are talked about by our president calling them names like sons of b***hes. I stand, and I will always stand, but I don't believe that making adult men stand up for something they are against is fair. On one hand, we say that we want a democracy Then, when it's convenient, some want a communist country. It doesn't show disrespect to anyone in the military or their country. It shows control on the ends of those telling grown men what they better do. Nothing was said when Tim Tebow made a stand for what he believed in. No one! He was applauded and still, to this date, his name is great. Mention Colin Kapernick's name and, depending on who you're talking with, you might have to nearly fight.

My husband, other men, and women that I respect dearly are ex-military. Some are still serving in the military. My nephew served in the Marines. His then wife served and still serves. I have friends who served and some are still serving. Before you even think to say that I don't respect the military – don't, please. I would not say anything that would disrespect their loyalty and commitment to the county, and if the truth be told, many of them understand what the problem is behind standing (or not standing) for the anthem.

To me, that is another one way that they can still be controlled and coerced to entertain. They might have a lot of leeway, but let them screw up...you'll see who really owns who.

Being Black Held Them Back

I can't help but think about all of the people who would be so much further ahead in life had times been a little better like it is [getting] now. How many beautiful Black women of years ago missed the opportunity of becoming flight attendants because they didn't fit the criteria that were set by a few who thought Black wasn't beautiful enough? How many pitchers and quarterbacks were looked over because the ones who made the rule said that a quarterback had to be smart, and Blacks weren't smart enough (in their opinion) to play the position?How many boys played other positions besides quarterback because they never got a shot at throwing the ball? You might be saying "Hey... at least had the chance to play". That's not good enough. If you have not experienced the biases and restraints that others have battled, then you won't understand. There have been certain things that I *ran my mouth* about before experiencing some things for myself too. I didn't even know that I didn't know.

Until recent years, models had to have a certain look that was created by White designers and the White population. Thanks to Tyra Banks and her show, "America's Next Top Model", some of those stereotypes changed. Maybe it wasn't all credit of Tyra, but she was definitely an advocate of different looks, shapes, shades and sizes for models. She couldn't change the minds of all of the designers, but I'm sure she impacted some of the small minds that once thought their clothes looked better on a clothes hanger walking on a runway. If women didn't have that made-up standardized look that many would say was acceptable and beautiful, modeling was not an option—especially for any woman with a hint of color to her complexion. That was especially true for Black women. I can hear it now… "If Black women wanted to model, they should have lost weight." Let me enlighten you for a moment. It wasn't as much about weight as it was skin color and bone structure. The shape they wanted everyone to believe was the desired shape was a thin ruler build. That was not the build of majority of Black women, and if it were, their skin color would cancel out their chances. There were a couple of beautiful Black women that made the cut later, and they made history.

Have you ever thought about how a young Black girl (like myself) as a kid thought about herself and carrying the feeling of not being good enough or pretty enough? I wasn't perfect enough. I was Black (first of all), I had a gap in my teeth, and I knew early on that I wouldn't be a skinny woman. I was skinny as a girl, but I knew I had what I thought or had been told 'Black in me' so I wouldn't be skinny enough to model. I had all of the wrong characteristics and features – so I thought. We were convinced that was true: a Black girl or woman wasn't pretty enough to model clothes and makeup because of the way that God created us. That lie convinced a girl that her body shape was not desirable and her skin color was not the *right* color. Individuals have fallen into depression and have thought that God didn't love them because He created them in a way that was unacceptable to the majority and the way He created them caused their lives to be a living hell. What we were taught was everything except the truth, because it was their truth and not THE truth. The enemy (our adversary, the devil) has been destroying the lives of individuals all of our lives through the willingness of others.

When I decide to watch a golf tournament, I can't help but wonder how many more Tiger Woods there would be if golf wasn't considered a 'White man's sport'. How many more professional golfers would there be in the majors if Blacks would have been welcomed on the course and in country clubs around the world? How many more professional

Black tennis players would there be besides Venus and Serena Williams and Arthur Ashe? The latter of the three names are oftentimes forgotten, I'm sure, because tennis wasn't on the list of Black sports back then. It too was labeled as a 'White sport'.

If the sport wasn't track and field, basketball, or football, Blacks weren't expected to participate outside of P.E. class. I will not get away from certain subjects in this book until you understand that which is going on today has everything to do with what we have been programmed to believe and accept. I want to bring to the forefront the thought of the many dreams that went to the grave with countless individuals as well as those that are still alive who never got a chance to live out their dream. Of course that statement holds true to people of all races today who choose not to go after their dream; but this isn't about that right now. I'm talking about those who were denied the privilege. How many would have been doctors or lawyers in the early days? How many more people like Thurgood Marshall would there have been? The dreams of so many people were mass murdered and others thought nothing of it, and some are still doing it right now today in a different and more subtle manner. In most cases, all they (Blacks) needed was an opportunity; and the bad thing is, the ones that kept them from that opportunity knew that was all that was needed.

Let's talk about professional race car drivers. According to ranker.com, there are fifteen noted Black race car drivers in NASCAR. That's more than I ever thought were out there. Compared to all the people in the world, that number is too small. Some of the drivers interviewed about race car driving noted that Blacks were not encouraged to drive. It was a sport that they didn't want Blacks to integrate. That stupidity has been the story of our lives...Will we be accepted? I am not impressed by the tolerance of Black drivers now. That isn't anything to applaud. It should have never ever been that way. I am so sick of people saying, "That's just the way that it was." Well, it doesn't make it right. In my opinion, well-known race car industries conditioned fans to not want to see Black drivers. I believe they prided themselves on remaining White, and their White fans didn't have to see Blacks out there or have to sit next to one in the arena.

When I first heard of Nicole Lyons, I was elated to read her story of becoming a professional driver.

Then there's Tia Norfleet who actually competed in NASCAR. Look her up for yourself.

Tell the History. It's Needed.

When I learn of something great, I share it with anyone who would listen. The problem of today is the fact that many of us share everything besides the good things that will edify individuals, and encourage them to dream bigger. Do the research and learn about people who have done things that went against the odds and broke barriers. I definitely share with my children, and I have been blessed enough to have children that reciprocate to me. I have learned that Blacks aren't the only people interested in the great things Black people have contributed to history as well as today's success, but others want to know as well. When people use the words "Black history", I now correct them and say *history.*

When my dad was younger, he was a great baseball pitcher. I have heard stories told by some of his friends. Sometimes I feel like I was there when the events happened because I've heard them so much. Unfortunately he didn't get to make it as far as everybody felt he could have made it. I had the pleasure of seeing Daddy pitch, but it was in softball on a men's team. I was impressed! We (me, my sisters and my mom) went to as many softball games as we could when he was playing. All we could hear from the fans was, "You should have seen *Blue* pitch a baseball!" I don't know where my dad got that nickname from, but that's what his friends and everybody in my hometown called him: Blue or Boy Blue. The stories that are told to us all end in, "No one could hit on him." Daddy was born in 1935—enough said.

Both of my sons played baseball too, and they only heard of stories of how my dad was good enough to have played in college and possibly the majors. It's quite painful to know that my dad was deprived of something that he could have done, only because Blacks weren't allowed to play on the level they can play now. The way Black men were done in baseball was downright cruel. They were treated worse than animals for no reason at all. I shouldn't say 'like animals' because animals were treated better than Black people. I've seen people allow a dog to lick them inside of their opened mouth, but they would puke if a Black person drank from their cup. Even today, the major league baseball industry has changed. I would be confident in saying it is probably because the drafts are more about recruiting from places such as the Dominican Republic, Puerto Rico, and other countries than our own citizens here in America. Young men in America are expected to go to college and be recruited, but the same isn't required for those outside of the country.

In early 2000, my husband assisted a friend of his in organizing a select baseball team. The team wore specially ordered uniforms that were replicas of the Kansas City Monarchs Negro League baseball team. Anywhere the kids played, their suits were the talk of the bleachers. They were so cool. As a parent it made me feel good to see my son rep that uniform.

The idea for the team was incomparable for several reasons. It was a diverse team, it was a teaching tool, and it gave us parents the feeling of giving back to those that gave so much. The least we could do was represent the name and make sure we could tell the stories behind the uniform. The coaches made sure they took the time to tell the boys about the men who paid a hefty price while wearing that uniform. There were many untold stories that their uniform represented, and those stories were way more than just the game of baseball. They learned how those men before them didn't get a chance to play the game that they currently get to play – freely and in peace. The only reason the guys in the past couldn't was because of their race. Their ability frightened the other leagues, but the race of the men was most frightening.

When we were in Hutchinson, Kansas in 2002, we occupied a banquet room and the coaches asked the parents if a film of the Negro League could be shown to the boys. We wanted the boys and their parents to know more about what I consider one of the best kept secrets to the young baseball players of today.

We watched interviews of the players as well as others that were able to tell the stories about the original players and the game. The videos included clippings of footage that revealed how the fans threw things at the players and called them names while they played. The White fans would boo the men for no reason at all. We saw teams being denied opportunities to play on the same fields as the White teams. Many of the men who were filmed talked about how they were hurt and injured by White players from other teams. Raw footage showed the injury that Jackie Robinson received when he was spiked on purpose by a White runner. If having to fight against other teams wasn't enough, Mr. Robinson's own teammates objected to his presence in the league, started a petition against him, and threatened not to play with him. It was a painful experience for him. Most kids and adults have heard of Lou Gehrig and Babe Ruth, and that's about all that most know about the former leagues. Reading up on other players, I discovered the outstanding talents of most of the Black players in the league. I have no problem believing they were great players. when they did get a chance to play against a White team, they always won.

I took it upon myself to start researching other Negro League teams besides the Kansas City Monarchs. I was overwhelmed with the talent those guys possessed. Men such as 'Cool Papa' Bell, Satchel Paige, Norman Thomas 'Turkey' Stearnes, Buck

O'Neal, Hank Aaron, Josh Gibson, Bullet Rogan, and too many more to name. I can't leave out Rube Foster and what he added to the league. It saddens me to know that almost all of these guys did not get a chance to live to see their names inducted into the Hall of Fame, or a statue built in their honor.

America was satisfied with giving us history about Jackie Robinson, as if he was the only Black major league level player. Research confirms that Jackie was not the best player of the Negro League, but he was the one that Whites thought would be accepted. He was educated and they felt he would be able to 'cross over' and be accepted by the White fans. I have a serious issue with that. We are always competing against one another because we have had to be better than the next Black person because they were only taking one of us. Once again, we have to be good enough by their standards to fit into their scope they created in order to be recognized. If we had an opinion or looked like they wouldn't be 'yes men,' they were not good candidates for the crossing over.

I'll talk more about what our brown-skin held us back from a little later.

Lights, Camera, Action!
"We're not going to see that!"

Remember the 1995 show Clueless that starred Stacy Dash and Alicia Silverstone? Amy Heckerling did a great job with that movie. Normally the mean rich girls are all White. I like the fact that she mixed that up. The original version that came from the 1815 novel *Emma* didn't include a woman of color. Heckerling put a modern-day change to it. All ages liked that movie, and I believe it could very well be because of the diversity in the lead roles. Diversity in movies I'm sure has its risks because White people don't go see movies that have a Black cast. Ask them!

Imagine this… Imagine if you are a White person and you grew up never seeing a White person on commercials, in movies or in magazines. Imagine that. You probably can't imagine that because you are probably thinking that it would never happen. You are right. It must be nice to be sure of that. I have lived that reality as a Black girl who grew into a Black woman. Before you think it is a complaint, it's not at all. It's a plea to ask you to try trading places in your mind since you have never experienced the reality.

Section One

"We've come a long ways, but we still have a long ways to go!"

Glancing at the television commercials while watching football, I am pleased to see more sitcoms advertising that involve Black actors – the seasoned ones as well as newcomers. That's cool.

It's important to include all races of actors in shows and commercials because I know firsthand how important it is to see people on television that look like you. That's something that I didn't have growing up. By now you're probably tired of hearing it, but it's the truth.

Viewers need to be able to see people who look like them on the small screen (television) and the big screens (movies). All cultures should be represented. When writers do not feel the need to capitalize on the opportunity, they are overlooking important populations and they are limiting talents. Majority of the world's population, at some time or another, use products and services that are advertised on television. Shouldn't all people be targeted if a company is trying to sell something? Absolutely!

Writers and marketers alike must change the way some of them view people. For example, anytime a drug addict, prostitute, or thug is needed for a role, the casting crew seem to solicit a Black man or a Black woman. If they want to show a guy who is coming from the penitentiary, they probably put an ad out there stating they need a Black man mid-twenties to early forties. If a prostitute is needed, they probably have their ideal woman for that role as well, and she must be Black.

Follow me here. You see, it's the picture in our minds that we've created. A prostitute or drug addict in their minds automatically goes to 'Black.' Why can't the casting crew look for a White man in his mid-twenties to early forties to be the drug dealer or the user? If a White guy is in a role that involves drugs, he is normally the mastermind who has the peons on the street. Unfortunately, a majority of the time the kingpin is Black too. Society has created a negative stigma on Black people in general, and it should have changed a long time ago. We (society) accepted that negative stamp.

Until recently, movie issues were pretty much the same. Most of the roles of Black people were either a cameo or a supporting role, and oftentimes their character is killed before the movie really gets to the plot. I remember when we used to be watching scary movies, and as soon as we saw a Black character we already knew they would be the first to go.

Several movies were released in the 1980s and 1990s that had predominantly Black casts that I have never seen. I will not name the titles because I am not here to trash anyone. The names of the movies are immaterial, but the reason I am mentioning the movies is very relevant. I was sick and tired of seeing storylines that I could not relate to in my own life. I didn't like the way I felt after seeing the few that I did see or after watching the trailers. The couple or so that I saw I either watched them after they came to VHS or cable. (Yes, VHS.) I understand that some people could relate to the story lines and it was necessary to target that particular audience, but not every movie should have the same plot. If I can be honest here, I can see why people believed what they believed. I'd be afraid to walk down the street with my purse on my shoulder too, because a young Black man might come and snatch it. That's what we saw all the time.

Same ole same ole...

I was fed up seeing the same loud, ghetto female characters trying to keep her guy from going back to the streets after being recently released from prison.

The only change in the movies were the actors. Black women were portrayed as being hard up, can't get a man, hard to get along with, and too demanding. That's not how we are!

Another popular story line goes like this. First, the guy comes home from prison after doing time for murder or drugs (sometimes a wrongful conviction) and tries to rebuild his life with the woman and child that he left behind. It's not long before he's faced with a decision: Go back to selling drugs or robbing to take care of his wife (or baby mama) and kids because no one will hire him with a felony. Does that happen in our lives? Yes it does, but that's not all that happens. I know some guys who fit that category of not being able to get a job because of their past, but only a few. That's not the only story that can be told about a Black person's life.

What about movies of successful men and women who did time in prison and chose a different path that actually worked? There are those stories out there!

I was tired of watching "baby mama drama" as entertainment. Those aren't the only subject matters that are relevant to all Black people. I was yearning to see a great love story - a family without drama. We all know that family dysfunctions are real, but is that the way that we have to be represented on every platform? Family drama and dysfunction comes in all races and family dynamics.

Stage plays adopted the same drama. Sure, they will include funny moments. However, if the audience didn't leave with tears in their eyes or feel the need to sob because they could relate to the pain of the script, people didn't feel entertained. Many of us have been accustomed to connecting with pain instead of happiness. I'm not saying that life is full of petals and blooms, and I am not saying that we should cover up the pains (because it is good that people know they are not alone), but I think we know that by now.

I can relate to the "baby mama drama" (unfortunately), but so can some of my White girlfriends. Maybe "baby mama drama" is more prevalent in the Black race because it seems that the Black people deal more with ex-girlfriends than ex-wives – unfortunately, because many of them never married their exes. That's another story for another book!

When I'd say something about the movie plots and songs, I was fed up with hearing, "Well, that's the truth! That's our lives!" Okay, I get that (for some people), but talent allows a person to write outside of themselves. I was always taught that reading was fundamental, and you could go anywhere you wanted to go in your own mind. The same is true for a talented writer. The movie can take people places they've never been. How about writing about ordinary people saving money to travel around the world to see places they've only read about? Okay, that was a freebie idea for someone to use and build on to create a story.

Section Two
Now...

I believe that the Black (and White for that matter) writers who would not write a good movie about Black people with a beautiful ending thought they would give what the audience wanted – so they believed. I don't think it was the storyline that drew the Blacks in. It was the fact they could see a reflection of themselves on the big screen (which a while back was rare), and they wanted to support movies written, produced by, or starring Black people. When a Black movie casting Black people came out, most Blacks would go see it no matter what the movie was about; therefore, I believe the message sent to the writers was false. It said we wanted to see more movies with negative content. There were many talented and brilliant writers out there. I believe they wrote what they wrote because they were serving what they thought we wanted to eat. I didn't have an appetite for it, so I didn't eat it. When I tried, I couldn't digest it.

I am not saying that it was the total responsibility of the White writers and producers to write about us, but when they did, it was the way *they* viewed us. The stories were told from a view through their dirty, judgmental, broken lenses.

The unfortunate and hurtful truth is that the majority of White people didn't go see movies with Black leading characters. It didn't matter who wrote, directed, or produced it. It didn't get their attention. I've seen movies advertised on TV for quite a while before coming to the theaters, but I'd mention seeing the movie to some of my acquaintances and they wouldn't even know what I'm talking about, because the trailers don't get their attention.

If a movie had more than one or two black faces in it, that was one or two too many for some White people.

Section Three
Black movie or White movie?

What constitutes a Black movie? How come more people don't say "White movie?" I wonder if the answer could be that all movies have been considered 'White' and that is the norm. I've heard the term Asian movie, Korean movie, but not White movie. Interesting.

Until recently, when it came to movies the issues were pretty much the same. Most of the roles of Black people were either a cameo or a supporting role. Oftentimes their character is killed before the movie really gets to the plot.

We Want Families Too

Can you think of a movie or two that involved Black couples that were planning a pregnancy? If so, can you think of five? Can you recall movies where the Black woman was struggling with infertility? Again, if so, can you think of five? On the other hand, I can think of many movies involving White couples wanting a child, as if they are the only ones who actually want families or plan their families.

A few years back Regina Hall and Morris Chestnut starred in *When the Bough Breaks*. That was refreshing! It was refreshing to see a married couple in love and wanting to bring a life into the world together. She was beautiful and he was as handsome as could be, and they were happy. They were a couple who had great careers, they were wealthy, and they wanted a baby. That kind of movie is rare to see because we have been conditioned to see a struggling single parent with a deadbeat dad that won't help with support or can't because he doesn't have a job. We have been subconsciously programmed to believe that Black women don't have a hard time getting pregnant, or they don't plan their children and that's not the truth.

In 2009, Idris Elba and Beyonce Knowles-Carter starred in a thriller film that turned the tables so to speak called *Obsessed*. Beyonce and Idris were happily married and new parents. Idris had an office temp who started developing feelings for him, and eventually she became obsessed. She was a piece of work! She worked tirelessly trying everything to seduce him, but it didn't work. I was glad the writer didn't allow Idris to start sleeping with the temp. That would have been an obvious plot. I didn't want to see another unhealthy relationship on television.

The other reason was that I didn't want the movie to have a typical ending with an unfaithful Black man leaving his beautiful Black wife for a White woman.

Let's talk about some of those movies that have been shunned because they were considered to be 'Black' movies.

It is crazy how the movies are separated the way that they are—so much so that you have to nearly beg a person of another race to check out a predominatly-Black casted movie. It is understood that we should all go and see movies starring a predominantly White cast. We have never felt that we can't or don't want to see a movie because of an all-White cast. We simply decide on whether or not the plot of the movie is interesting. If we had waited to go to a theater to see a 'Black' movie, we would have waited a long time to see our first movie!

Best Man (Directed by Malcom D. Lee and produced by Spike Lee)

Best Man was a phenomenal movie! It was a movie that almost anyone could relate to and enjoy. The movie was about a group of friends reuniting for a wedding after graduating college. Two of the friends in the group were getting married. There was one little problem though: The groom was marrying one of the girls that the best man had had sex with.

In the movie, one late night while they were studying together and listening to music, it just happened. The best man had sex with the groom's soon-to-be wife. I know...I said that on purpose, but nothing just happens. They must have been thinking about it at some point in time. No one knew the two had made out. It happened, but they remained really good friends from that moment forward.

The best man (Taye Diggs) was writing a book which anyone who would read it could gather that the storyline was the story of the friends. In the book, he vividly describes a night of passion with his best friend's (the groom – played by Morris Chestnut) soon-to-be-wife. I mean, I don't know a lot of scenarios like that one, but I can think of some drama-filled pasts of myself and some people that I know. The show was relatable for any race.

I appreciated the portrayal of the characters in the movie. They were all well-to-do and had great careers. Contrary to popular belief, that's possible!

Morris Chestnut's character was a professional football player and the other actors in the movie were doing quite well for themselves as well. They weren't thugs just getting out of prison. They weren't deadbeat dads that we tend to see on the big screen where Blacks are portrayed. They were from different backgrounds and different socioeconomic levels, but they were ideal characters that showed

Black people in a positive light. The movie was great. It was a movie that dealt with secrets, friendships, some would say betrayal, brotherhood, forgiveness and a wedding. I mean, how many weddings in real life that you have knowledge of didn't have some kind of little secret or two? Maybe you don't know about the secrets, but it doesn't mean they didn't exist!

The *Best Man* was way more than I can or will try to explain. It's a must see. A recent interview by TV One with the cast and director of The Best Man revealed that the movie did not test well with White audiences. When Malcolm D. Lee wrote the script, he wanted anyone (regardless of color) to connect with the movie. When the movie premiered, Blacks went in droves to the movie to support and watch this great feature.

Unfortunately, a lot of White people I know do not really go to see movies with African American casts. There have been several great movies that I have asked White people that are close to me if they had ever seen the movie advertised. They'd say, "No. I haven't seen that. I've never heard of that movie." They haven't seen it advertise because their brains turn off unless it's something to criticize or categorize as "look at them" or "I told you so." It's not that they haven't seen it advertise, they don't pay attention to the advertisements because movies with a Black cast don't get their attention. Needless to say, they hadn't even seen the trailer! I'm not being negative here, I'm being truthful. Real. We don't mind seeing other movies. I really liked *Maid in Manhattan, A Walk to Remember, Nights in Rodanthe, Urban Cowboy, When Harry Met Sally, Something Borrowed* (one of my favorites), and too many more to name. I wish Black movies would get the same respect and desires to be seen by all audiences. When *Black Panther* came out, it took the movie to go global before people started paying attention to it. That's sad.

The movie, *Best Man*, was like any other feel good movie I've seen, but it didn't get the credit it deserved nor did it cross multicultural boundaries as it should have. It's not the first movie in which that has happened, and it sure won't be the last one. The movie was beautifully written, classy, and packed with talented actors. Many of the actors stepped on the scene of acting even stronger after that movie. If you haven't seen the movie, you should. And check out the tearjerker sequel *Best Man Holiday*. Totally awesome movie!

Something New (Not to us)

I have talked a lot about educating others about who we are as individuals, and there are certain tools that can help us do just that. A friend of mine that I talk about throughout many areas of the book was one of several that I educated. I shared the movie Something New with him and he loved it. He didn't want to give it back. When he watched it, he never thought of Black character or White character. To him, it was just a good movie. During that ordeal he learned more than I could teach him. I should say what I shared with him was confirmed by watching the movie.

The movie *Something New* starring Sanaa Lathan (Kenya McQueen) and Simon Baker (Brian Kelly) to me was great. I can't count the times I've seen it because after seeing it at the movies a couple of times, I bought the DVD.

The movie is about Sanaa Lathan (a career-minded Black woman) who went on a blind date, but she had no idea the guy she was meeting was a White guy. She never wanted to date a White guy because she was like many people with closed minds. She had never thought about whether or not she could be attracted to someone with a few shades lighter skin. It was, well…something she was brought up believing. We can't down her because that is how many of us feel at times about dating out of our race (or color I should say). We forget, however, that we are all people. Yes, we have our differences culturally, but we are more of the same than we are different. Yes, we can fear how the rest of the family would accept us and that is an understandable fear, but we shouldn't allow that to hinder us from the possibility of experiencing true love.

I like movies that do the unexpected and step out of the norm. Remember the movie *Unfaithful* with Diane Lang? A lot of guys (including my husband) didn't like this movie because it was finally the woman cheating in the movie instead of the woman always being hurt and betrayed by a cheating man. *Something New* is the same way. It's a 'turn the tables' movie. It shows what it is like for a person who isn't accepted just because of their race. Black people are used to hoping that a White family or friends will like the person they have chosen to date if he or she is of another race or ethnic background. I understand that feeling. Not only have I experienced something similar when I was a teen, but I had thoughts about my son being accepted by his wife's family. Honestly, I am sick of having to deal with those kinds of issues in life.

In the movie, Something New, Kenya finally gives in and dates Brian, but she was hesitant to let her friends and family know. When they found out, Kenya's mom and brother didn't accept him— especially her brother. In their opinion, he wasn't good enough because he was White and nothing more than a groundskeeper. Brian happened to be a professional landscaper. It wasn't the profession itself they were not pleased with. They thought she should date a Black guy on her level of professionalism and same race. They had their eyes set on business executive, Mark Harper (played by Blair Underwood), who happened to be Black.

The movie was so impactful for me because the entire storyline was what we normally see in movies, but the other way around. We usually see the Black person not being good enough for the White son or daughter.

Her family had to try to see him (Simon Baker) for who he was and not the color of his skin. Honestly, it was refreshing for me for others to see what that looks like.

Something New was a fantastic movie and a timeless one. Check it out. You won't be disappointed. If you are, then check out the real reason you feel that way. You might find out that it's not the just movie that you don't like.

Gold vs. Black

As far back as I can remember, I've always had a love-hate relationship with the Oscars and other awards shows. I hated the fact that they didn't recognize or award Black actors and actresses, but I loved watching the glitz and glam of it all. Fashion and beauty was always a part of my dream, and the award shows were pretty much the only time I could get a full dose of what I loved in one night.

Although I didn't feel that anyone of color would win, I watched for many years. Still, I never felt comfortable because I felt that I was contributing to the problem. I was supporting something that didn't recognize or appreciate people who looked like me.

We all know that the Oscars weren't about anyone outside of White actors. Before you think I am saying that Black people should win because they're Black or they should be 'given' something they didn't earn, I'm not saying that at all. I'm saying they should have been given a fair shot at winning, but they weren't.

I believe the Blacks that showed up did so because it was an opportunity to dress up and relish the atmosphere where they had earned a place. After all, whether they were receiving an award or not, they were still stars and were privileged as such.

Something's a brewing...

The heat from the Oscars wasn't turned on overnight. It came from decades of disgust from the people that were never addressed openly. Some of those people went to their grave never having an opportunity to be appreciated or acknowledged for their work.

In 2016, people were finally tired of keeping their mouths shut about not seeing a Black actor win an Oscar for outstanding roles, as well as tired of the roles being limited to Black actors. I'm not much of a movie watcher, but I try to see a good one that I think I will like. I didn't have to be a movie critic to know that some of the Black actors were amazing, but never had the chance to put that gold trophy in their Black hands.

It wasn't until 2001 that an Oscar was won by a Black woman. Are you kidding me? That's way too late! Unfortunately, the role Halle Berry won an Oscar for was one in which many Black people didn't respect and agree that it was Oscar worthy. It wasn't about her acting in the movie. It was about what she did in order to get an Oscar. I watched a small portion of the movie, but I didn't care for it at all.

Noteworthy: While doing research, I learned information regarding ONE Black woman by the name of Hattie McDaniel who won an Academy Award in 1939. She won the Best Supporting Actress Oscar for her role of "Mammy" (a maid) in the movie Gone With The Wind.

Also, according to information I recently gathered by reading an article on line from *Time.com*, I was informed that , in 1941, Almena Davis Lomax founded a newspaper that highlighted the disparities in Hollywood and in the world. Lomax was known for her boldness and her ability to speak out about movies that portrayed Black women as *'happy'* servants and content slaves. It was said by her son that his mother was frustrated with Black women being portrayed as 'oversexed and primitive' and the black men portrayed as brutal. Seems like Lomax was far ahead of her time, and little did she know that these things wouldn't change. This article was full of information that I had never heard of, but it has caused me to have a desire to learn more.

Marvel Was Marvelous

Now you already know I couldn't leave out *Black Panther.* That movie was one of the best movies I've seen. To me *Black Panther* wasn't the typical movie that involves Black actors. Although the role of Michael B. Jordan was one of an angry boy who grew up still holding the anger over his father, it wasn't the 'hood' movie that the writers could have so easily transitioned to. *Black Panther* was refreshing. It exceeded the normal expectations of the movies that have been written for a predominantly Black audience. Mr. Ryan Coogler and Mr. Joe Robert Cole did a magnificent job. The costume designer, Ruth E. Carter was justly awarded for her astronomical, astonishing work.

To me, *Black Panther* crossed the lines that have been subconsciously put into place in our minds of what can and cannot be done. They slammed the box office with their one-of-a-kind hit. Finally a movie that showed the faces of strong, powerful, smart individuals that were in front of the scenes instead of behind the scenes. They were up front and not a bunch of extras in a movie. Well done!

Every person I talked to had heard about *Black Panther*. Undeniably awesome! Unlike other movies that didn't even get the attention of our White movie goers, *Black Panther* did. It was undeniably well done and well written. A movie that was family friendly, and gave our young Black boys and girls as well as others a superhero to be like and to imitate. For adults, it was an empowering moment to see outside of themselves. *Black Panther* took us to Wakanda (Forever). That place doesn't exist, but it allowed us to be okay with Africa. It allowed us to think bigger when we think of Africa and the richness of the earth and the people there.

The movie included a past love story between Nakia and T'Challa (Lupita Nyong'o and Chadwick Bosman respectively). Their relationship had history and it wasn't a bitter one that interfered with their priorities of working together for a common cause. The movie showed strong family roots and family values which are missing in the majority of movies today. Although the thuggish angry Black man character played by Michael B. Jordan was a more familiar one, it was for a specific purpose. The writers showed it but it didn't build the complete story around an angry Black man.

Awesome, bravo! Come on *Black Panther II!*

We Read and Write Too
Don't Judge Every Book by Its Cover

I enjoy reading a good book, and yes, the front cover is something that I take into consideration when I am choosing a book. I keep that in mind when I am thinking about writing a book of my own because it is unfortunate, but it happens...the cover of a book can be a turn off.

The latest book that I bought has two women on the cover, facing each other while holding martini glasses. It didn't bother me or turn me off because the front of the book didn't have two Black women on the cover. So what! It doesn't matter to me. That is something that I can answer right away. If the book sounds like it's going to be a good one, then I'm all for reading it. I don't care who graces the cover. Maybe it's because I'm accustomed to not seeing us on a cover of anything, so it's nothing new. I am used to the characters in the book being described as a woman who doesn't look like me.

If you're not a Black person, have you ever picked up a book with intent to buy that you believed to be a book about someone Black or written by a Black person? I'm not talking about a Christian book written by a famous preacher such as Bishop T.D. Jake or others. I really would like to know.

I used to be a devout reader, so people would recommend books to me all the time – that's why I can say what I'm saying. One time a great friend of mine who happens to be Hispanic told me about a book that a former Black pageant queen wrote. I have recommended books and movies to my Caucasian friends, and a few of them took my recommendations and read the books or took the time to see a movie that I recommended and enjoyed them immensely. It's all about stepping outside of yourself, in which so many people won't do. How many movies have you seen that appeared to be a Black movie? What about a book? Do you want to know why there is so much separation even when it comes to something as simple as a book? It's because of the buried mentality that is carried from years back. No worries. I'll get back to the book in a minute, but I have to say this right quick. I was watching a show on CNN, *United Shades of America* hosted by W. Kamau Bell. He was traveling to different towns in several states meeting with klan (I don't capitalize on purpose) members. I could not believe the ignorance of those people still today. They were burning a cross in a ritual. Each time they would light one's torch (as if it was a candle), they'd say, 'doing it for Jesus.' Jesus don't have anything to do with that mess. It's about hate and God is love. The love for us is why He sent His only son to die for us on the cross. Those are my beliefs. I mentioned the klan because when interviewed each of them would make references of staying with your own kind. They didn't see Black people as human for the most part. They feel that they (Whites) are pure. Newsflash…they're not! They have given Christianity a bad rap because of their evil ways. They are murderers but also cowards. If you can't show your face, you don't want to be seen. If you don't want to be seen, maybe you're not that proud of what you're doing after all. Back to the klan and people not being interested in reading books or watching movies starring Black people…they feel they can't relate to the content. They too think that we should stay apart, although they don't really know or realize it. And if you consciously think that way my dear, you are a racist. I don't care how you take it either.

It is sad that the people in America have so much freedom and access to anything we want, but yet we limit ourselves because of something as petty as color. Religion separates us as well, but I can understand that more than race. For me, I am a total Christian, but I am not afraid of the beliefs of others (I do have my limitations in what I would participate in concerning other religions.) In our beautiful country, we have opportunities to explore any and everything we would like to explore. Although that can be scary, it's true. I am just sorry that we are color struck and judgmental when it comes to race.

My B.C. days, (that means before Christ - a true relationship, lol), I used to read books that you wouldn't ever take to church and leave them in the backseat uncovered! One particular author that I liked was Zane. She was one of the best authors out there. I found myself reading everything that she published. I even pre ordered her books before they were released, whenever I could.

A friend of mine, a former baseball mom friend, told me about Fifty Shades of Gray. The way she described the book was exactly like the books that Zane had written and published for years **already**. We were used to the 'smut' books – as we call them. When *Fifty Shades* came about, I couldn't believe the attention E.L. James received for writing the same type of books that Black authors had written for a while—especially Zane.

In most stores, Black authors are separated from White authors. Why is that? I honestly feel that I would be safe in saying that it is true for the majority of the stores. I believe we subconsciously or consciously allow that to happen and that is destroying integration and unity in America. It feeds the beliefs that we are so different in every area of our lives. Black people might be able to walk in the front doors of restaurants or sit anywhere they want to sit on a bus, but we are still so segregated . What hurts more is that I don't believe enough people see or care about that variety. I don't want to have to walk to a section in a bookstore where Black authors are off to the side – alone. Hairstyling books are the same way. Black hair products – the same way. I believe we are just habituated to the separation and possibly feel that there is no other way. There is a way though.

Could you get into a book that has a Black cover? I know I asked this earlier. I did it on purpose. I wanted to paint a bigger picture for you to see what I am saying and then come back to the question. How many books have you skimmed through or even picked up to read the back cover that had a Black person or a Black couple adorning the front cover?

If Zane had the supporters that E.L. James had with her book, I can only imagine where Zane would be in comparison to what she was capable of doing. I am not advocating Zane or belittling E.L. James, I am only using those names to make a point since both are known in their own rights for writing erotic fiction. I am also pointing this out since it has come to our attention that women [seemingly] were hungry for erotic entertainment. I can give some of

Zane's no-rise to the top blame on the freaky in-the-closet Christian women. Yes, I said it. Many of them wanted and enjoyed what Zane was writing, but they didn't want anyone to know. They sat up in their beds at night and read Zane's books like anyone else, but many probably wouldn't admit it. I wonder if they would have supported Zane on the big screen. I don't know, but I doubt it.

Who would have thought it? An erotic movie on the big screen gave women permission to watch soft porn without the guilt of feeling they were watching grit and grunge pornography in secrecy. Could a Black woman have gotten away with it? I am still asking myself that. We always have to be ten times better. Even if we are, we have to have the right people backing us up. Even then, sometimes it's not quite enough.

Take the movie, *Magic Mike* for example. I had never seen the movie at the theater. It was a good movie, but that was another movie that I raised a brow over. With a movie starring White actors, the boundaries are so much broader than they are for movies starring Black actors. I never saw much of the movie, *Players Club*, but from my understanding from other people, sounds like the plots were similar—erotic dancers getting caught up in a less than pleasing lifestyle for money. Either way, anyone can see that White movies and books are praised for their eroticism, while Black movies are limited to Black audiences or considered raunchy.

"It is unfortunate that some have sidewalks while others have highways."

~Angel Tucker-Carr

Part Four
March On

People have been marching for everything for decades. Depending on what the march is about will determine the level of change. Stand up for this or stand up for that has been the slogan used for any and everything from bullying to fatal diseases, to things in between such as keeping music and art in public schools. There are groups that stand up for saving trees and animals and even Monarch butterflies. I am all for standing for your cause. What I can't understand is why it is so much easier to stand up for everything except justice and equality for Black people.

Protesting has been the way Blacks have used their feet (walking) for a change. With an organized boycott, they changed the way the bus system was run. They went from having to sit at the back to sitting wherever they wanted. Their 'change' that they kept in pockets hit the economy hard, and that brought about a major change. No matter what anyone says, a seated bottom and a closed mouth doesn't get anything done. Faith without works is dead.

For years upon years, the Black race has been in a disarray and suffering from emotional distress from fighting and asking for something that no one should have to ask for: to be treated like a human being. Time is up on saying that you don't understand. Time is up. We haven't been heard, and we no longer hear you when you say that you don't get it.

The Word of God tells us in Amos 3:3, "Can two walk together except they be agreed?" That question is true because the Word of God is true; but let us talk about that in terms of the marching.

Let's talk about the different marches that have gone on around the country. I am not a liberal, nor am I a complete conservative. I am not a radical by any means because I agree with topics from both sides. I don't feel that I have to choose according to a party. If I am out marching with the liberals, expect that I am marching for what I have on my sign. I should not be categorized as one who is marching for everything on the agenda. Many people get upset when people insinuate if they voted for Donald Trump, then they must be a racist. Well, it's the same thing. If they are not indeed a racist in some form, they must agree with some of the issues that he promised to address. You see, categorizing doesn't feel good when it's turned around. I have learned that the hard way, and I'm still learning.

I feared for my life!

How can you protect what you are afraid of? I know that I'm not supposed to end a sentence with a preposition, but in this book, it becomes necessary in order to get my point across.

I have my own opinion, observations and true stories from others as to why people are afraid of citizens they are supposed to serve and protect. It's because people (other races) have been informed to

1) Be afraid of Black people

2) Don't ever get into a fight with a Black person because they will beat the *you know what* out of you

3) Black people are strong and like animals

4) They (Blacks) are dangerous

If you have been told this lie all of your life, that will automatically create a fear in a White person's life about Black people. What happens if that White person happens to be a police officer? Oftentimes, death.

It is nearly heart stopping to see young Black men gunned down by police officers on a regular basis. The only explanation we get as a community is that the officer "feared for his or her life". That has become the award-winning phrase. Maybe the

officers are afraid for their lives, but I don't think
for one moment it is because they feel threatened
by the situation at hand. They are hearing the voices
in their heads that have warned them about a Black
man (or woman in some cases) is dangerous. Maybe
it is the sister of the same voices that Black people
hear in their heads that warns them that their life is
about to end because of an encounter with a White
police officer or a racist. Either way, hearing voices
are frightening, but when the power is in the hands
of the one who has the authority and the weapon,
only one of the situations is more deadly.

I am tired of seeing the faces of Black young
men posted on the television news. Listen, I am not
talking about the ones that are killing each other or
have committed a crime. Not all Black boys that are
on television because of death are criminals. I have
to say that because too many are being thrown in a
barrel labeled 'criminals' Therefore, justice is almost
impossible for them. Just because the verdict comes
back not guilty for the ones who take their lives
doesn't mean that it's correct. Why do I say that? I
say that because there's a judge and a jury making
that decision—not God. I promise to talk about this
more in detail later; and I also promise to talk about
the Blacks who do commit the crimes. I know some
of you were already making statements in your head

or underneath your breath about it. I will get to that because that too is a problem.

I didn't have a Black husband or a Black son laying in a pool of blood fighting to see another moment even after doing everything the officer told him to do. I do have a Black husband and two Black sons. I can't relate to the pain of those families who went through the pain of losses, but I can sympathize and empathize with them wholeheartedly. I'm learning to start trying to see things from the view of others instead of waiting for the issues to come to my front porch. I don't want to be that person. I want my heart to always feel for others. Most people say they don't want to get involved, but might I remind you that you are already involved. You're not involved directly, but indirectly.

No Justice No Peace is the chant we will hear until a real change comes. For many people the words 'no peace' means rioting and having a shaken spirit. Courage and boldness is an outcome of inner peace.

Black Lives Matter (BLM)

Several years ago a friend of mine was going through some painful issues with her son. He was addicted to drugs and if that wasn't enough, she was dealing with the fact that he would take anything that wasn't nailed down. It was the addiction that changed who he was completely.

She was working, trying to be a great wife and mother to her other two children, but was challenged by her son's addiction. One of a few reasons I am sharing is to enlighten this audience (the readers) of the disparities between how Black guys are treated versus White guys. My friend is White. Her son could go into any store and fill his backpack with items and walk out of the store and never would anyone address him. He was never a suspect. If he was, no one ever stopped him and questioned if he was stealing. If a Black guy walked into a store with a backpack, he would be told that he couldn't enter the store with it or he would be followed around the store to make sure he didn't take anything. I have been a victim of being followed around the store—especially in the local beauty supply stores that are owned and operated by people of other races and nationalities. I can't blame them for being watchful, after all, they have been warned about Black people and 'their' stealing and other non-trustworthy habits. Stereotypical beliefs.

My friend's son was a perfect example of being privileged because of his race.

One incident she shared with me was when he was riding in a stolen car with some of his minority friends. They wrecked the car by slamming into a tree and the car caught fire. The boys jumped out of the car and ran, but her son stayed. He was the type that would take the punishment. If he did the crime, he was willing to accept the consequences. I don't know if he was so willing to accept the consequences because he had never had any stiff penalties or what. I believe he would have had a different outlook on what he did if he had ever had a real punishment for the things he had done. After he stayed and the other guys fled the scene, Mark waited with the car. The police officers that showed up to the scene took Mark home like a good little victim. The other boys all received five years in prison for their involvement in the stolen car incident. That's what we have witnessed all of our lives when it came to drugs charges, stolen vehicles, murder...you name it. We don't have to ask ourselves why her son never faced any charges. He is White! That's reason enough. Honestly, we are sick of this and we are sick of living in this country of inconsistencies and maltreatment.

Black Lives Matter is a phrase that I even got tired of hearing at first. Even though the majority of the world was tired of hearing it, I understand why the phrase was created in the first place. I'm not saying this because I happen to be a Black life that matters. I am saying it because I believe that all lives matter.

Until the world can show that they agree, we will always have issues surrounding race relations. We will always question if our lives really matter as Black people. When a person doesn't think he or she matters, they will either fight to get the respect or allow themselves to be what others have said they are. Black Lives Matter folks chose to stand up and fight for their respect and dignity.

Let us get to the root of the Black Lives Matter movement. There has never been a question as to whether or not all lives matter. To pretend that you do not understand that no one was insinuating that a particular life didn't matter was absurd. In addition to all of the times Black people have been looked over and seen as nothing and no one and killed for no reason, it makes many of us question whether or not our lives matter to anyone else. It baffles me that people will go all the way to Africa or other far away countries and continents to save the lives of animals that are hunted and killed for their skin (hide), tusks, teeth, and anything else of value (of that animal). Some people are furious about the animals being ripped away from their carcasses after killing them for their own gain. Some people spend fortunes on saving trees or donating to shelters, but these same people will allow the slaughtering of human beings in our own country.

I have heard all kinds of excuses and reasons why the murders are happening, but let us be real and truthful here. A rap sheet or flawed background is not authorization for killing a person when the current traffic stop or arrest is not related to the crime at hand – or no crime at all. Let me point out some things that I don't think we as people 'get' sometimes. I say 'we' because I have been guilty in the past of thinking a 'certain' way about people also.

A few years ago, Alton Sterling was shot in Baton Rouge, Louisiana. Reportedly, he was outside of a store selling CDs and had used a gun to threaten someone. Reports reveal that he was shot close range by two police officers. Eric Garner was killed outside of a store selling cigarettes. Is it a fatal crime to sell the cigarettes? I don't think so. What I do know is that selling the cigarettes isn't what got him killed. It was an excuse to approach him and it led to killing him. The New York City Medical Examiner's Office report stated that the cause of death was compression of neck, compression of chest, and prone positioning during physical restraint by police. Contributing conditions listed were acute and chronic bronchial asthma, obesity, hypertensive cardiovascular disease. The officer denied choking him though. Instead of the 'system' trying to figure out how we can get a handle on murders during traffic stops and arrests, those in charge spend more time trying to dig up a person's history and past mistakes to justify being killed today.

The bottom line is that Black men and women have been killed for drummed up reasons and no one is paying (through convictions of the courts) for the murders. Every time we look around we are seeing police officers walk free after taking the life of a Black man. Then I hear people sounding like some of the people on some of the 1960's shows talking about the people marching. Rioting is not cool, and burning down places of business in the neighborhood they live in doesn't make sense to me. I know they try to make a point and get attention, but burning down the mom and pop stores in the neighborhoods isn't the way to go about getting the attention. It only gets more negative attention. The White people there don't care about them destroying their own. That's just one way that Blacks contribute to being held back from something better.

Do you have any idea of how painful it is to tell your sons how to stay alive in this world? Do you know how it hurts to tell them if they get pulled over, "Do this. Don't do that, and don't reach for your phone or anything at all?" Believe me, I want my children to call me so that I will know where they are and in case that will be the last time I hear their voice. I know it sounds crazy, but, if you are not a Black person, then you have no idea of what it feels like. The boys used to get tired of me telling them step-by-step of what to do if a police pulls them over, but I couldn't help it. I still tell them when they leave the house going somewhere especially when they travel. They would say, "Oh Mom! Okay, okay! We know." After the killing spree that went on, they started saying, "Okay. We will, Mom. Thanks." I don't like having to do that with my kids. I want to be able to pray over them before they leave and while they're gone because it's the right thing to do – not because I fear for their lives being taken away from them at the hands of someone else because they are Black men.

Black Life Red Blood

We have always been held hostage for what other Blacks do. So many times we watchTV. If we saw a murder or robbery or something, we'd say, "I sure hope he's not Black." It's not that we expected a Black suspect. It's because we knew White society seems to always be looking for an excuse to feel the way they do. They have used any and everything to justify locking their doors when a Black man passes or backing into a corner when one gets on an elevator with them. Black men have told me their stories of how it makes them feel when that happens to them. They find it degrading.

When my oldest son was a little boy, young Black men were killing other young Black men on an alarming basis for petty things. They were being killed for their shoes, car rims, or even the color they were wearing. Gangs were taking colors as a representation of being a part of them – or against them. That was so stupid. It showed no respect for a Black man's life anywhere. It was a vicious cycle. Some of them would give reasons like "someone disrespected them". Really? Is that how disrespect is handled? Is the consequence of so-called disrespect death? Unfortunately, they thought it was. That was a superficial reason that stemmed from childhood trauma: The root of hating themselves and where they are in life. No excuses, just my truth.

It is dispiriting and saddening that Black on Black crime has been about senseless issues that were created amongst themselves in their own 'hoods.' Division came from what was once a union. Not many people realize it or they have chosen to be okay with the division. Without going too deep into religion, I will stay surface and say *an enemy hath done this.* That phrase came from the scriptures regarding the enemy planting the tares amongst the wheat. The tares can be used metaphorically for the drugs, colors, and other nonsense that have separated Blacks. The drugs have been thrown into the Black neighborhoods like pieces of steak in a backyard of pits and someone says, "Go at it." The pit bulls or any dog for that matter will fight over the steaks until they are no more. Countless lives have been lost for reasons that probably can't even be intelligently explained.

According to documentaries, the murders were happening in the inner cities and places on the West Coast far before it hit Texas in the late eighties and early nineties.

Let's go deeper into the Black on Black crime issue in America. I've said it, you might have said it If you did not say it, you thought it. I have heard it more times that I can count: "Well what about the Blacks killing Blacks!" What about it? It's sad. It's wrong. It needs to be stopped. I addressed it a couple of paragraphs ago. People need to be held accountable for murdering whether it be Black on Black, White on Black, or White on White, etc. Murder is murder! There's a subtle tone in the question about Blacks killing Blacks that I pick up. The underlying message to it is, "Why are Black people worried about Whites killing Blacks when their own do it? I can't help but feel that the killing epidemic would come to an end or at least an attempt to end if it were White children and young men dying like Blacks. Putting a stop to it would be at the top of the agenda.

Until It Hits Home

Opioids have gotten America's attention because it's affecting more than Black kids. A majority of society doesn't care about Blacks dying much like human trafficking and prostitution that I mentioned earlier. It's not a problem until it hits their homes. They don't care about how many young Black men are filling up the prisons over something others get probation for or no charges filed at all. They sure don't care about Blacks filling up the funeral homes and cemetery plots.

How many times do you think a Black young teen/man would walk away from a mass murder? NEVER! White boys/men either take their own life or go peacefully to jail and brag about why they killed innocent people the way they did. When White boys and young men kill, they want to study their brain or blame it on bullying or parenting. When Blacks kill, they call them animals. I am guilty of calling all individuals who commit heinous murders animals - not just Blacks. I wonder how many robberies and murders are committed by non-Black people. I am sure we will never see the actual numbers if we are waiting for the incidents to make it to television. I have never gotten so tired of seeing Black and Hispanic men in the news alone for crimes. I would think my race is perfect too if I was young and hardly ever seen anyone who looks like me on the news for committing crimes.

Dylann Roof went into a Charleston church and shot nine innocent Black people that he sat side by side with during Bible study and then took their lives. Black people don't find it strange when a White person wants to come and join anything (especially worship) for the most part anyway. A majority of Blacks are welcoming to other races. He wasn't questioned or barred from coming in and joining in Bible study only to end the lives of the unarmed, caught off-guard church people. Some of the people were too old for us to imagine them trying to get away from that animal. His interviews were non-remorseful. He didn't care! He chose to talk about why he did it and how White people need to take care of each other. Dylan killed nine people, but he is still living to see another day.

Columbine High School Massacre. Enough said.

That massacre occurred on April 20, 1999. It was a school shooting and attempted bombing at a high school in Columbine, Colorado. Eric Harris and Dylan Klebold murdered twelve students and they also killed a teacher. Another twenty plus were injured, and a few were injured trying to escape the school. The two trench-coat wearing murderers committed suicide. We seem to focus on the children, as we should; yet in any comparison at all those monsters are never talked about as being cold-blooded killers.

The Las Vegas mass shooting that happened on the night of October 1, 2017 might have happened one night, but it destroyed lives for years to come while ending the lives of others. Stephen Paddock was that murderer who took his time preparing for the mass shooting from his Mandalay Bay Hotel and Casino room. He killed 58 people and wounded 869 others. Once again, another coward committing suicide after taking innocent lives. We are so busy talking about Black on Black killing, but we fail to talk about the ones who take out dozens at a time that also look like them in race and skin color.

The Sandy Hook Elementary School shooting on December 14, 2012. Elementary school is a building full of little children and those caring for them. Then 20-year old Adam Lanza shot and killed 26 people, 20 of them being children and the others were staff members. He killed his own mother before he went to the school. He too committed suicide after his heinous crime.

Stoneman Douglas High School. Nikolas Cruz was charge with capital murder for his actions on February 14, 2018. He opened fire in a high school full of students who look like him. He killed 17 and injured 17. He made it out without incident and alive to tell the story if he chose to do so.

In 2012 at the Century 16 Movie Theater in Aurora, Colorado, James Holmes used tear gas grenades and shot people in the audience of a movie theater. I remember it was a midnight screening, (one in which I'm not fond of doing as I get older and wiser). He was said to have been wearing tactical clothing, which makes sense for the grenades. He opened fire and killed 12 people and injured 58 others by gunfire. He was arrested without incident and made it to see another day alive after taking so many lives and injuring dozens more.

Santa Fe High School shooting on May 18, 2018 in Santa Fe, Texas. Eight students and two teachers were murdered, and another thirteen were wounded. The shooter was a 17-year old student of Santa Fe High School, and he was taken into custody without incident. His name is Dimitrios Pagourtzis.

The named individuals killed masses in one setting. There was a time when I was afraid of getting on an airplane. It was something about being in the sky in something as big and powerful as an airplane without being able to control what happened that would scare me.. I don't like the idea of not knowing what is going on in the cockpit or not knowing the pilot. There were so many things that I would think about, such as not knowing if he was having a bad day or if he was sleepy or just wanting to end it all. People have said to me,

"Angel, more people die in car accidents every year than in airplanes." I tell them that it might be true, but the airplane takes out sometimes hundreds of people in one crash—so it evens out. I look at the mass shootings the same way. Those killers take out or injure dozens of individuals at one time, but we focus on the one person a Black man kills. None of it is condoned. I am only highlighting what is normally looked past.

There are other incidents and mass murders in churches and schools that have happened on United States soil, and I can't recall or find in research where officers shot and killed the suspect. If they did, it wasn't without negotiation first. We have witnessed many apprehensions of murder suspects calmly walked to a squad car and given water or in one case given food. I just wonder why a Black man can't get the same leniency after committing a petty crime of maybe stealing something from a store or selling cigarettes outside of a convenience store.

Freddie Gray was a 25-year old Black man arrested by the Baltimore Police Department and charged for possessing a knife on April 12, 2015. Interesting enough, while being transported in a police van, Gray fell into a coma and later died on April 19, 2015. He had injuries to his spinal cord (believed to be caused by excessive force). The officers from the

Baltimore Police Department that were involved were suspended with pay.

Eric Garner died in New York after being arrested for selling cigarettes outside of a convenience store. He was 43. This event took place in July of 2014. He was placed in a choke hold by police while pleading for his life. The infamous "I Can't Breathe" phrase came from Eric Garner's last words as the world watched him die.

It baffles me of how a person's physical limitations or existing conditions seem to always play a determining factor of a Black man's death when it comes to being murdered. We never hear about an officer's health when he or she is killed in the line of duty. It is probably hard to recall any other murder that has taken place in any capacity, where the victim's health is talked about more than the crime itself.

Philando Castile was killed in front of his fiancé and child. Instead of addressing his murder, society wanted to bring up his priors. I don't understand it. That's one of the reasons Black Lives Matter started! Whether Black lives matter or not was and still is in question. There are so many other names, but I'm going to move on after I mention Trayvon Martin. I believe Trayvon's death hit harder because he was a baby to me. A child! He was younger than my boys and younger than my daughter is right now.

He was walking alone not bothering anyone, and a citizen on patrol confronted him and killed him in cold blood. George Zimmerman had no right to kill Trayvon Martin or anyone else. He was not in law enforcement and had no authority, but yet he wasn't charged with any crime whatsoever. He was an ordinary citizen who decided to murder a Black boy that night. He has had many prior interactions with the law, but none of that has been brought to light in the media. He openly hates Black people and identifies with racist hate groups. I don't know why because looking at him he definitely doesn't look White by any means. That doesn't matter, and I probably should have left that out; but then again, many people from other countries identify as what they are not. George (not worthy of calling him Mr. Zimmerman) is known by many (according to a television special) for being racist. Acquaintances of his were on video saying that he called Black people "monkeys". That was his name for Black people other than the "N" word.

He was another animal who killed an innocent Black person and got away with it here on earth in our justice system. I remember watching the documentary and I saw on a piece of paper that the camera zoomed in on, that the jurors were told that he had a *right to defend*. Defend who? Jurors tend to forget about what is right. God is the ultimate judge, but we do a poor job in America with justice. That's where the changes need to be made. Ordinary people are chosen to sit on a jury to decide the fate of individuals that many of them might hate or dislike.

When President Obama said Trayvon was him or could have been his son the world went crazy! The world who couldn't see past Trayvon being Black or Barack Obama being a president. They already hated having sympathy and empathy for that child's parents. Some people said he should have stayed out of it, while others say he went against police officers. Are you kidding me? How? How did making that statement go against police officers? I know. He was supposed to be on the side of the police no matter what (yeah right). That's how many people stick together even when they know a person is wrong. That's the way of the world we live in. *Don't commit the crime. But, if you do, I'll have to help you cover it up!* That's exactly what I get out of that behavior. President Obama saw himself as a young Black boy who could have been killed like Trayvon because of his race. That's what he was saying, but it was twisted to mean something else. Now, we have a president in the White House who jumps into every situation. He even demands law enforcement to get involved in certain issues because that is who he is. Nothing is said about that other than he is a different type of president and he's not a politician. So, we are supposed to be okay with his silliness.

In the same documentary, I heard about a twelve-year old that was shot by a police officer while he was in a park with a toy gun. That is not a good idea anywhere and I know that. Not long ago, in March of 2019, a White man with a gun went into an open garage of a house that the police had followed him to, jumped fences, and did several other unlawful things. He was arrested without incident. They had clear shots at him over and over. I'm glad they didn't kill him, but I wish Black men and kids would be able to get the same patience and understanding in a chase or arrest.

Find the holes that you wish…the fact remains the same—lives are being taken and no one seems to show that they care.

During the time I was writing this book , Jordan Edwards was murdered and it wasn't looking promising that the officer who killed him would be convicted. I can't believe how many people tried to justify the officer shooting an unarmed fifteen year old in a car. The only defense we often hear is "I feared for my life or my partner's life." Finally, that phrase didn't work. So far it hasn't, but of course his murderer is appealing. I understand him appealing – that's normal.

Take a moment… Close your eyes and be still. If you're not in a place where you can take yourself to a still place, then try it later, but by all means please try it. Think about your own sons or daughters if you don't have sons. Imagine them being in the place of any of these men and boys that I mentioned (or didn't mention by name). What would you feel? Would you try to dig up their pasts (rap sheets) and get citations that turned into warrants? Would you be eager to mention they've had run-ins with law enforcement? Would it be fair to talk about their prior arrests if any to justify why they got killed for being pulled over for something as simple as a blinker? Let me put this out there right quick: If a person has a history or has committed a prior offense like an assault or if they have an active warrant, dispatch will receive an alert. The dispatcher will inform the officer so the officer can approach the suspect with caution. I get it. They are supposed to be aware at all times. I'm not talking about those kinds of stops. We are quick to speak because we have no connection with the lives that have been taken. They were not our children, our nephews, our neighbor, our dads, or our uncles. I know Jordan Edwards' grandmother. His death nearly took her to her death. Everyone who knew him personally said he was a kid with a promising future. I know we don't have the power to say when a person dies, but in the natural world, he had a promising future because of the track he was on in life and the family he came from.

Recently, I was talking to my husband, and I told him that I can't help but see the resemblance of slavery days in today's times. I wasn't there, but I've seen movies. I've also heard stories of how helpless Black people felt when they saw their loved ones hanging from trees. I heard them talk about how it felt to see their loved ones with gashes on their bodies oozing with blood; and there was nothing they could do without becoming a victim too. Actually this was still true of the days after slavery as well. I recall hearing stories of how it felt to watch your loved ones arrested for defending themselves. If they were lucky they'd spend time in prison and have a felony on their record.If they weren't 'lucky', they were killed. We all know that receiving a felony for a crime not committed isn't lucky, but it's better than the alternative. My grandmother, great uncle, and great aunts spent time in prison for a charge that I just described. I grew up believing they had committed a crime, but somewhere in my mind I always figured it was probably something race related since they were all born from 1902-1912. They were very mild mannered people. There was no law **for** Negroes. The charge went as assault for my family who was trying to defend their father from being murdered by a White man. However, for a White person it would have been self-defense. I was glad to finally find out the truth. I don't know every detail, but I found out enough to know that my grandmother and her siblings were not out looking for someone to assault.

My mom tells me that it was *nothing* (meaning common) to see Black dummies hanging from trees with a noose around its neck. I heard that two small towns near me were notorious for the black dummies hanging. They tell me that in places such as Mississippi that it wasn't just the dummies. Sometimes, it was the real thing. As far back as history goes, Blacks have always watched White men have their way with Black people – from raping them to killing them. Whatever they wanted to do, they could do it, and nothing would be done. Reminds me of what we're going through this day and time. We watch and nothing is done. Please don't bring up Jordan Edwards' murder finally getting justice. He is only one of too many to count.

I don't think anyone in their right mind would say White lives don't matter, Hispanic lives don't matter, or Asian lives don't matter.

The majority would believe the phrase holds true because of what we have witnessed (on TV, and sometimes in person), time after time that a Black life does not matter—especially to the small percentage of dirty police and hate groups. It's not just the police officers who are making the bad decisions to kill unarmed Black men and women for that matter. Think about it: the police aren't serving as the judge and the jury. They are only having *their* cases presented to our fellow citizens, and they (the citizens) are the ones confirming that a Black life does not matter.

I feel confident in this matter to speak for the majority of Black people and to select others who understand what I am about to say. All lives matter, but we are just addressing the lives that are in question right now. If you are any race other than Black (maybe Mexicans too at this point) ever felt that your life didn't matter because of your race? I rest my case. *Case dismissed.*

It's Your Duty, Not a Choice

Let's take a pause break and talk about jury duty. I was once an individual who despised the thought of being called for jury duty. When I'd get the card in the mail, I would cringe. I can't even tell you why it made me feel that way other than I felt I was being inconvenienced. I had to miss work (like I didn't want to), find parking, sit all day, wait to see if I would be called, and God forbid if they pick me! I used my 'legal' excuses every chance I got. Seems like I always had children that were under the age of ten and had no one to keep them, so I didn't have to serve.

Finally, there came a time when I decided that it was a privilege to serve. I thought about the people who couldn't serve because of their background (today), but the skin color long ago. I started to realize that if I want to see a change in anything, then I need to contribute to that change. Many Black people won't serve on jury duty, but they wonder why the convictions come down as they do. I've said it again and again, the judge can only work with what they have in front of them. Of course they decide the sentencing.If you're in the room when the decisions are being made, the difference is made right there. It's not that I think we should go light on someone because of their skin color, but we see things differently. Majority of us aren't ready to lock up a child for the rest of their lives for a crime that carries a sentence of fifteen to twenty years or so for a White person.

We don't have time for everybody to go to school and become lawyers,judges, and district attorneys, but we do have time to serve on a jury. Oftentimes, we think the differences are made only in the areas of power and titles, but jurors have major power. Look at them when you think about cases of Black men and women who are sitting behind bars. I am not saying all are innocent in prison. I know better than that! I'm talking about the ones that are innocent and have been framed or mistaken for someone else or those in prison with maximum sentences that don't fit the crime.

Allow me to leave you with this:

Stay clean to be able to exercise your right to vote and serve.

Understand you have the power to create and promote change.

Change your perception of what jury duty really means.

Go to school to educate yourself and know your rights.

If you don't do it for yourself, do it for your kids and the future generations. After all, someone did it for you.

Next Generation Policing (Will it get worse or better?)

No one knows but God. I can only guess. My hope is that it will get better, but my guess is that it won't. I'm not a pessimist or a one hundred percent realist. You don't have to be neither to tell the truth about what you see. I can be an optimist when I am thinking about things that I can control. I have zero control over the people in the world. I don't even have control over myself, but thank God I do have control over my thoughts because thoughts become things. If I didn't know who God is in my life, my thoughts could bring about some things that might not be so nice and pleasing to Him.

Much of the world sees only what is available to us on television. Another part of the world has firsthand experiences because they live in certain areas that they can't get away from it. I would say that I am in the middle (give or take). I live in a part of the country that I see what others see on television, have experienced some painful situations myself, but the most difficult part is I get to witness people saying things in private that they won't say in front of a television camera or in the face of others.

"What do you mean by that, Angel?" I'll tell you what I mean. When I asked would policing get better or worse, I had my own answers in mind. They are strictly my opinion from personal observations.

Sometimes I sit and cringe when I hear people talking about Black people as if they are nothing. The most painful part of hearing the words that proceed from their mouths is that they really believe what they are speaking. Anytime someone can justify a mother being held at gunpoint and a cop using expletives threatening to pop a cap in her head while she is holding her child...that is despicable. There was an incident that none of us know the full story, but from what we all could see by camera footage on the news, the cop wasn't right by any means. I watched him ask her if she is f'ing deaf. Then he goes on to tell her to get out of the f'ing car several times. She explains that she is holding her baby and can't put her hands up. He let her know that he didn't care if she was holding a baby. He goes on to shout more derogatory expletives in a tone that was harsher than one you'd use with a bank robber. The woman was being ordered out of her car because someone in the store called the police about a four-year old girl walking out of a freaking dollar store with a doll. I haven't heard much talk about the man who was with her. I didn't see him being taken from the car or getting out on his own. The footage I saw was him being handcuffed against a car while the officer kicked his leg out from under him (acting like he was spreading the man's legs) causing him to nearly fall. How can we expect people to have respect for a person in a position that abuses his or her position as such? Many people think that an officer should be obeyed and given a pass no matter how filthy his actions are, and that is what I am sick of hearing – justifications. I have heard more justifications for killing and roughing up people than I care to hear in a lifetime.

As I sit and hear those who believe the officer had a right to talk to a woman in that way about *a $1 doll, I am in tears. I am dumbfounded that people would actually side with someone like that. What values does that person have of his own? I wonder what part of him is saying these things. Is it his heart or just his mind? I want to say it's surface speech, but I don't know. A huge part of who I am doesn't want to believe that he really feels that way. I'm struggling to keep my mouth shut and just listen, and my God, it is a struggle! I'm hearing phrases 'feared for his life' and 'the guy had something'...only to find out everything the person talking had heard was what others had told him. He had not even seen the video of the incident. His entire story was one sided and negative regarding the woman because she was Black. That alone is what scares me about future policing and the citizens in general. It's not just the police. It's our society. They believe anything you do to a Black person is justified because the authority and truth lies in the hands of anyone except for the Black person – always! How can the officer fear for his life when the woman doesn't have a weapon and she's holding two babies and pregnant with another child? How? That crap sounds good and it has gotten more officers freed of charges than I even care to research and name. It hurts me to know that the people that I know and deal with would justify someone taking my life just* *because I am Black. I say my life because it's the same thing. What makes me any different from the people out there? Once I am on the streets, I'm still Black.There are more individuals that see me like some of them see other Black people. They see me as a threat and guilty as accused without a trial. I believe to my heart that Black people are guilty to the prosecutors and the jurors before they ever step foot on the stand in court. Their complexion determines their fate.*

The future of policing will have to take a major turn to get better. History is repeating itself - slowly but surely. It seems that the police of years past when Blacks weren't considered anything more than property, would kill a Black person for no reason at all. If they even thought he had done something they wouldn't hesitate to kill him. Then the country became more integrated and people were trying to get away from racism because they knew it was wrong and destroying our country. No thanks to where we are today with social media and all ages are mixing, the ones who have heavy influence are turning the waters bitter once again. They are spewing out what their forefathers believed and they are taking hold of the minds of young White people. They are brainwashing the young to carry out what they started with racism and bigotry. You see, until social media graced the airwaves, many of the children and their young parents were taught by what they heard and saw in the house. It wasn't always pleasantries, but they were saved because they would mingle with Blacks in school. Now children are going to charter schools and private schools with more kids who look like them; When they get home, they are in the clutches of those who have been in conversations on social media all day with other racists. The younger people in the country that are in positions of authority are different now. They are brainwashed. Many of the ones I have seen in person mirror what I have seen on television and in the news. I feel a change is coming again, and this time it won't be for the better.

I hear the stories of people fearing for their lives just like the world does, but I get to hear the hearts that spill out something totally different. Remember, I am never talking about everyone. This is not a blanket of blame and shame I'm using to cover anything. I am just sick and tired of hearing the defense talk about how an officer or someone else who kills a Black person is fearful and innocent, but I'm not hearing matching stories face to face. I see one thing, but hear another. I feel that society is hearing people say one thing in front of the cameras and the press, but they are witnessing what really lies in the hearts of the ones claiming to be in fear.

Justice or Just-us

I watch prison and cop shows that include criminal activity and the sentences handed down to those allegedly committing crimes, and I notice a pattern. When a victim is black, it seems blacks get less time for murdering someone black. That is another reason people question if Black lives matter: a Black woman killed by a Black person just doesn't hold the same weight.

Wrongful convictions is just one of many dilemmas that we face in America, being Black.

Start with the Central Park Five. In 1989, five teenaged boys were wrongfully convicted of rape of a woman that allegedly took place in the Central Park in New York. The boys were coerced and coached to even lie on each other, and only two of them actually knew one another. One of the boys was fourteen years old! How does this happen?

Some sources say they spent between 6 and fifteen years, while others say they spent between five and fifteen. Either way, they lost their freedom because of the INjustice system. If it weren't for the true rapist coming forward, those [now] men would still be locked up. No movie or any documentary could actually make us feel what those boys went through in prison. Day in and day out, beat, raped... Only God knows what else happened to them. We can't fathom what they felt.

According to Attorney at Law Jarrett Adams, he too was wrongfully convicted for rape at age 17 and sentenced to 28 years in a maximum security prison. After serving nearly ten years and filing multiple appeals, Jarrett was exonerated with the assistance of the Wisconsin Innocence Project.

Why is it so easy for Black men to be accused of rape? I wonder does it have anything to do with the lies that we have been told about Black men being oversexed and are vicious when it comes to sex. I have been around many Black men and I haven't witnessed that to be a true statement. There are nymphomaniacs of all races, but I haven't seen that trait in Black men. I guess it's safe to say that they are not all that way. Trust me, I have been in some compromising areas at vulnerable times, and I didn't experience anything like that.

I am not a judge, a lawyer or a police officer, but I have had close relationships with individuals from all of the above professions. When people argue things like 'beyond reasonable doubts' and what the penal code says (that they even disagree with), I can't help but feel they are not being human at that time. We can all go by book, but sometimes the book is too broad of a brush to paint with. Another thing

I must point out is that defense representation for all individuals aren't available, so their chances of reasonable doubt aren't on their side.

It doesn't take a district attorney, a judge, jurors or anyone outside of an ordinary person to know that the justice system doesn't always seem fair when it comes to a person of color.

For example, sentences for the use and distribution of crack are harsher than cocaine. Cocaine is crack depending on who the user is will determine what it is called. White people are said to be more of the cocaine users, and Black people are said to use crack more.

Bill Cosby was sentenced to prison for charges many of the Hollywood men and our president of the United States of America and others have been allegedly accused of committing. I don't have a heaven or a hell to put anyone in, and I am not judging anyone. I am only speaking about what has been in the news for the past couple of years . It took very little time for Mr. Cosby to be tried and sentenced at eighty-three years old, while the others are living their lives in the free world. Losing a job or a career is definitely a penalty, but the men who lost jobs still have their freedom and can easily go somewhere else and work. Most of them have held positions high enough and 'gotten' enough money over the years that they won't have to go out and find jobs. We can easily say that Mr. Cosby admitted to the allegation(s), but the case here is justice isn't for us. Admitting or not, most of the others haven't even been indicted and formerly charged for anything.

I am not an advocate of committing crimes, so allow the 'defense to rest.' I am not siding with anyone, and my opinion about the cases is that the crimes should carry the same weight/sentence – not depending upon which set of jurors the court chooses or who the judge is for that day.

I am not going to do play-by-play crimes and the sentences they carry, but the crimes that we are privy of by way of the local news, the penalties are not the same across the board. You know it and I know it. I've known people who have served multiple years in prison and some are still doing time for violations that White guys would get a slap on the wrist for doing. I have heard individuals blame the jurors, and I can agree with that, which leads me to say that is a problem. I know it is our civil duty to serve on a jury for our peers, and it is unfortunate that our peers cannot be *trusted* to make decisions from hard cold evidence, or the lack thereof. So many times we have heard of men and women, especially Black men who have spent their entire adult lives in prison for something they did not do. Many of them met the description of what some White person gave that was a blanket description for almost any Black man in America. Look at Susan Smith who drove her children into a lake and said that a Black man did it. She gave a description and said what the man was wearing, only to find out there was no Black man! She was that Black man!

The Coin with Heads on Both Sides

Approximately thirty-four or so years ago Vanessa Williams was crowned Miss America, but she had to give up her crown less than a year later. Mrs. Williams was allegedly forced to give up her title due to nude photos of her that were published in Penthouse magazine. I was one of the many disappointed fans. I was disappointed that she did what she did and the fact that she would no longer be titled as Miss America.

I was in my early high school years when it happened, so I never saw the pictures and I was not interested. I am still uninterested in seeing the photos now because the photos were shameful to her. It is unnecessary for me to put any negative thoughts in my mind about someone who has done everything she could do to live that incident down. I can respect that effort.

Times have changed drastically.Mrs. Williams isn't the only woman with a celebrity status to have taken nude photos. She might have been the only woman with Miss America status to have taken nude photos. If that was the problem, I get it. The

Miss America title should require high standards. I just have a hard time believing she was treated that way because of the pictures without her race being a factor. After all, she was the first Black woman to be crowned in 1984. It doesn't seem like being Black should have been a problem in the eighties, but it was. It is still a problem now in 2019 to many individuals.

When a Black woman does something vulgar and unacceptable, she is criticized—especially prior to today's times. When White women committed vulgar and unacceptable acts, they were and still are considered sex symbols. Why is that? Probably the same reason women of non-color descent are praised for their bodies, looks, and strength while women of color are criticized for the same. There are well-known White women who became famous for showing their bodies and having sexual intercourse on video. That same sex act opened doors for others and started what would be known as an empire. No one knew they existed hardly before the sex. Numerous celebrities have become icons and household names for their provocative, sexual ways. It seems to be okay because they are expected to be that way. They are in their places so-to-speak. A title such as Miss America wasn't for us, and as with anything else, we are held to a much higher standard while standing underneath the microscope.

I'm sure she went through hell and probably even times of depression or worse, but she didn't let it show. She held her head up and continued to sing and act. We never saw her look as if she had been defeated, and I am sure not everyone was pleased that stripping her of a prestigious title of Miss America didn't break her publicly.

In 2015, members of the Miss America Pageant offered Mrs. Vanessa Williams and her mother a public apology for how the scandal was handled back in 1984. I am glad that she finally received an apology, because believe me, a late apology does help. It won't change what she went through, but psychologically, it changes things.

Together We Stand

In America, we have been so fixated on a divide and conquer mentality that it has trickled down to every generation for hundreds of years. When I started thinking about what we stood for (verbally) in America, I couldn't get away from the thoughts that were being downloaded to me. I kept hearing the word *united*. *United* where? We haven't been *united* in hundreds of years.

In history classes, we were taught that we were not united with anyone, as Black people. I realized why that was probably true. They believed that we were not full humans. We were considered a fraction of a human. Therefore, when humanity was being spoken of, it didn't mean us. We were taught that there is everybody else and then there's the Black race. We were set aside. As I shared that statement of being set aside, it was revealed to me that we were set apart as Believers.

Black people were only given one month that we could actually celebrate being Black in peace. We should never have to celebrate our race. We should be embracing ourselves as human beings and not being Black. We bought into the idea that we were given a 'time' to enjoy our race, culture, and the few people that we were taught about who had accomplished great things. We were allowed and encouraged to dress in attire that represented the African culture. Little that many of us knew that we didn't have to dress as an African to celebrate who we are. We are Americans. In my opinion, it was a way to make sure that we knew (or believed) we were different. We were not from America, and we had 'permission' to like ourselves for 28 days. It was our *pass* (so to speak) to be able to say *I'm Black and I'm proud*. Only then it was okay for a magazine to put a Black face on the cover because the editors didn't have to explain or justify why a Black face graced their covers. In many ways that did so much damage. We were still being controlled, and no one was preparing for damage control. There is a cause and effect to any and everything. America is seeing the effects of what they caused.

During Black History Month, the teachers would struggle to scrape up books to read to the class about Black history so that they could fulfil their curriculum for February's Black History Month.

As I think back on those times, it was fun for some to come up with new material but a dreaded task for others. I'm sure it wasn't fun teaching about something you had no interest in learning or teaching. We were deprived of so much information during my years of K-12 into college. I am just now learning about people pre-slavery who were powerful, wealthy, respected individuals. It angers me that White people got rid of the books that showed us being more than housekeepers and slaves. They changed the history books to reflect them being on top and us working their fields and being controlled. It was a way to keep us believing that we were nobody without them. Even with them, we were still only a fraction of a human being.

Once our ancestors were enslaved and later died, we began a new curriculum. We were being taught about the weaknesses of Black people. We were shown pictures of Black people being beaten and hung. We were shown Black people serving in areas and in jobs that were degrading and belittling. Every now and then a teacher would make a comment of how hard they worked or they'd say something about how loyal they were to their owners. I guess it was supposed to make us feel good when a 'good Negro' would be mentioned and the teacher would say something like, 'he was trusted.' I was never impressed. I just dealt with it like a good little Negro girl.

Always fighting for attention and a position in a self-proclaimed White man's world.

You Reap What You Sow

There's a biblical principle that is actually a life principle: You reap what you sow! If a farmer plants okra, he should not expect to harvest corn. The seed that we plant will produce its own kind. It might be an abundance of harvest or a single item, but rest assured there will be something unless there is something that inhibits its growth.

One morning I was listening to Pastor James Merritt, and what he said captured my attention. He said, "America sowed into slavery and is now reaping racism." Wow! Did that get your attention? I never thought about it that way, but he sure is right. That right there was a revelation for me because it actually answers some 'unasked' questions for me. If slavery was sown, then the harvest couldn't have been good.

If we want to change the America that we see now, then we must be willing to start sowing seeds of love, truth and compassion for one another. We've seen the results of sowing the opposite, and it's not good.

Section One

Our current White House administration is what I would call 'toxic' for the American people. I am sure many of you immediately thought of Donald Trump. He is not the entire administration, although he is the head conduit of all that takes place. A person in charge could never say that they had nothing to do with anything, good or bad.

One of my few reasons for pointing out the toxicity and making a statement as such is because the White House (administration) should be a place where America looks up to and wants to follow. It sets the tone *if you will.* During the past few years we have seen issues that took years to overcome be overturned. For example, women finally started coming forward regarding sexual assaults. They became more verbal and bold in speaking up for themselves and other women around the world. Women started with requesting equal pay and treatment as men, then they started demanding it. What happened next? They were met with pushback. Not just pushback from supervisors, companies or the individuals they were making complaints against, but from the president himself. Women were called liars and taunted and verbally attacked because of their voice.

Women were first given their voices by being allowed to vote. On August 18, 1920, the 19th Amendment guaranteed All American women the right to vote. This was only about 50 years after the Amendment for Blacks to vote was established. So women have come a long way, but with just one White House administration term, we felt thrown back into time. I wonder if our president had not been a person many allegations had come up against, would he have felt the same way towards women and working diligently to shut their voices down when speaking about their pain and experiences.

The same administration led by way of modeling retaliation. We had come so far with being able to speak up about mistreatment on our jobs and in our schools, and in life in general. Americans could tell about being bullied while feeling fear and retaliation, but there were existing laws in which we placed our confidence. The laws are still in place, but when we see the highest office in our country firing individuals for speaking truth, an invisible muzzle gets passed around to places of business all around the world. If the words that sounded like our president's voice during an interview can say that he can grab a woman by the vagina and even kiss them in the mouth because of who he is, that statement alone sends messages to all. Young men and young women heard that. Womanizing men in high places and positions heard that. Women and girls heard that. What happens on both sides of the gender line? Some are empowered and others are afraid. Sometimes people do things without even thinking, but subconsciously they feel they have a right to do whatever they want—especially when people in positions of authority call it natural and okay.

We can't afford to lose the great things that America has fought so hard to achieve together as a whole, not just on one side of the house, but in the entire house. Let's not lose decades of work in just a few years that will last decades more if not changed. America can't afford it!

The Divided States of America

Make America Great Again is the popular slogan that we are seeing and hearing these days in America. We're seeing the slogan on the back of vehicles, on ball caps and t-shirts, displayed on yard signs and on the signs carried by protestors and just about anywhere people want to project their voices. Hey, I'm just fine with people having a preference and sharing it respectfully. That's not my concern or issue at all. If I can even say 'my issue.' It's America's issue. My question has been, and still remains to be this: What was so great about America (then) that isn't great now? Was it great because we didn't get to hear the voices that we hear today coming from all sides instead of just one side? Is America not great (now) because the lack of control from only one side is now challenged?

Most of us love America (I know I do) and think it is the greatest country in the world because of our freedoms, opportunities, and democracy. Here lately, in the latter part of 2018 I am beginning to question if the slogan is referring to those freedoms or are they subtly speaking of oppressing Black people again as in the days of slavery and the civil rights era. When the same slogan (*Make America Great Again)* is used as it was used by a past leader that was obviously a supporter of broken America, my question gets answered. They are wanting America to be great for *them* again. Was it really great for all people or just White people? Is it that great today for everybody? Not completely, but it's a start. I guess we are supposed to be okay with the changes that have been made such as no more *open* lynching and burning of crosses in folks of color yards. I don't have to say go and ask someone of color who lived in the days of slavery or during the times when slaves were free but couldn't live free, how it was. I know.

I've already heard. I have been told what it was like for a grown man to be walking down the sidewalk (first) and a White woman decides to walk down the same sidewalk, the Black man must cross over to the other side of the street, and he'd better not make eye contact with her. I have been told how an adult man had to say ma'am to a White child that was barely over the age of a toddler. Was that great? It wasn't great for my people, nor is it great thinking about it. That Black man who told me addressing a child with ma'am no matter what age she was, happened to be my daddy.

Was America great when Black people couldn't be served in any restaurant around town? (Well, unless you stop at a Kountry Kitchen or some other place in a little kkk-run town in Texas, that idea of not serving Blacks is still a practice). Back then if Blacks were allowed in an establishment they had to use the back door! Was that great? Was it great that a Black man could be sitting down trying to eat his food and a White man starts to taunt him and belittle him calling him Nigger or boy?

One night my husband and I were watching television together, and they were showing a firefighter attempting to extinguish a blazing fire. The force of the hose got our attention almost simultaneously. We looked at each other and said, "Isn't that what they used on Black people?" We just stopped for a moment and thought about how awful that must have been for White police officers and sometimes ordinary citizens to use high powered hoses on Black people whenever they wanted to or *felt* the 'need.' So, was America great then when they would tell the dogs to sic'em in a crowd of Blacks of any age? They didn't care how old the victims were. Was that the great America our president is trying to promise to Americans today? Maybe those 'wanting America to be great again' are striving to make the only jobs available for people of color to be in fields chopping and pulling cotton from sun up to sun down. I mean, that was the America that correlates to 'making America great again.' Surely (I hope) that isn't what they really mean. Maybe they are wanting Black people to sit at the back of the bus like they had to long ago. I guess making it great means going back to the times when Blacks were denied an integrated public education, beat for reading, or attended schools where they sat in a classroom with grades 1 through 12 all in one room. I don't get it because I am still trying to figure out which part of America was so great that they are trying to return this country to.

When I see people openly boast about how much they hate other races and how they are determined to not allow people of other races and religions to take over, I wonder what will *make* America great.

When the group of White males (I don't use the word man unless it's earned in many instances) were marching in front of the Jewish Synagogues in Charlottesville, Virginia chanting "Jews will not take over", I couldn't imagine what they were thinking. That's what the Germans thought – they were racially superior to the Jews. They felt the Jews were a threat to the German community. The Charlottesville protestors went to that extent of violence over the removal of a Confederate statue! It's the same riot where a precious young lady by the name of Heather Heyer was killed by a car attack. I wonder what makes them think the Jews can take over or even want to take over. How can the Jews take over when the majority of their race was assassinated at the orders of Hitler whom many of the ones marching hail with reverence? Many young people are mimicking the hail Hitler sign and using swastikas to prove their loyalty to White power. I guess they don't realize that Hitler wasn't White, but I guess the skin color was enough to categorize him as White. What do they mean by 'take over' anyway? I wonder if they are referring to taking over as in the way that White people did in the sixties and prior. I don't believe any other race outside of some racist White people are wanting to take over. Most people just want their fair share of what belongs to them and the opportunity to achieve that which they acquire without incident. I feel confident in saying that the people they fear are people who are wanting to be treated fairly and left alone. Left alone as in not picked on and killed for uncalled for reasons.

I sit and watch tug-o-wars over flags being removed as well as statues of individuals that clearly stood for racism. It is easy for some people to say that it is all a part of history; therefore, these historical items should keep their places in the middle of American cities. I disagree. I wonder would the opinions be the same if those historical statues and idols represented innocent blood shed, lynching, beatings and oppression of *their* race and *their* ancestors. They were the Whites' (some) heroes but the Blacks' enemies. I can only wonder, but for my ancestors it wasn't a wonder at all—it was a reality.

I think about my daddy who passed in October of 2012, and was able to see the first Black president majority of America has known. There has been a sharing of another Black man who supposedly was a president in America, but he isn't known by many. His name was John Hanson. Since my daddy had to die, one good thing I can think of is that he escaped the disappointment of the setback America has taken and its current path to destruction. When he left here President Barack Obama was still in office. I know how many of you can't stand to hear the man's name, but it is what it is. Why is it so hard to understand why some Black people were happy to see the first Black president of the United States of America take office? Switch places! If we had never had a White president, wouldn't you like to have seen one? Of course you would. Many of my Caucasian brothers and sisters can't understand what I am talking about because they believe the only way America should be is underneath a White president; so their minds can't even go there and fathom a president never being White. Am I right? Of course I am!

My dad was a man of love and held a high regard for others. My dad would treat everyone the same. He would have a conversation with the homeless, shake hands with the crackhead (a term used for people who are believed to be using or have used crack cocaine), and feed the hungry. He would have been sorely disappointed in the rhetoric coming from the leaders of America and from the highest position in this country. I can hear him saying it now, "You know, that fella is going to ruin this country, isn't he? He's a silly outfit!" My dad called idle, worthless talk 'hurrahing.' Don't ask me what that means, or even how to spell it, but that's what he'd say. He felt that ignorant substance-less talk got people into pissing matches which were unnecessary and dangerous. He would always tell me and my sisters, "Don't stand around and argue with people. Just watch them." He was so wise. He was right. Too much talk is unhealthy and can be dangerous. Don't talk – just do.

I hate that my mother is seeing this country fall into a reverse. Our elders have come too far to see such a setback. I remember how many of them cast their votes for the presidential candidate in 2008 with such a sense of pride. There were some who were still leery of having a Black president. I don't know if it was because of the same-sex marriage that President Obama backed or if it was because he was Black. Many people (even Blacks) still had the mindset that being Black wouldn't allow him to be smart enough to run the country. This country of Black people have been brainwashed to believe that White is right.

I won't give up praying for peace and a turn around. Will these states ever be united? I am not naïve enough to think that we have ever been where we should be, or even close; but we were able to live in peace with one another – for the most part. Now people aren't afraid to kill a person just because they are of another race or religion. I guess when you hear hate and division spoken from the highest and most notable secular pulpit of the country, why not! I put it in the same category as this, a child hears his father bashing others and upholding the wrong that his siblings do or the father does those things himself, a child would not be afraid of the consequences. In fact, that child is praised for his wrong doing. That is what we are seeing in our country today. Bad behavior gets rewards.

Our president has been noted for asking people to do illegal things for his gain and promised to pardon them if they were sentenced to prison. Our president has even bragged about paying legal fees for someone if they assaulted others as long as they were doing it all in his name. A reporter was body slammed for asking questions to a high-ranking official and he was praised for the assault. Bombs were sent to innocent people around the country and our president couldn't even publicly call out the names of the targeted victims and give them empathy. There is no 'bigger person' in that. I don't have to like a person to be able to say, "I'm sorry that you went through that." Standards are a must, but they are not present for all sides. Democrat or Republican, a bomb sent or threatened to be sent should be addressed and empathized by the president. Will this country ever heal or has too much nonsense hate and division taken place and too much rhetoric spoken?

In these divided states of America we have seen more hate amongst people because of a difference of opinions and beliefs. Isn't that what America was all about? I have come to a tough realization that at one time I tried to make myself believe differently, but I've come to believe that our president of the United States of America isn't about Democrat or Republican. He has shown us time and time again that he is for anyone that will have the same agenda regarding race as he does. I don't believe for one bit he is so concerned about Israel as much as he is concerned about the White people who call themselves Evangelicals. That's MY opinion and my belief that I get to express in America as an American. I have heard statements about people that he once disliked, but then if they say anything remotely close to leaning his way about making America White again, he's all for them. They soon become his confidant and team member. A vote against Mexicans and Muslims is a vote for him. I don't think he cares about Black people, but he doesn't talk much about Blacks because I don't think he has a fear of Black people taking over or taking a lead in America. He is all for the Blacks dying at the hands of supposedly respected authority because that will eliminate any issue with the Black race. He sees that many Blacks are holding themselves down and he doesn't have to do much work to make that happen. That's why I cringe when a Black person (especially a man) does stupid, petty things that will land them standing before a judge because that is almost all the time a trip to prison and a blemished record that will keep them from becoming upstanding men and women who can use their voices. I believe that he feels he has a handle on our potential as Black people, so he's okay with where they are right now. His agenda right now is to keep the fastest growing population out of the United States.

I can't say that I disagree with everything he does, just how he says some things. I too believe that people should become citizens and do things right before they benefit from what America has to offer to American citizens. I don't believe that a child should be conceived on another country's soil and then many more children are conceived and born in America without the parents attempting to become legal citizens so that they and their children can stay together. As parents we have to set the example in doing what is right, and also leading the right way in our communities.

Okay, I digress...My bad.

Divided States Of America – Us Against Them

I believe we (people) categorize the importance of some things according to the amount of knowledge that we have regarding a particular subject. Some of those subjects that I am referring to are subjects regarding Blacks. I will discuss my stance on Black

Lives Matter (BLM) later, but let me use that for example. I absolutely do not agree with everything people do all in the name of the movement, and I am careful about what parts are actually the movement and which parts people are taking that title and running with it for others issues.

I absolutely cringe when I hear people say, 'the Democrats' or 'those Republicans' are this or that. When evangelicals or other religiously affiliated individuals make loose statements about the 'Dems' it bothers me to the core. They should be the ones bringing people together instead of separating them by their words and categories.

I wonder do people really think that all Democrats believe in abortion and gay marriages. I wonder if they think Republican women don't have abortions, or haven't had abortions. Before you think that I don't understand the argument, let me assure you that I do. I know we are not talking about who has had what, and we are focusing on voting people in office who wants to stop abortions. I get it; but I want the language to stop that sounds like all Democrats believe and support abortion. That's not a fair statement. Are there any lesbian and gay people who vote Republican? Are there no Christians who vote Democrat? I believe you can see where I am going with this now. It is unfair to group billions of people into two categories. Not only is it unfair, it's foolish.

It's also foolish to think that one side has all of the answers. We are bigger than a cookie-cutter remedy.

As far as I've been taught and have read, America was founded on Christian principles, but not all Christians (especially back in slavery days) followed God's agenda and principles. They twisted the Bible to make it sound like God condoned who they were and their behavior. It's much of the same thing today. Many people of color have decided to move away from the Christian religion because of the lack of love and compassion some Christians are pawning off as Christianity. Not only are people of color choosing other religions, but so are people who don't understand what the 'love' is all about that they are seeing portrayed by many Christians. That's not an excuse, it's the reason for some.

There are people in the world today who believe that our God can only be found THROUGH once race of people and their beliefs. Nonsense. Read for yourself. The same mentality that is being spewed on everyone today that says one race or one party knows it all is the same mentality that enslaved millions of people centuries ago. Unfortunately, some people still have those beliefs and that is why it has been and will continue to be difficult to change the world as we know it.

I have been blessed by Christian radio and Christian television, so I will not allow the opinions and beliefs of some of the hosts and their guests to change that. I am smart enough and wise enough to know that the enemy would love for me to believe that God isn't for us. If he can't succeed in making me stop watching, he would try to make me dislike the ones speaking about issues in the way that they do. Some of the guests will be people of color who have been sought out to believe the way they believe, instead of having a healthy dialogue to come up with what God is saying to us all. The enemy will use anyone to try and turn us against each other – even if it's one of our own (Believers). I have talked to a few individuals already regarding Christian television, and their response is, "I'm done with..." I tell them that is exactly what the devil wants. We can't be done with it, we have to stand in love and in truth against the adversary; yet I understand where they are coming from on that subject.

Some shows on television (news and Christian television) regularly promote one party over another. In fact, most of us are divided by what we watch and what we listen to. I don't think they quite comprehend all of what they are standing for when they make certain statements; and whenever it is brought to their attention, it's always, "I know, but..." They say they are not listening, but their talk and behavior reflects otherwise. How do I know? I know because in my household we turn the television to different [news] stations to make comparisons. I am floored by how many people believe it is okay to uphold the beliefs of individuals who are racist or indulge in racist behavior as long as they are for saving unborn babies. I am not saying that either is right but what I am saying is that both are wrong; so why can't they say it is wrong and stop saying, "I know, but..." I've heard and continue to hear more excuses as to why President Trump is the right person for the position of president. They say that he doesn't agree with abortions, same sex marriages, he is for Israel and he is a businessman. I wonder how much of his idea for 'saving' Israel was his idea and how much was about keeping the White Christians on his side. I can get behind (support) the fight against all of the same things the people voting Republican are for, but if a person votes Democrat, according to the Christian community (on TV and some radio stations), I would be considered on the side of the Left! Why are we labeling people as left and right? They claim that we are one body in Christ, but many treat other people like they are an infection of the body. I absolutely boil inside when I hear some of the hosts say 'the left' does or 'the left believes...' The left, the left, the left! Stop it already, please. Pounding that phrase in the heads of people (especially Christians) is wrong. That's wrong and it needs to be corrected. We should be seen as people.

Many shows will feature guests that are there to explain why the Right (their words) is right, but it seems they are there to prove they are right. There's not much explaining going on at all. I don't feel they are interested in listening to understand more than they are listening to respond. I would love to hear a true dialogue instead of hearing a panel of guests there to prove their point. I am going to say this again, I am not saying the issues at hand are wrong. I am asking, do we continue to look over things that are done and words that are spoken about and towards Black people (and others) are less important issues? I don't get it. I don't think I ever will. To me, it's much like slave owning back in the day. People who owned them thought it was right and they justified it. I honestly believe these people love God and they believe they are doing right in their hearts, but when it comes to Black people and racism it is clearly misunderstood. We have been expected (by many) to understand all issues except for racism. I can't help but believe that it is because Black people have never been considered a priority.

I stopped listening to one radio station because each day on my ride home from work, it was nothing but political talk. It wasn't enough about God unless someone called in and asked specific questions about the Bible. Every single day during the election period and leading up to it, all of the talk was about President

Obama and President Trump. What finally got me is the ugliness of the two men hosting the show. It was beyond me. They hated President Obama for no reason other than he was Black. I used to look up to them for being so savvy in the Word of God, but that could no longer override their talk. They would say things about President Obama that wasn't Christian like at all, and then try to back it up with scripture. That's not right and things like this one has caused so many people to steer away from Christianity, because they are choosing to watch people instead of reading for themselves. They are taking the words of White Christians whom many of them still believe negatively about Blacks deep down. I tried not to allow myself to go there in my mind because I didn't want to believe that mixing politics and religion could come between Christians loving one another.

I've heard White Christian leaders urging people to pray for the leaders of this country, which I agree with that because that's what the Word of God tells us to do; however, I can't say I heard that plea when President Obama was in the White House serving as our leader. Once again, and I can't say this enough--this is why many people don't believe in the Christian religion, because they are not looking at the true representation of who He is. They are allowing bitterness and biasness of people (flawed human beings that we are) to represent who God is, and that is causing major failures.

Check Black on the Ballot

One of the most disturbing and angering things that happened to me regularly during the 2008 presidential election was people asking me ignorant questions regarding how I would cast my vote. Asking someone who they will vote for is not the ignorant question, but when someone asks if a vote would be cast for a candidate simply because of his race then that is stupid. I think in some cases it wasn't what was asked, it was who was asking. When people I didn't think would think something like that ask me, then that's scary. I say it's scary because I never knew those particular people would think that way. I had known them for years and some were actual friends, so it surprised me for them to ask such a thing. Then again, if you want to know something, then the only way to know the answer is to ask. I believe it caught me off guard because we've never asked someone if they were voting for someone because they are White. Oops! That's right—we've never had an option. I guess that's what they were thinking. By the way, these people and others had never asked me who I was voting for pre-Obama.

When I was asked if I would be voting because there was a Black candidate on the ballot that would imply that Black people have never voted before. Granted some people had never voted before because either they were too young to vote or they never knew the importance of voting. Some Blacks started voting when they felt there was someone who would have something in common with them and would fight for the issues that mattered to them. I sure can recall my parents and my grandmother talking about presidential candidates and voting when I was younger. In the 2008 presidential election, that person happened to be Barack Obama. As I stated earlier, Black people never asked whether or not a White person was casting their vote because the candidates were White because that has been the case our entire lives leading up to President Obama. I know people personally who didn't vote for President Obama, and yes they are Black. To think so shallow and believe that President Obama received votes from Black people solely because he is Black is ludicrous. Excuse me; but many White people voted for him as well. The voting was about the citizens of the United States believing that he was capable and the man for the job.

I have personal knowledge of friendships destroyed when President Obama was elected for office. Yes. For real! Maybe they weren't true friends in the first place – even if they had called themselves friends for more than thirty years. A long-term friend of my family told one of my sisters that they were afraid when President Obama was elected. My sister asked why, and her friend said that she was afraid that he would make White people slaves. First of all, that's dumb. Second of all, that would be another war. Lastly, that tells me that people know that slavery was wrong. These people are the same ones who would say, "That's just how it was" whenever you talk about slavery being wrong. So, if slavery was so normal and that's just the way that it was, then why be afraid and why would you fear retaliation?

What it comes down to the fact is that President Barack Obama was not hated for what he did or what he stood for, the man was hated because of his skin color. I've come to that conclusion because I am a person who did not like everything he stood for, but it didn't make me hate him. It didn't make me jump in every conversation and bad mouth him. The hate goes much deeper for many good ole Americans. Whenever you can hate a person that you do not know, the reason isn't just surface or what they stand for politically – it's personal.

I will be really vague with the next statement on purpose, but follow me here. Someone gave me a letter that a friend of theirs had sent to them via email basically threatening that person about voting for President Obama. He called this guy 'N' lover and said how disappointed he was that he would vote for Obama. He went on to tell the person via email that they could never be friends again because for him to vote for Obama tells him who he is. These two individuals had worked side by side of each other for many years. The one receiving the letter had no idea the other one felt that way; and that my friend, is scary.

I was watching an interview of President Obama and some of his staff on a special, and the staff were sharing with interviewers some of the experiences that the president had while in office. They gave insight on the bills that he tried to get passed as well as ideas that were never addressed—only because of who he was. Many credible individuals have talked about how the House went against everything he wanted to do without even discussing it. This information came out after his presidency because of the respect that he (Obama) had for himself and the position that he reigned in for eight years, he never addressed all of those issues publicly. He didn't tweet about his problems. Unfortunately, he is not the only person who is or has been hated because they check the Black/African American box on forms. Many of us have experienced that first hand, but any reason (other than Black) given for disliking President Obama is a lie.

The Truth behind the Disagreements

I wonder how much of the division is about differences of opinions and not our differences of skin color. How much anger is present because someone supports another race or an issue that many believe will benefit someone of color? It looks a lot like the days of Dr. Martin Luther King Jr., when he and others would march down streets standing for equality, while dogs were tearing at their clothes and people were hosed down like a burning house. People such as J.F. Kennedy, who didn't think like the average White man back in his time. (According to History).

I am reminded of how anyone (non-Black) who would be against slavery and inequality was considered an "N" lover and treated how they think an "N" should be treated. It seems today if a person votes democrat they might as well be an "N" or an "N lover" since to most people in the Republican party the Democratic party leans more towards helping those in need and who are oppressed in some way. Anytime we speak of people in need or oppressed, they are automatically believed to be Black.

Before I go further, I must include something that came to mind here recently. I am replaying in my head the chants of "We will not be replaced" that were shouted as the individuals flooded the streets of Charlottesville, Virginia. For the life of me, I don't understand anyone thinking they own America. I don't understand that. You can't take back something that isn't yours. The majority might feel they run the country, because of the privileges that are given or should I say, taken. If the ones wanting to say that no one other than White people belong here, then my message to them is, go fight for YOUR country. If America is yours, then go get suited up and get on the front line and fight the war and the battles of freedom that the BRAVE men and women fight every single day of their lives. Even if we are in peace times they are still fighting because they can't leave. Their presence is keeping the peace in many areas of the world. They talk a good game and pick fights spewing their hate upon the ears of anyone who would listen, but they only want to fight domestically. I know why they won't go fight for the country that they claim and bash anyone else for so-call disrespecting...they have a slavery-day mentality that they can reap the benefits of the people they hate. They get to be free and march with their burning torches and hiding underneath sheets while men and women of all races fight for their freedom and the freedom of the hate they speak. They want the 'deeds to the land' that others work. That is also a slavery-day mentality.

Much of that kind of thinking came from them believing what they were taught about Columbus discovering America. [It] wasn't lost and it was already occupied.

The Color is Green

I have a very rich friend that I spent several hours with one night as we crashed Super Bowl parties of the rich, which were friends of hers. We went from house to house like giggling high school girls. We had another car of friends following us, but somehow they got lost and decided to turn around and go back to my friend's house. She and I kept rolling and visiting. Each house owner was as welcoming as the last. They loved her and me as well. I must say that it was pretty cool. I was in awe of the homes, the cars and the butlers and maids who actually wore uniforms and bowed with the white cloth laid across their arms. I didn't know whether to be offended or what! That thought didn't last long. We just kept it moving.

We visited the homes of heirs of billionaires, drove by her neighbors' homes which were professional football players, and the homes of her multi-millionaire friend who owned world-renown companies.

We had so much fun, but then we finally sat at one of the homes and we had a conversation. It didn't look strange because there were many sidebar conversations going on. She said, "Angel, what do you want to do?" I knew that question wasn't about whose house would be next, but about what I wanted to do in life. She knew I was all about entrepreneurship, but I wasn't there yet. I had missed some trains in life that fear kept me from getting on, but she knew that I had that 'it' factor that she wanted to see come to fruition. I was breaking through some barriers, but I was still allowing barriers to remain in front of me. She shared some personal things about *me* with me. That sounds crazy, but it's true. She then made a statement to me that I will never forget. She said, "Angel, there comes a time when all 'they' see is green." I knew what she was talking about and I got it. Evidence was all around me that they didn't see this beautiful, bubbly, brown woman. They saw a beautiful, bubbly personality woman who happened to be brown but was filled with green. Not envy, but dollars. So many doors have been closed to us because of our skin color, but she was a witness who had lived what she was telling me. Whenever I see a professional athlete or high-profile person who is accepted or sought after who happens to be Black, I think about what my friend said. She was so right—all they see in the rich is green.

As they would say in church, "Can we go deeper?"

Let's look deeper into the power of the almighty dollar. If you ain't got it then you ain't got the power—at least by today's standards.

Our president (Donald Trump) is a great example of that statement. Right now he has a 39 percent approval rating and without taking an actual poll to find out if the statement I am about to make is true or not, I'd say *I bet* that approval is linked to the few individuals that are still expecting him to do what he promised on the campaign of making America great again. By the time this book comes out, his rating will probably be different.

Although when he makes the statement *Make America Great Again,* he makes it clear that he is referring to the times of racial inequality and injustices. As for the other approvers of the president, I'd be willing to say they will stick by him simply because they believe what he believes according to race relations. He says what a lot of people think but aren't bold enough to say. I get that. I'm that way in a lot of ways; but the scary thing is *what* he says. If these people are believing in their hearts what he is sharing, then we are in trouble, America. (In the thoughts of Bernie Mac when he talks to the camera and addresses the viewers as America). In all seriousness though, it's scary to think that he is the leader of many corrupt minds. I guess anyone who would have the kkk (I won't capitalize on purpose) and its members backing them is saying something that some people aren't hearing or not wanting to hear.

Much of the 39 percent might be stuck on how they think he handles business – only going by 'face value.' I have learned that business men with power are attractive to many individuals due to the influence they have and the stature they portray.

For many years people were known by how many people they owned and how much money and land they acquired. They didn't care if those things were purchased, taken or stolen. Even though much of what we have been privy to be exposed to such as the truth about illegal loans and non-payment to employees, unpaid bank loans funded much of the president's businesses. It doesn't matter because he is still seen as powerful. Maybe they see themselves, their fathers, grandfathers and spouses in him, or they see who they'd like to be. I don't know.

While on the subject of money and power, I am reminded of how women would stay in abusive marriages for the assets and public privileges. Stories arise more and more about women staying with men who travel more than half of their lives and some even lead double lives, but it's okay as long as their husbands are in positions of power and they get to live like the queen they feel they deserve to be. Power and status rules.

The Perfect Disconnect

I believe the majority of the disconnection in America, in addition to so many other problems is that people are shouting from their surface. If you want to know what gets attention, think about the lion whose roar shakes the entire jungle. They mean business. Marches, protests on the streets and disruption of city halls are coming from many of the people's surface pain instead of their heart stories and experiences. Many of them are speaking from broken places that were never mended, and it is hard to speak from a space in which you are still sitting. Of course they are passionate about their involvement, but until we (people) are forced to, we don't talk from our own stories and platforms. We can relate, but we stay in a comfortable zone of, *"I'm here for my friend."*

I am directly involved and positioned about individuals who just don't get it. They don't understand the protests. They sit back and get angry over people wanting to be treated fairly. They are bothered by the people that are bothered by the pain. Instead of seeing the people's pain they see it as a complaint. I have seen people get so angry at people marching after a loved one's life has been snatched away and all they get is a 'we're sorry' or 'he feared for his life.' They are saying they are sorry, but the grave is still being dug for the individuals' loved ones.

I am well aware of how some people don't know how to do anything in decency and in order, but I cannot group a mass of people as one. I don't care if they are all women, all Democrats, Republicans, all Blacks, Whites, Hispanics or all anything, as long as they are not trying to hurt or kill others. Some of the same individuals that I mentioned get upset so quickly in discussions about seeing the other side of the coin. Why? I don't know why, but I wonder if they would want someone to hear their point also? Many of them have always been on the side of making the rules or having the rules made in their favor instead of having to abide by the rules. They don't get why 'they' (those people) won't just shut up and go with it. It's like they are saying, "The rules have been set, so follow them or else [go back to where you came from]. I mean after all, you don't have a voice! We have spoken for everybody, so go with it." These people who act like that are accustomed to being the only voice and never taking the other side's opinions and problems into consideration.

In 2018 my son informed me of a documentary that he had seen and thought that I would appreciate its contents. He shares my desire to grow and learn about issues that affect our community and our people. The documentary was called 13th. I remember cringing at times while watching, especially when one of the guys in the documentary, who happened to be White said something to the effect that Blacks go to prison and go back again a second and third time again because they have a need to be controlled and told what to do. He said Blacks need someone (a White person) to tell them what to do. The saddest thing about his statements is that he believed them. He honestly believed that we (Blacks) have a desire and a need to be told what to do by White people. How could anyone convince themselves to believe something like that? What we have seen in America is alarming. There are so many educated scholars who do just enough research and analyzing to build a case to actually convince themselves and others that their theories are true. If you don't believe me, how do you think generation after generation believed that in order to be a baseball pitcher or a quarterback in football you couldn't be Black because Black men weren't smart enough to play the positions? It gives my heart a sinking feeling to think about how many young men of color missed the opportunities to play those positions because coaches believed that lie. I know things have gotten better and more Black guys are filling some of those positions, but I am talking about the ones who never had the opportunity in their times. The ones that are finally making the cut (chosen), they are being watched harder than anyone else, criticized and critiqued for every little move they make or don't make. It's that familiar comparison that we will never get away from – in my opinion.

Taking Sides

For every cause there is an effect; however, not everything is the fault of someone in particular – even though it's in our nature to feel that we have to lay blame somewhere for anything that happens. Some things just happen and some things aren't intentional. Everything that occurs in today's time, someone has to be at fault causing people to automatically take sides. I believe if we would sit back at times and see what the problem really is before blaming someone, we would see more clearly and get *somewhere*. We might even find out that many of us are on the same side of things – even if some would hate to admit it. I have stated time and time again that it's a root issue. Our mindset(s) have deep roots that are entangled with wreckage of our past. If you are on this side, you are already guilty, and if you are on that side you are innocent or a victim.

Caught ya! You're probably already doing it. Doing what?

You're probably wondering who is who. Which would be considered the victim and who would be guilty. I bet you immediately started thinking of which side I was referring to as being this or that. We all do it, but the problem is that the majority of us won't admit it and those who will admit it won't change or aren't willing to change.

Go Back To Where You Came From!

Several years ago I saw something that I had heard time and time again, but that particular time the phrase that I saw posted on social media stood out to me like a red spot on a white wall. Someone posted "Go back to where you came from." They weren't talking to me, but it included me indirectly because they were arguing with a person of color telling them to go *back* to Africa. I find it interesting when someone says that to a person that has never been anywhere other than the United States. I guess that's why I took a personal interest in what was said, because it wasn't the first time I had seen or heard that statement made to someone. I've heard others say they had been told that, but I had not. I guess when people say that they feel that it ends the conversation in a victory. I'm just guessing. I'm not sure.

After reading and pondering over that phrase and what it actually meant, I had to blog about it.

I've never been to Africa and neither had my parents and grandparents. Growing up I would really take offense to someone saying that because I had such a negative view about people in Africa. I would always think of starving children and women walking around without shirts and bras on with nappy hair and buckets on their heads. Don't judge me. Every movie that was filmed that I saw while growing up and as a young adult characterized Africans that way. I had never been there.

I had never witnessed the beauty of the dark, smooth, flawless skin of some of the people in Africa. I had never seen the caramel colored women with beautiful eyes in different shades of brown. I had never witnessed or been taught about the riches of the motherland. I had never been told about the some of the most precious gems in the world originated from Africa. I had never heard about people that travel there to steal resources and come back to the states to build wealth. I never knew about all of the natural herbs and healing medicines that came from the earth of Africa. I should have known, but I didn't. I was so blinded that I didn't recognize the colors of fabrics and materials that only they can put together the way they do are magical. Much like the people in India, the colors associated with Africa are electrifying and alluring. If you can't tell already, I wish I had known about Africa and maybe I would have taken it as a compliment when someone says or writes, "Go back to Africa" or "Go back to where you came from" insinuating I came from Africa because of my race. Granted everything isn't good over there (I've heard from credible sources), but it's not all good in America either. There's a history of witchcraft and darkness over there, but so it is here. There is definitely starvation there, but as it is here. I'm not making comparisons as a tip for tap I'm just saying it to prove that we have been taught false teachings about who Black people are and where their ANCESTORS came from. I feel that one day the Black race will be so far removed from their African heritage that they might not be able to name anyone or trace their roots that far back to actually find Africans in their lineage.

One day I was at an event and I and some of the parents were talking about all of the biracial children that we see, and one of the dads said, "One day there will be a new race." I said, "I was thinking the same thing." Races are crossing the color and race line so much that a whole new look of people are being born. I think that's the coolest thing yet!

I wouldn't care (now) if my grandparents or great grandparents were from Africa. There's not a thing wrong with it. I would proudly represent them now that I know better. When we know better we do better. I'd like to say that Maya Angelou said that, but it has been stated so many different ways that I'm not even sure who to give the credit to for that statement.

I hear Africa is a very special place. It's a beautiful place where the lions, elephants and giraffes walk around with human beings. My husband has been to Africa and lauds its beauty. One day I'll go visit and take it all in.

At this point in my life I have a different reason for taking offense to the statement telling us (Blacks) to go back to Africa because of the intent behind it. It is said in a derogatory manner and as a way of belittling Blacks. I now know it's an ignorant statement because maybe they're like I was – uneducated about Africa and the ingenuity of its magnitude.

I've come to know that racist people in America would say that about someone to attempt to hurt them and make them feel like a visitor in their own country. They want people (especially Blacks) to feel like they don't belong. Saying *go back to where you came from* makes them feel more powerful and that America is owned by them. They feel they get to dictate who comes and who goes. That's not true, although we are seeing that happening right now with immigrants.

Immigration is an ugly topic right about now, and I believe it's bringing out the worst in a great part of the population in all races. Before it seems that I am all for immigration, let me be clear on something. I support **legal** immigration. Illegal immigrants came over to the United States in the 1800's, but now that they are all here from the countries that are acceptable. I'll talk about those acceptable places shortly. I don't agree with open borders and people coming over without being accounted for in this country. What I mean by accounted for is that we have resources, housing, medical, etc. that could cause a country to go bankrupt for sure if immigration isn't handled properly. There is a way to do it (immigration) right, only if people would get on one accord. I have friends that have different opinions about immigration and borders than I do because they are closer to the problem than I am. They have relatives who came over through illegal immigration and some still have family members trying to get here. I understand and I respect their opinions. In order to make the right changes we must talk and also listen to one another.

Is immigration such a bad thing? I guess it depends upon who you ask. I would answer with an 'absolutely not!' America wouldn't be America if it weren't for the immigrants who came over in the 1800's. Many Americans have a bad taste in their mouth about immigration because of the recent ignorant rhetoric about who immigrants are and the dangers of them being in our country.

The foolish bigotry talk has been yelled from the highest office in the United States and backed by the followers. I am by no means saying that the talk of immigration started a couple of years ago, but it has been highlighted the past couple of years. The talk of ridding America of illegals was the message of the campaign, so the message had to continue and get louder in order for a select majority to continue to feel that promises are being fulfilled. The negativity has grown more and more.

People are seeing immigrants as Mexicans only. That's not fair. They might be the larger number of people trying to come to America at one time, but they are not the only immigrants. America has people from all over the world here. It's a melting pot, and that's the truth. The times that I visited New York with my family I was surprised at how many times we came across people who looked Black or White and then they would speak a language we had never heard. They were speaking languages that were new to me in sound. I'm thinking…it doesn't sound like African, German… The accent didn't even sound familiar. I couldn't even pretend that I knew. I was like, "Honey! Did you see them? Did you hear them talk?" I was fascinated with the different dialects and languages. That's what America is all about. That happened over and over, so finally I just smiled and kept it moving. Recently I was attending a conference in Dallas, Texas, Conference on Crimes Against Women, and I was blessed to be in a class that a couple of women from Queens, New York were teaching. Those women knew their work! I was so impressed. Anyway, they supported what I had witnessed for myself when I was in New York. They said over eight hundred (yes, 800) different languages are spoken in Queens. The speaker said, "Don't find it strange when you say something to someone and they just nod their heads." I jokingly said to myself, "Where were you before I went to New York?"

My earliest memory of talking about immigration was when I was in the eighth grade in social studies class. We talked about the pilgrims when I was in kindergarten, but what I remember most about them and the Mayflower is how I colored them on my coloring sheet. Humorous, but it's the truth. I bet you thought I was about to say something all profound, but nope, it was the coloring I remember. I couldn't wait to get my handout with the picture of the feast on it and the cornucopia that I couldn't wait to use my earth tone crayons to color with. That big juicy looking turkey, I made sure I colored it the perfect shade of brown. I remember the picture with the guy wearing the big hat with the buckle in the front, sporting the high boots and a coat looking top. I can't forget about coloring the

Mayflower! Enough about all of this reminiscing. I can tell you all about that, but I was never taught that it was wrong for them to be here. No one said it was wrong. Here lately I'm asking the question in my head, "What makes it okay for your ancestors but not mine or theirs?" Is it because when they came here they all fell into the White race no matter which country they came from? Is it because of the color of their skin? Still to this date, unless someone who looks White specifies his or her race, they are automatically categorized as White and to America that makes it right. They're welcomed and their children are welcomed. I wonder how many came over here without obtaining legal citizenship and had children that grew up and made lives in America. Much like the Dreamers. I wonder how many illegal immigrants' used their skin color as their pass, causing them to never have to show proof of their status. I know we have to show our birth certificates and social security cards for most legal transactions now, but I'm not sure when that actually started. I am also aware that not everyone had it easy coming into America. I'm not saying that and I'm not contradicting myself. I am only talking about how people of fair skin don't seem to be questioned about where they originate, and they are sure as heck not told to go back to where they came from.

I have listened to interviews of several people who are in agreement with illegal immigrant Mexicans coming to the United States, and their motives for illegal immigration is for selfish reasons. Many of them say they are good workers and they can work their farms. It's not a compliment that they say they work hard. I think what they mean when they say *they* work hard is that they can work hard and do the work that no one else will do for the little pay. Some employers say that Mexicans are the ones that will work and want to work; but I think they should tell the truth and just say they are the ones that will work for the pennies on the dollar, and the employers can get away with doing whatever they want. I'm not belittling anyone when I say they will work for pennies on the dollar. I say that because everybody knows these people are desperate to get here to the United States because any conditions in this country is better than where they came from. Many of them have worked for below-minimum wages or way less than what the jobs would normally pay because they want to stay in the country. They can't report labor abuse and the employers know they can't. The employers know that the illegal immigrants fear being sent back; and from news reports, there have been individuals (rescued) who were being held as slaves in homes to provide free work while being threatened to be turned over to the authorities. That's just low down and dirty.

A few years ago (if it has been that long), a couple (Mohamed Toure and Denise Cros-Toure) had a five-year-old girl from Guinea which they kept her in their home as a slave for sixteen years. The girl was unlawfully taken from Guinea, where they were citizens themselves before coming to the United States.

They made her work, didn't allow her to go to school and God knows what else they did to that child. They were arrested and sentenced to seven years. Wouldn't it be great if they were sentenced to the number of years they kept that child in bondage?

Think about it! If you're here illegal, who would you think you can report to? If it were me, I would think the labor law doesn't cover me since I wasn't supposed to be here anyway, so I would probably take the abuse too. I don't know.

Sex, Labor and Human Trafficking

I have been afforded a number of opportunities to receive training about victims of sex and labor trafficking. The trafficked victims are most of the times coerced and paralyzed with fear of being beaten, deported, or worse—killed. Who would miss them? No one knows that many of them even exist. They are in a strange country and have no identification, no experience in anything, no family or loved ones to call for help. They are not accounted for since they are not citizens of the United States. Many of them become sex workers in massage parlors, strip clubs and even as street workers. Not long ago, a report was released about the New England Patriots' owner who had his share of patronizing a spa or parlor where trafficked women worked. I won't feed into that right now because he's not the only person guilty (allegedly) of that activity. Some of the women are right in our everyday paths possibly working in the sanitation departments on our jobs, in restaurants and hotels cooking and cleaning.

In or around 2018, I attended a conference that then Dallas County District Attorney Faith Johnson and Sheriff Marian Brown were guest panelists discussing human trafficking in Dallas and surrounding cities. I met a young lady who was trafficked for almost ten years. The survivor stated that her trafficker not only impregnated her twice, but he also sent her to college. He later became her pimp, but there was something that no one knew. She worked on a daily job in a high-profile office and no one ever knew her story. Although women aren't the only individuals that are trafficked, women make up the largest percentage of victims. It's awfully sad when you take the time to actually think about the suffering that victims of trafficking go through.

I've had individuals who have been cleaning up buildings and offices come and tell me how poorly they have been treated. It's only because of who they are on the outside. I know what that feels like to be treated poorly because of your outer covering. I say outer covering because they don't know the person inside. They're not interested in knowing.

It has been several years now since the company I work at started contracting out for janitorial services, and most of the employees are Mexican. I would say approximately 99% of them are, or at least the ones I've seen. Some of them had not been in the country for very long at all, which tells me they are illegal. At one time they had a few more Blacks working in that department, but that didn't last long after the contractors took over. A lot of those companies hire illegal immigrants to do the job and possibly have one person they'll appoint as supervisor to watch 'the help.' You know how that goes... Get the one slave to watch the rest of the plantations workers.

Majority of the cleaning crew work very hard. They work hard without having any benefits. Whenever some of the employees would come to the office and act as if they were trying not to be seen or heard. They won't try to converse if their English is broken. I made sure that I would talk to them anyway, whether they could speak English or not. I have seen other employees talk as if the cleaning crew wasn't even in the room. They would ignore them completely. One time, one of the women drew close to me, and when she felt comfortable enough she told me that she was embarrassed to try to speak. I told her she could practice on me. Every day she would stop by my desk and talk. Her English became better and better. She and a friend came out to an event that I had away from work. I taught her make-up tips and she would even borrow my beauty magazines that I sometimes had on my desk.

We have a great crew in my department; we communicate with the cleaning crew and treat them like they are what they are – our colleagues. Ignoring them and treating them like second-class citizens causes them to shut down and feel like less than a person. I don't like to see anyone standing in the shadows of other people and treated poorly.

You Know You Have A Shoe In!

I'm old school, so when I use certain phrases that some of you might not know what I'm talking about. What I mean by a 'shoe in' is that it's 'a go.' If a person applies for a job or tries out for a team and someone says they are a 'shoe in' that means that person doesn't have to worry like the other applicants because they will be getting the job or the spot on the team. I've faced the 'shoe in' scenarios all of my life. I can't tell you how many times I've witnessed people being hired just because of who they know or who they were connected to, while others were promoted solely because of their relationships over their skills. The not-so-funny thing is when a Black person gets promoted or even hired there's all kinds of scrutiny around the decision. Oftentimes the votes are recounted (if there are votes), the credentials are rerun as if someone missed a flaw. I remember being part of a 'team' (that's what I'll call it for now), that we had to make a decision regarding someone to choose, and one person was adamant about the Black man being 'too good to be true.' That person didn't even hear herself talking. She got so caught up with her argument that she forgot we were all in the room. She even said that he was too perfect. If we're not good enough it's no surprise. If we're good, then it must be a mistake. Reminds me of the drama behind President Barack Obama during his presidential campaign and during his time in the White House. He was too good to be true. He's a Black man, so he must have had some kids somewhere outside of his marriage. He had to have been on drugs at some point in time or something! When they couldn't succeed with the birthing card idea something else had to come up. I don't know what ever happened regarding the lie that the female came up with trying to convince people to believe that President Barack wanted her over First Lady Michelle. Well, that fell through. Had it been true, it would have still been on every platform on the internet. President Obama was just, 'too good to be true.'

People of color don't have it so easy when it comes to being given anything—especially a job. It must be nice to be able to hear 'you're a shoe in' so often. I've seen individuals who didn't even have to hear the words to know they were already chosen. It's just the way the world of the majority has been, so why would they start sweating it now? Whenever someone of color says we have to be ten times better than the next person who isn't of color, you can rest assured they are telling the truth.

I've had my years prior to my current job when I had to worry about being hired or even getting a call back, because someone else was already chosen. When I went looking for a job, I was tired of hearing, "We'll call you."

The saddest thing is that no one sees anything wrong with it. It has been an understood game that not all of us have been invited to play.

The New GOP - The Good Ole Boys (GOB)

If you scratch my back, I'll scratch yours, your children backs and your grandchildren backs. That simply means, when I take care of you, I'm taking care of your children, your grandchildren. It's called generational wealth and generational changes.

My dad used to say, "It's not what you know, it's who you know." It took many years of having dealings with people to know that daddy was right.

He wasn't just talking. I should have known that because my dad was a talker, but he wasn't a person that used 'idle' words, or spoke just to hear himself talk. When he would talk, he was saying something that was important and a wise person would want to listen. In order to make that statement as often as he did, he knew something we didn't know. He had personal experiences. He knew that life was about who you know as much or more than what you know. As I've gotten older, I have caught myself saying the same thing to my kids. "It's not always what you know, kids. It's who you know." You could say that I too have had my own experiences. I've been passed over for who someone knew over what I knew. Time and time again I have seen jobs given to people because of who they know. Many have had under-the-table interviews set up before a position is even posted. I've witnessed individuals being trained for positions that were coming up, even if the job itself was supposed to be a secured place that the outside world was not supposed to have access to. I remember a specific situation of a supervisor that I knew hired her best friend. The best friend was allowed into a secured area every night being secretly trained for the position that was going to be posted. Needless to say the friend aced the interview and was handed the job. I've seen things like that many times.

Whatever happens to one person in a family, affects the family's entire bloodline in one way or another. The decisions some of our parents and grandparents made have affected us directly or indirectly – whether we know it or not. Even the Bible clarifies that truth – generational blessings as well as cursing. If you don't believe me, check this out. What do you think happens to families when a loved one dies and leaves an inheritance? The person or persons the inheritance is left to will benefit from what their family member left. That is life changing within itself! I'm not saying everything left behind or passed down is always good. I believe in generational blessings as well as generational curses.

Some families are reaping the benefits of what their grandparents sowed. Individuals have built vacation homes on property that their grandparents once controlled. Whether it was bought or taken, their offspring benefits. Streams of income have been generated for families, children and grandchildren for decades if not centuries. Back in the days of slavery, slaves didn't own property – they were property. Listen, I am learning about a few people (slaves) in history who actually owned things, but when I have to dig into history to find one or two or a few who were owners, then that alone says it wasn't enough!

I have to insert this information here. I like to watch Island Hunters on HGTV. Every time I watch the show, I can't help but wonder where do these people get an island from that they have the deeds to sell? An island? Where did you get an island from? Interesting. That will be something that I would love to know more about. How did a real estate company, or broker or whatever they would be called, obtain an island?

Imagine having a piece of land that you don't need for yourself and your family to live on. The land can be leased or sold for income, creating generational wealth. Imagine this if you will... Imagine how much of a difference that would make in a person's financial status if someone was paying you for the use of something that you didn't have to work to obtain. Imagine coming of age without any experience at all and you are invited to work at your father's firm doing some 'behind the scenes' work. That opportunity can position you for a life that you weren't fully aware even existed. Imagine that. To some people, that will seem normal, for others it's a big wish. For many it is the norm because either you know someone this has happened to (should I say... happened for), or it happened for you. Either way, it's no big deal and oftentimes taken for granted. That doesn't just happen for many Black people because our families didn't have much to leave. Much of what they did have was taken away from them by White people who wanted what they had.

We didn't have anyone leaving masses of wealth or ways of making money for our families, because our ancestors started out in the negative. Many of our ancestors were killed, so they never had the chance to build unless they were building things for Whites. They built places like the White House that they couldn't even enter inside of unless they were working. Each generation was starting from 'now.' We're always starting from the first generation. I know people who have had jobs where several generations worked at the companies. Where were our people? Working in the cafeteria of the companies or cleaning the building? Possibly. Don't get me wrong and think that I am saying this statement holds true for all Black people because it doesn't, but I am speaking as a majority – a large percentage, and that alone makes a difference in our present situations. When my dad died he didn't have anything to leave to my mother and us. He had been cheated out of his portion of what he inherited, so he didn't even get a chance to enjoy the fruits of his father's labor. My mom just turned eighty-four years old and sad to say, she hasn't seen any of her husband's wealth either. This time, it wasn't the White man that cheated my dad. I'll just leave it as that. That particular issue reminds me of the slaves that actually owned other slaves. There's always one or a few that have no problem keeping the next person down as long as they are 'up.'

When we moved to the city my dad ended up working for a company nearly thirty years before his death and they were nice, but they cheated my dad out of all of his benefits. He was from the country and didn't know, and wouldn't let us tell him those 'nice' people were being dirty and using him. All he had to leave material wise was a paid for home for my mother to stay in. I don't want to sound as if that wasn't something of value, I'm just saying that it could have been so much more had he not been cheated by the nice White people that he worked for the greater part of his years on this earth.

I am proud of the friends and acquaintances that I have that are making the difference in their families and their bloodlines by setting up wealth through entrepreneurship. They know what works. They understand that if their families will get wealth, it will come from the decisions they are making right now. They are setting the stage for a comfortable lifestyle for their children and grandchildren, as well as setting up funds for college if their children choose that route. That is where the changes will take place generationally across the race. We have a long way to go, but it's possible.

Majority of Black people just want an equal opportunity. They don't want handouts.

What you don't know can and will hurt.

Knowledge is power! What you don't know will hurt, and can kill or leave you in poverty. The Word of God tells us that people perish for the lack of knowledge. If you don't know better you don't know to *do* better. I remember when we had a family discussion about the business. My children didn't want to have anything to do with the business after graduating from high school. Since graduating from college, my oldest still has no interest in the business. I understand why. He was burned out from that field when he was a little boy, and he saw the time that my husband spent away from home building the business. He didn't want that life for himself; but we have talked to our children about the importance of running the business from a distance later. I don't think it is forcing them to do what they don't want to do, I believe it is opening doors for their future to learn the importance of building for themselves. We are fully aware that God's plan most times isn't our plan, so we are open to following His lead.

I could name quite a few people that I know personally, who were hired based upon whom they knew/know. We call it the 'good ole boy' system. The good ole boy system allows people that are sometimes unqualified for a position to fill it because of who they know. Sure, not all the time, but a lot. On occasion, hiring is justified because of a piece of paper (degree); therefore, hiring the individual doesn't stand out as being a *favor*. There have been many cases where degrees came later! As I mentioned earlier, oftentimes individuals are hired to work in different areas of a corporation or business while they go to school and the company pays for their education. They are becoming qualified while they are working in the position.

"Hey there Jim! Ole John oughta be graduating pretty soon, shouldn't he?" "Uh, yeah. He's got about another year and he'll be finished." "Tell'em gimme a call when he gets a chance. I'll put him to work!"

That's how the story goes. It happens all the time! Unfortunately, if Blacks get into a position, they are seldom in a role that will allow them to bring in other qualified Black employees. Notice I said 'qualified.' We already know that we have to already be equipped for the position when we get to the door. Doors are hardly ever opened for a less than qualified Black person. Even the qualified are turned away at times for less qualified Whites and other races. One Black is enough, in most cases according to some companies. That's not a figure of speech either.

The good ole boy system lines up jobs for whomever they want to give the chance/job to - either as a favor, or to get that person started on their path in life. They don't even have to be majoring in a particular field or already degreed. It doesn't matter. I have known people to have their education paid for while they were working on a job that was handed to them by a family friend of their father or another relative. A number of people got their start that way. I have personal knowledge of companies that have held jobs for young women and men that will be graduating from college in particular fields; therefore, they step right into a career they want, making a great salary with benefits. Is that fair? It's very fair if you are on the receiving end. Others are working in chain stores checking out groceries, with a degree. I've known people who were hired for jobs that others have waited years and years to get an interview; but the others were given a chance because of who they knew. Sometimes it was a payback or a favor. A favor? A favor gets paid off at the expense of others waiting in line to get a job they are qualified for, while another walks right in without any experience at all and starts working. It's wrong, but it happens all the time. I am in my late forties now, and I have seen this type of good ole boy system since I was in my twenties. I have had to train people to supervise me. I understand training someone to know the policies and procedures of the company, but that wasn't the case. I had to train someone who had no experience or knowledge whatsoever; but instead of hiring me to be the supervisor, I was told to train the new supervisor. This happened more than a couple of times. It was sickening to put it lightly. Would that person have the same stories to tell that I am telling? Probably not, because it was normal to her. She felt that she was *supposed* to be over me. She didn't feel any remorse about me training her to be my boss. Help each other... I get it. Although I get it, I wish others would get it, instead of making excuses for the favors. It's easy to talk about people and say what they should and shouldn't be doing when you have never had to hustle and get anything. I am not saying that this fits everybody's story because I know personally it doesn't; but it is more likely to fit the story of the majority than the minority.

It's the same way when buying a house. Black people have to have so much more than anyone else in order to qualify for a home. Many of our children end up growing up in apartments because of it. It's not that their parents can't pay the mortgage, they can't qualify to get the house. It was set up that way. Loans, houses, cars. You name it! I can tell you at least one story of this happening for someone I knew or knew through someone else. When a loan officer says, "We're going to give you a chance. You're a young couple and we want to help you get started." Oh yes. It happens. Remember generational wealth and favors that are obtained and passed down. It also happens in banking. Loans were given to individuals because of who they knew no matter what the credit score looked like. There's a situation that really floored me one time. An individual drove three different cars in a matter of months, because each one this person bought (with her bad credit), she decided she didn't want to after keeping it for a while. She took them back and the dealership accepted them. A Black person would have probably had some charges filed (they can always find something that fits the situation when they want to). The dealership employees would have thought the Black person was in some kind of scam or trying to commit a theft of a motor vehicle. It might sound humorous to some people, but if a guy in a hospital gown hooked up to an IV trying to get some fresh air [at the doctor's orders] can get arrested for looking like he's trying to steal hospital equipment, I know they'd arrest a Black man or woman at a car lot.

My story is a polar opposite!
You Can't Afford That!

In 1991, my husband and I went to a car dealership in Fort Worth, Texas to buy a car. The dealership was a huge place on Grapevine Hwy in North Richland Hills, Texas (where my White boyfriend and I went to the movies that I talked about earlier). If you recall, I mentioned this area of town wasn't the friendliest area for Blacks back then, but we stopped anyway. Our credit was A-1. There was only one problem. We were young, Black, and we were driving a new car already. I had a 1990 Mitsubishi and I was looking at a 1991 Chevrolet Cavalier. I could afford it, but the salesman didn't know. He came out to greet us and asked what we were doing. We shared with him that we were looking at that Cavalier *over there* and my husband expressed to him that he wanted to buy the car for me. I was never materialistic and into the latest anything, so it wasn't an extravagant car, but I wanted it. The salesman asked what we were going to do with the car we were driving – assuming we just bought it since it was a 1990, and we were in the year of 1990. We had actually purchased the Mitsubishi in 1989. Still new, but we bought it early. My husband told him we would be keeping both. We didn't want to do a trade-in, we wanted to just make that second purchase. He said, "Y'all can't afford that!" We didn't know what to say. He caught us both off guard with his statement. He had never even seen our driver's license nor had he run our credit. He assumed since we were young and Black we couldn't qualify. He said, "Give me a moment." We were offended, but hey, we weren't shocked. People felt they could say anything to Black people. Remember, I was born in 1970, Dr. Martin Luther King died in 1968! Blacks had not been far removed from segregation when I was born. I was in the fifth grade when I was bused clear across town to an all-White school. Everybody hadn't received the memo! We waited, and out walked another guy who happened to be Black. I still remember how he looked and his name. He said, "Can I help you guys?" We told him that we had been helped and we were waiting for the guy to come back out. We thought maybe he was going to get keys for us to test drive or something. The salesman [new one] said, "I'm sorry, but he told me to come out and help y'all." Well, my husband and I knew what that was about. My husband said, "Oh really? He didn't tell us he was going to get someone Black to help us." He asked us what happened, so we told him that the guy told us we couldn't afford another car payment and he would be right back. The salesman (we'll call him Jim) said, did you get started with your credit check. We said, "No. He didn't even get our driver's license." Before he knew it, he said, "What? Are you serious?" We said, "Yes." He said, "Let's get you this car that you want. Come in with me." I started to leave the place without buying that car because of what the other jerk had done to us, but it was my goal to show him that we were somebody and we had money. We filled out the paperwork, went to the finance office and started the paperwork on my brand new car that

I drove off the lot that day after a brief time in the finance office and making a down payment that was next to nothing. What was even more disturbing, is the fact that the man in the finance office was Black and happened to have graduated with one of my sisters, and I graduated with his sister. My sales and finance guys were surprised that their coworker felt that way and had done such a thing. They learned about their coworker that day! It amazes me of how racist people can pretend day in and day out around their coworkers. The worst part of it all is that if they were asked about being racist they'd say they're not. Some of them really don't know that they are because they have never been on the other side of their racist ways. The first salesman probably thought the Black guy could break 'no' down to us better than he could. Our first sales guy never came back over to see how we were coming along, since he was so sure that 'Jim' was wasting his time with us. When we finished up with the paperwork, the finance guy said, "I'll be sure to tell him you bought the car, but he will probably see you driving off in it."

I have had credit issues (years after that incident) over the years due to things that were beyond my personal control; but that one event made me want to do better and keep myself in good standings. You see, my (our) good credit standing made the difference that day. Our good standings allowed us to keep our heads up and be proud of who we were and what we were able to do. Some would say, "Well, it made you do better!" No. That alone didn't make me want to do better. It could have made me angry and grouped all White people the same, but it didn't. It made me understand that ignorance of prejudices and racism runs deep—so deep that it becomes a part of that person.

That type of behavior has been around for too many years to date back, but they honestly cannot see how that can and will cause one group of individuals to be at an advantage over another. Now don't get me wrong, I know some people go to college, get their degrees and never receive assistance from anyone. I applaud those people. Well, I will never say anyone made it alone, but you know what I mean. I think it's great to be helped by someone at the top, but I wish people of color had that type of advantage also. I wonder how much different would corporate look if the opportunities were equal. How many corner offices in high rises would be occupied by educated Black people, or Black people in the process of getting their education? How much difference would it really make? How many diverse neighborhoods would there be? It's not that Black people don't want better. It is the fact that everything is twice as hard to achieve, or to even get in the door. I have never been to Atlanta, but I hear it is much different there than in Texas. Maybe that is why so many Black people have a love for Atlanta. It is described as a place that Black people get what they work hard to get.

Racism and unfairness isn't just a Texas issue though, it is an American issue. I hate to report this, but it has gotten worse in the past almost two years (2017-18). America hasn't been as divided by race as it is now, since the Civil Rights Movement. Hate crimes are on the rise, and people openly talk about races that they hate. There are social media groups that are formed to talk about racist ideas and people. Many of the members of the groups are said to be high-profile individuals in positions of authority at various organizations around the world. How scary is that! I already shared why I think open racism is on the rise. It is said to be a choice, and I agree. It's a choice to show how much you hate another race or folks of another religion, and it is okay. If a child is misbehaving and the parents know about it and does nothing but make excuses, then that child will only misbehave more. That is what we are seeing in America today. Without getting political, it is a mess!

Redlining – Systemic Racism

I had heard of gentrification several years ago, but redlining I wasn't familiar with what it was and what it entailed; so I did what I always try to do when I am introduced to something—I find information regarding the subject at hand. I also learned a lot about several topics dealing with Black people, from my education professor in college. I'll share what redlining is for those who are like I was and aren't sure of what it means.

Years after the civil war, government agencies started to divide cities into desirable and undesirable areas for investments. Black people were blocked off from being able to access investments. It is said that the maps were used by banks and insurance companies as a way to deny Black people loans and services based on race. Of course being my age, the people who affected were my parents' age! Remember what I talked about earlier regarding the school districts and the taxes that go to the school depends on the area? Redlining could be responsible for the poor schools and lesser quality of education.

When our grandparents and parents wanted to buy a home, they couldn't. Once they put in their address, the banks already knew they were 'redlined.' Houses and education were denied to Black people. Education aids in getting better paying jobs; so if our parents and grandparents couldn't get a college education (some couldn't get high school education), because of segregation, how would they ever be able to get wealth? They couldn't! White people were able to get into colleges and get great jobs and create wealth. The wealth they created was passed down to their children and grandchildren, and they are still passing it down.

I have friends who bought their first house immediately after getting married in their early twenties. Many Black couples still live in apartments and many of them have had to raise their children while living in apartments. There is nothing wrong with living in an apartment, but it's the reason we were in apartments longer than White couples. Of course it's not the only reason, but some of the other reasons stem from bigger issues. Jobs or the lack thereof have everything to do with being able to obtain credit. Prison systems are another marking many get that keeps them from the jobs that keeps them from obtaining credit that keeps them from buying homes. Sounds like I was reading an excerpt from *Chicken Little* the book, but that's the best way that I could create a visual to see to cycle.

I talked about it earlier in the book and I will continue to mention it whenever necessary – White people get opportunities that Blacks don't get. The uneducated or should I say uniformed White people think that Blacks want a hand out. What they fail to realize is that we all need help, but they have been set up by their ancestors and parents, but they think they have done all the work on their own. Many have been given land, livestock, fields, businesses, and money to fall back on or to help them. If a person has help with a down payment for a home, that's huge. If a parent can cosign for a car for their children, that's a big push. I am thankful that we were able to buy all three of our children's first cars in cash. Then we cosigned for both of our boys' second vehicles.

Back in the day people had to walk into the bank and present themselves to the bank president or branch manager for loans. Are we really naïve enough to think that people weren't turned down because of their race? Do we not think that people were also approved because of their race? I've seen couples who had nothing for collateral buy homes and cars; but Black people had to have A-1 credit to have the same opportunity. We inherited our circumstances – good and bad.

Family wealth, incarceration, education, and legal representation is part of systemic racism. Unfortunately, systemic racism is as old as mostly all of us living beings—if not all. We have been screwed by those before us. It's hard to get past it because people don't see anything wrong with what has gone on. They (Whites) think Black people are lazy and they don't see what history has done to the present and how damaging it will continue to be to our future if we don't wake up and smell the coffee. Many of them don't believe that we should have equal education because their money had 'paid' for their children to get the opportunities they get; and they are not willing to put an end to education inequality. Honestly, I believe to my heart that most of them like the gap being there because it's a way to keep Black people underneath them. I believe that gap is something that many human beings like having – the haves and the have nots—not just White people.

It is believed that redlining is still affecting the value and sales of some homes in some states. I am not at all surprised.

What's In a Name?

A simpler form of redlining came in a different way – it was in the name. On applications and documents, people have been judged by their name. The Name Shambalitha -Jaquita would not get the job back in my day! Oh, I'm sure it still happens now, but not like it used to. I feel weird saying back in my day because I'm only 49, going on 50. My parents used to say *back in my day*, and now I get it. They weren't referring to the 1800's, but times that were more recent than I could imagine back then. When I use the phrase, I am only talking about maybe 20 years ago. That's it!

Shambalitha is a red flag. It's a flag that waves in color—the color black. I'm sorry, but you know

I'm telling the truth here. I'm not stereotyping the name, but if the truth be told, we know that names on applications make a difference. Unless it was a fast food place, color mattered.

If the name Shambalitha-Jaquita is on a resume, chances are the person going through the resumes will not pull her resume unless that person doesn't have any implicit (unspoken) biases. A funny thing I'll share. Long time ago, White women were given not-so-popular names too.

Sometimes we don't even realize we think the way that we do. I have gone through applications before and without even thinking, I have pretty much sized up the person's race by the name at times. I didn't care one way or another, because I am a Black woman and I have hired all races of workers, but it's normal to do that. It's only hurtful and shameful when your decision is made from the name. I've had Pakistanis, Black, White, Hispanic, Bi-racial, French, Jamaican, Indian, and those are the known races. I'm not afraid of color; but I can't say that for everyone.

You don't know what it's Like to Be Me

If I am my brother's keeper, then show me who my brothers are...

I often admit that I don't know what it is like to be someone I'm not. I think it's important for us to allow

that reality to sink in every now and then. I don't know
what it's like to be a teenage boy, a Black boy of any age,
or a sixty-year old White man. I don't know what it's
like to be a White woman my age or any age; therefore,
it is important that we all understand that. What I do
know is that we are all human beings and that should be
enough. I don't know what it's like to be an inner city
youth who only knows survival. I don't know what it's
like to go without necessities and have no idea of where
to get my needs met. I have been without nice clothes to
wear, but I had food and a place to live. I don't know what
it is like to live in an area where there's a young Black
boy's funeral almost every week, sometimes every day of
a week; and nothing is done about the murders. I'm sure
many of the murders go unsolved, or no one is arrested
for them. I don't know what it's like to grow up on the
system (government assistance); so I must be careful when
I speak and care before I share. Oftentimes we believe we
say things in a dense mode in order to justify our words
and thoughts instead of thinking and acting from an
empathetic heart first.

God, please grant me a heart of compassion, love and
of kindness. Please give me the vision to see beyond my
own four walls, and past the color of my skin. Help me to
see things the way you see them, and not the way I have
been taught to see them or have read about, because I know
everything on this earth that man has created is of [Hu]

man. *Only You can give me the discernment to see clearly. In Jesus name. Amen.*

One of the best ways to learn about people is to be willing to step outside of our circle and talk to people who don't look like us. By doing so, we will learn so much more than what the 6:00 news tells us. Nowadays we have networks that feed us news 24/7 if we're willing to tune in and be filled.

My husband and I purposely float between news networks to see who will say what on the news, and it's amazing how different the stories are told. What you put in, you will get out. I can always tell who watches which outlet.

Everybody has asked the question, and they learned to ask it early of the abolitionists, 'What shall we do with the Negro?' I have had but one answer from the beginning. Do nothing with us! Your doing with us has already played the mischief with us.

Frederick Douglass

They Don't Get Us

What does that mean? Why do we say it? What is there to get? Oh, I am asking because I have caught myself saying things like that only to finally stop and say, "Get what?" For what reason does anyone of a particular race have to be 'gotten' and understood? There's nothing to get! Let us be! We are people and we want to be seen and treated that way. We are imperfect as all people are imperfect. It is so normal for people to think and to communicate to others that we are some *'thing'* that needs to be understood. We are people. No other race (that I know of), continuously say, "We just want to be understood." Do you want to know why they don't say it? They don't say it because they don't feel that anything is wrong with them, and quite frankly, they don't care if anyone thinks something is wrong with them or not. Society has made White people to be the standard. If someone talks correctly, then stupid people will say they talk white. If someone of another race says they are dating or married to a White person it's like they've reached a goal. That is crazy to me, but we've done it as a society. Those of us who didn't do it allowed it.

White people have programmed Black people to automatically think that we are different and need to be understood on every level. It will take generations (I believe), to change that way of thinking. That stinking thinking that we are different did not start yesterday, last year, or even in the last one hundred years – it started with our ancestors. Our ancestors had no choice but to believe deep down something was wrong with them since they were treated like a plague; therefore, the mindset has to be reset even in some of those of our own race. It will take time to deprogram all human beings. Deprogramming will allow future generations to begin with a clean slate on a level playing field.

Let me clarify something. We are all different from each other. We are different culturally and obviously on the surface, but we are all unique individuals—all of us; but to believe that different is wrong is what we must get away from in our society.

The majority has named things and labeled issues, so they have created what they call the 'norm.' Whatever they didn't name doesn't exist. I will elaborate on what I mean shortly.

Call me rebellious, call me whatever—just be truthful about whatever you call me. Recently I was completing yearly mandatory training, and I just stopped and made a statement that got the attention of those around me. I said, "Why are we having to study and test over something that someone came up with from an idea, created a company and made it mandatory that certain employees around the country learn the material and pass a test? That doesn't make sense to me. Who says they are correct in their way of thinking? That's what I want to say when I think about the standards that have been set, and I go back to who set those standards and called them golden? I'm just saying.

Carry on…

To be real here, Blacks make up a small percentage of America. Blacks have never been seen as a significant part of the human race by other races anyway (in America); so what Black people feel isn't honored or respected by the majority of White people. When we think of how insignificant we are to the majority you can see why our voices are silent, quietened and seemingly powerless. After thinking about the small percentage of the population that make up this country, now think about the incarcerated citizens. If we have a voice in any matter, what we say is grilled until it passes inspection and confirms that it is not volatile. The individuals with the big voices that have made an effectual impact on our country in history were often seen as rebels and uncontrollable. The key term is *uncontrollable*. Anyone (oftentimes Black) with a voice (something to say) who stands up for something is seen as negative if they are not endorsing what the majority says or thinks. Countless Black teens have been ousted and seen as troublemakers because they want to say something that will make a difference in their lives, but because of who it comes from or how it comes out, they are seen as troublemakers. If only people will listen and allow them to speak, they might hear the truth. Maybe it is hard for that individual to convey their thoughts, but when what they are saying is already wrapped in anger and bullcrap according to the listener, it's hard to be heard.

A few months ago, I was looking at a show on TV One, *Uncensored* featuring Nick Cannon. As I listened to him talk I had a conviction of my own. I was guilty of some things that I had thought about him regarding *his choice* of wearing a turban on his head. Thoughts is the proper word because I do not believe in sharing all of my thoughts on social media, so I kept what I thought to myself. I preconceived that it was some weird reason he was doing it or just trying to set a new trend.

I think sometimes people forget that those people are real human beings when we get on our soapboxes and talk about them on the internet. We talk about celebrities, their families, their looks, and other personal things and areas of their lives that they are unable to keep private. Some celebrities I will speak about because after all, they made their stardom by exploiting themselves and what they do isn't a secret anyway. You know the ones who leave nothing to the imagination. I'm not talking about them.

During the interview, Nick Cannon shared how the folks behind the show that he was hosting did not agree with some of the jokes he had made while doing standup. He also mentioned his turban wasn't exactly welcomed on the show either.

When I first saw Nick wearing the turban I didn't like it, because personally I think he's quite handsome without it on, but I also thought he was switching over to some other religion. I know; I'm guilty. That would be his choice, but again, I'm pointing out how many thoughts I had about him wearing the turban. When I heard him talk about the feeling of royalty that he gets when he wears it and what he had come to learn about wearing a turban, I was impressed. You see, I can respect that. Nick chose to believe in something and go against what others thought was acceptable and presentable in their eyes. It goes to show that we are oftentimes controlled by what others think is acceptable behavior.

The only time they 'get us' is when we look and act acceptable in the eyes of others. I don't get a lot of people of all races, but what I do get is that we are all unique individuals created by one God. It is not my place to *get* anyone. With the exception of hate, bigotry and racism, people are people and should be seen as such. I am not here to start categorizing and analyzing when a person shouldn't be seen as just being who they are, because I am not qualified to diagnose psychiatric or psychological issues. I am not an expert in those areas.

I am not a Bible scholar either, but I am a woman who believes in God the Creator and I have a foundation in Christ; therefore, I know that God gave man dominion (power, authority) over everything. In the book of Genesis, He said we will have dominion over the fish of the sea and over the birds of the heavens and over the livestock and over all the earth and over every creeping thing that creeps on the earth. I don't fly nor am I a fish, so he wasn't talking about any human being having dominion over me. He did not say that he will give one race dominion over another; although in slavery times people practiced, taught and exemplified that behavior, it's not what He meant.

Without going deeper into the Bible, what I am declaring is that in the early days of man, Adam was tasked with naming animals and the things that he saw. Let us fast forward past the days of Adam. Man is still naming things such as diseases, plants, new animals, trees…everything! When some things were being named by historians, doctors, inventors, etc. we have to ask ourselves, who gave those things the names that they have now. Many labels and names came from research labs and classrooms that Black people did not have access to and collaborate with others for several generations. I can understand why Blacks were left out and have been treated insignificant, but it does not make it right. Let me clarify the part that I understand. I understand that Black people were working out in fields, inventing tools to make their job easier, but the White man came, took and named those tools and received credit. It wasn't just tools that they took ownership and credit for, it was everything. So when Black people do not fit in the mold that was created for what White people named, there's a problem. It has been that way since the days of slavery. A great deal of what has been done was done while Black people were banned from publicly learning. They were beat if they were caught reading. Black people around the world might have started behind the curve, but many have succeeded their amazing efforts to do and become what their ancestors did not get to do and get credit for (publicly) before they died, or before they could be recognized for what they have done.

Hidden Figures

Black people invented the traffic light, touch-tone telephone, thermostat temperature control, suspender, reversible baby stroller, portable pencil sharpener, the pacemaker, the mop, the mailbox, the lawn mower, blood bank, automatic elevator doors. The list goes on and on, and I would spend too much time and space listing everything Black people created. The reason I listed what I did is because it is important that society stop seeing Black people as a bunch of people that showed up on this earth benefitting from what our dear White people invented. Young Black men and young women need to know these things because it sure wasn't taught to us in school. Even now, I don't know of any schools that teach Black history as a class that is mandatory. It was great to learn that the first person to perform open heart surgery was a Black man. His name was Daniel Hale Williams.

Madame C.J. Walker was born in 1867, but she was a successful entrepreneur. She invented hair products of her own in 1905, and became a self-made millionaire. My daughter researched her and wrote about her one year during Black History Month.

Annie Minerva Turnbo Malone was another Black businesswoman, born in 1877. She also created and marketed hair care products.

Mary Eliza Mahoney was the first Black woman to study and become a professional nurse in the United States. She was born in 1879. I just want to keep naming, but I need to move on. I am naming these people because if these people had the brains to do what they did, imagine what others would have done if they had been able. Our people are not dumb! I want my children and other children, young adults and folks like me (who didn't get to learn about anyone outside of the few people we were taught about during Black History Month) to know there are more awesome people to learn about. We have so many people of color to be proud of, and I want to know why these individuals were hidden from us. We didn't have the internet and resources that are available now, so we had to rely solely upon the teachers who taught what they wanted us to learn. Maybe some of them didn't know what they didn't know, and their intentions weren't of malice. Maybe they were only teaching what they had been taught.

We have not been able to share our knowledge and contributions to this world because of our outer coats. When I say we, I mean Blacks in general, because I cannot even take credit or sit on the same level as the mastermind geniuses that created household and major devices that we use every single day of our lives. Many of those items are life-saving as well as life changing and created by people of color.

I am not making a contribution to the 'us' or 'them' problem or attempting to make an argument. I won't hesitate to say that we are overdue in our learning that Blacks are more than criminals, thieves, murderers, felons and waiting on government assistance. Those are the things I was exposed to believing when I was growing up; or at least they wanted us to believe that.

Chapter Two
Get Outta Here!

I have been curious about a town within the city of Fort Worth, I guess you could say it is within the city, for quite some time. That quite some time equates to about thirty-five years – since coming to Fort Worth, Texas to live.

White Settlement, Texas is the town that I am referring to. I remember being so afraid to even go near the town. Honestly, I didn't know a thing about the town firsthand; I just knew what I had heard from the older Black people who lived here in Fort Worth. I heard them say how the town got its name, and although I thought that was a little off track (to say the least), I believed there had to be some truth to what they were saying. I can probably count the times I've been to White Settlement on purpose, and those times were for business reasons only. I believe the FWISD (Fort Worth Independent School District) home office building is actually in White Settlement, and I've been over there to watch one of my sons practice baseball. One time I went to a funeral that was held in the chapel of a funeral home there, and that's about it. Recently I was in White Settlement to have my picture taken professionally for work, and those are the times that I recall going to White Settlement on purpose. It's a place that I didn't feel was inviting to me as a Black person, and the things I had heard made me feel that Fort Worth was a big enough place that I could do what I needed to do without going out there!

It wasn't until nearing the finish of this book that I decided to search for what the experts versus other citizens had to say about the town. My elders were right. The town's name was given for the exact reason they said it was given. It was named White Settlement because the pioneers largely from Kentucky and Tennessee 'settled' there. Although Indians were already there, they came in and settled and took over the town and named it White Settlement.

Reading a couple of articles online, I read in an archived article from the New York Times, written by Simon Romero, dated November 13, 2005, that the townspeople didn't want to change the name. In fact, they love the name of the town. They don't care that the name is bad for business and investors from other places. It runs some people away, and business can be limited when the words White Settlement is used. Those words are not welcoming to anyone other than White people. No one! The mayor wanted to change the name of the town because of the way the town is seen for its name, but instead the town wanted to oust the mayor for his thoughts. Interesting, but not surprising at all to me that they would feel that way.

It's disappointing that people would take over a town that was already occupied by Indians, and somehow buy the land that was already taken. Many Whites back in the day were always *takers*. They felt if they wanted something they could take it, buy it and pass it down to their heirs – and they did. When their heirs grow up they feel that Blacks don't have anything and never had anything because of the lack of working or wanting something better; but they never tell how they took what they wanted and that's the reason many of them had what they had. They were the law, so who could the people tell? It was allowed because no one seemed to be considered human beings except for them (White people). I am not excusing the behavior of the generations of today, but I am saying that I understand how the White people my age, older and much younger can be persuaded to feel the way that they do. Majority of them have never been told the truth from start to finish. I can't say everybody took and didn't work for what they had. Those that know some of the truth still says, "It wasn't right, but that's just the way that it was." Unfortunately, people are still suffering from things that were just the way they were.

I'm not saying that because I don't think the word 'all' is fitting, because there could be the one or some that I don't know about, and I do not like 'grouping.'

Another article that I read THE STORY OF WHITE SETTLEMENT, prepared by Frances Colwell and Y.S. Morgan of the White Settlement Historical Society and was presented to the City Council in celebration of the Bicentennial Anniversary of the American Revolution was a good read.

I like reading the work and words of others because it's an inside look of what they feel and how they see things. In the article there were words that were hurtful to me and if I was a Native American, it would be total disrespect and disgust. One statement refers to the area being 'heavily **infested**' with Indians. Another statement uses the term, *Indian problem*. I am not saying that the writers were saying *they* themselves felt that way, or they were talking about the people in general felt that way; but I thought it was necessary to point out that somebody felt that way. Somebody felt the words 'infested' and 'problem' was the best way to describe the Indians or dealing with them.

Have you ever had someone tell you not to come to their house after dark? Have you ever been told that if you come they will protect you from the others that don't like you? I have.

Small Town Big Problems

"Mommy, will I be safe?"

My husband and I spent half of our daughter's senior year taking her on college visits and researching towns that she had been invited to possibly attend college. Our research and deciding factors included the diversity of the colleges as well as the towns as a whole. I have never been an advocate of an 'all anything.' What I mean by that is exactly what I said. Anytime there is an 'all' anything, I am not in favor of that ratio. I am more approving of an HBCU than I was in my younger days because I was ignorant (lacked knowledge) back then about colleges, but even with that, I still like diversity in a school. Now that I have been traveling to different colleges, I see that diversity is hard to find.

Now that I am older and wiser, I wish I had taken the opportunity to learn more about HBCUs and supported them, since I now know why many of them were organized in the first place. It wasn't necessarily the fact that Blacks didn't want to go to colleges with Whites, it was Whites not wanting Blacks to attend schools with them.

If a school happens to have a higher population of one race over the other, and most colleges do; then I want to make sure that it's not a racist school or town. I want to make sure that no one race will intentionally make the minority of the school feel as if they don't belong. If a person doesn't feel like they fit in, it shouldn't be because they're rejected for their race.

One day my daughter came to me and asked me about the college visit we were scheduled to take to Oklahoma. We'd been on a few trips there already, but this time it seemed to be more important to her. Her concern was as if she felt that she was going to a place where she would not be welcomed or wanted. I saw an underlying fear within her. Normally I would give her that pep talk that goes something like, "You can go wherever you want to go! You can do anything you want to do"; but this time was different. I figured if I had done that she might have kept what she was thinking buried inside, feeling that she couldn't share her thoughts with me; and I never want her to feel that way. I felt a genuine concern of hers, and my pep talk of who God created her to be needed to be given after I gave her the truths of this world. I don't feel that anything should supersede God's truth by any means, but there comes a time when we have to address the immediate issues that we are facing first. I'm sure there are a lot of kids who felt they were just as good as the next person but that still didn't shield them from the evil acts of others.

These problems are only a tip of the iceberg of problems that our children of color and their parents face every single day of their lives somewhere in the United States of America. My daughter should never have to wonder if she would be safe or accepted somewhere because of her race. Never! I am perturbed by the entire thought of it; but there's nothing I can do about it because there are too many individuals that are still holding on to the hate and ignorance of racism that started way before our time; yet, many individuals won't put it to rest.

Small Town Big Problems II - City Girl Country Living

I am a small town girl living in a big city. I am not what I would call "country", but I can be if I was in the right setting. I can slop hogs, feed cows, ride a horse, gather eggs from the coop and milk a cow! I can go to the garden and pull a fresh onion from the ground, pick some tomatoes and load up the bottom of my shirt with cucumbers to make some fresh homemade pickles from scratch. I would love to have that life. I have wanted to live that life for many years now, but there have been circumstances beyond my control that have kept me in the city.

When our children were smaller, my husband and I talked about moving to a small town similar to the one where I grew up, with the addition of some other amenities. We wanted our children to be able to enjoy the innocence of life. I have always been connected to simpler living. I am all for a fine home and fine cars, but a part of me is drawn to the *Little House on the Prairie* life. I know...I know. I'm just different, and I have known that for many years. I am in touch with who I am, and I can appreciate that about myself. I enjoy the quietness of the outdoors; and the ability to see the stars in the sky at night have been an attractive incentive for country living.

In small towns people are actually people instead of a credit score. Maybe all of that has changed, but that's what I remember about growing up in a small town. My father could go into one of the banks that he banked with and get a simple signature loan just using his driver's license – not for identification, but for paperwork. The schools are smaller and everyone knows each other in small towns. Sometimes that could be a deal breaker, but for me, I like it. Nothing's perfect, but when the good outweighs the bad, I can handle that.

Over the years of traveling here and there, my husband and I would always revisit the thoughts of country living; but that one problem still exists, and unfortunately the probably isn't going anywhere anytime soon – if ever. As we'd drive and enjoy our time together, we'd find ourselves asking the question of where we would move to if we decided to move. Where could we go where our children would be treated fairly? Where would we be comfortable living and could sleep peacefully at night, and shop in the local stores with ease and comfort. We wondered if our children would be liked or just tolerated. Where could they live and not be made spectacles out of whenever a teacher wanted to make a point or reenact slavery in history or social studies class? You've probably never thought about that. I mean, who would? It's hard to think of those things when you have never been faced with the said issues. Do you think I'm making this stuff up? Well, I'm not.

Have you ever thought about relocating? What did you have to consider? Career, job, kind of house, amenities in the town... Have you ever had to consider your race first? I have. I will be honest with you. It makes me angry and hurt all at the same time. It is overwhelming and heart troubling to know that we still live in the days that people judge according to the color of our skin and not our character. It is sickening.

There are small rural towns and suburbs that are still known for racism where the citizens brag about their bigotry ways and how Blacks aren't welcomed. This is not hearsay, you can look it up on any news outlet. Many people will not hesitate to warn a Black person not to go to certain towns because a Black person is subject to 'come up missing.' A couple of true stories that I can give as examples are things that happened in the town that my son attended college. I'll also talk more about that town later. During one of the college visits with my daughter I learned of another incident that had taken place in that small town of Ada, Oklahoma where he graduated college. When I asked someone about the race relations in the town that I was visiting, I was advised that *it wasn't like Ada!* We had already talked about Ada, so that's why it was mentioned again. I was then told about an incident of a Black guy being run into the woods by some White guys in the town for no reason other than his race. Black people didn't tell me this story, other White people did. Another incident that I found online about the same town happened several years back, was a vandalized church. Threats and racial slurs and a klu klux klan symbol was spray painted on the church that was in a predominantly Black neighborhood. The words white power were spray painted on the church sign along with the kkk symbol. That is unacceptable in America, and I can only speak for myself right now...I'm tired of it.

Restaurants and gas stations are owned and operated by klan members. (I chose not to capitalize klan on purpose. I will not give the name respect that way). There are towns right around Fort Worth, Texas that are known for their racial biases, and I still get a bitter taste in my mouth when I think about those towns. The populations have changed somewhat, but the culture is much the same. Thanks to the old folks in the town who do not want to see change, nor do some of them respect change. They are still in charge and either running things or teaching their offspring to continue what they started. Racism is everywhere! It has even made its way into the high schools and colleges where students are videoing themselves calling Black people niggers and chanting songs that they have made up about Black people. Groups of White boys are photographed saluting Nazi style.

I'd love to move! I dread fighting city traffic every morning going to work. The past several years my husband's business would not allow us to move, but now we could work around that problem. The major dilemma that we face (one that hardly anyone of another race would have to think about) is finding somewhere to go where our children would be in a safe environment. They're young adults now and wouldn't have to deal with 'school' racism, but they are just the right age to get into real trouble if in a racist town.

Because of fear I feel that my children missed out on experiencing the life that I wanted to give them as young ones. There are a list of things to be concerned about when raising children in the city, but being treated poorly because of their race hasn't been the biggest concern unless you live in the suburbs or predominantly White areas. Unfortunately, for the past couple of years with the rise of racism, it has gotten worse. I can only imagine what it's like in the smaller towns now. Seems like many people got the memo that it's okay to show how you really feel about people of color, and nothing would be done.

Speaking of small towns, while on another college visit, we had the displeasure of seeing confederate flags plastered on cars, license plates and in the windows of businesses. By the way, it is the year 2019! Some of the towns we've seen that display are towns that don't look like fifty dollars could be gathered in the entire community as a whole; but those are most times the worst individuals when it comes to racism. Society has placed Blacks so low on the approval poll that a wealthy Black person is looked upon lower than low-income Whites. Personally I don't think anyone should be categorized by their money status, but I'm just sharing what I've read and seen.

When my husband and I took my daughter to Portales, New Mexico for a college visit, I actually liked the size and the feel of the town. I can't say that I liked the town because I didn't get a chance to eat there, go to any stores, encounter anyone off campus, etc. Many of the small towns between here and there were appealing to me for size and appearance. I guess they reminded me of what I've always wanted and what I've talked about wanting for a long time in a town. I crave that small town simple life and community feel. I feel that I have been deprived from that experience for one main reason – being Black. I'm not saying that life in smaller towns is a piece of cake, because they have their own issues, but their issues are different from city issues. The trip to the college, which took almost seven hours gave me a lot to think about. There were times that we went over two hours without anything in sight, and then we'd come across a small town. Although we try not to stop much when we're traveling because we like to make good time, we don't want our trips to become so rigid that the trip turns out to be more of a job than fun and adventurous. On that trip we made sure we had gas in the car because some towns we knew weren't safe for us to stop in at night. That's awful, but the feeling and knowing the reason it wasn't safe is even more awful. Each time we stopped I gave my daughter the same talk. I try to talk to her in a way that she will be aware of what could happen, while trying not to make her afraid of people. It's bad that we have to make our kids aware of the dangers of trafficking and also for being Black in this world.

I am tired. I'm tired of having to see if we were in a town that would welcome shooting Blacks as a sport and wanting to put them on display to say, "Look dad! Look what I found wandering around town!" It might seem comical, but it wouldn't be if you've been in my shoes or the shoes of others who know exactly what I am talking about. Sometimes I wonder if city people feel that way too or is it just small town alums who know what that feels like. I think about it in those terms because some city people believe it is what it is, and they can go wherever they want to go because many of them have been protected from that reality. They have never even been out of their own neighborhoods, their communities, or their city limits. Whenever they do, many travel by plane so they don't know what it is like and tell you the truth, oftentimes they don't pick up on racism the same ways that I do because they can't spot faking. I've lived it, so it's easier for me to see it.

Small Town Big Problems Part III
Blacks in...

I can't seem to get off the subject of small towns. I don't think that racism is worse in small towns, I sincerely believe that it shows up more because of the size of the town and the ability for others to have negative influence over another. There are several suburb areas around the city that I reside in, and it is not a secret that those suburbs (that are considered small towns) do not want folks of color in them. In fact, many of the areas grow so rapidly because the people who moved to the areas did so in order to get away from the diversity of the neighborhoods in which they were living. If you think for a moment that these things don't exist, please think again.

Another nearby small town within the city, I guess some would call a community, is known quite well for their racial biases. Whenever a Black is seen driving in town by police officers, they use an acronym on the radio to alert other police officers that a Black is in their town. They would use the term, "Blacks in ..." I wonder why it is important to make the others aware that a Black person is in their community. Sounds unreal I know. It's not. I wish it was made up, but it isn't. Once again, this is firsthand information from an individual who was directly involved in the foolishness, but soon got out. The facts given weren't from another Black person, but a White person who witnessed this evil behavior. "Either get out or become toxic like the others", he said.

I'm sure some people are thinking to themselves and wondering if what I am saying is true, and if so, how can it be without repercussions. One reason there aren't ramifications of the behavior is because oftentimes the approval comes from within a community or from the head. I think it's safe to say that you will possibly never know what I am talking about because chances are you will never have the problem of finding a 'safe zone' instead of living where you want to live or driving where you want to drive. The most fear a White person can announce is that they fear being robbed in predominantly Black areas; and most of the time it's because of what they have been fed and seen on TV. I admit things are bad in a lot of areas now with robberies, but it hasn't been as bad as they have thought it was in the past. To a majority, Black people have always been out to harm or take. You might not ever experience looking over your shoulders or rearview mirrors hoping that someone doesn't feel like harassing you that day, but if you should ever experience such a thing...think about those who experience it every day because of their race. Again, I can't make this stuff up!

Directions to Death

There are many small towns in Texas that I never knew existed; and those towns have been the topic of conversation recently, by people that I know and trust. Even though some of the towns aren't openly racist or known for their racism, we must travel through some of those towns to get to our destinations. That is where the real danger comes into play.

I can't remember what year it was, but I estimate the year to be around 2000 or 2001, but I know it was the year my nephew had started college in Corsicana, Texas. My husband and I had him so spoiled, along with my dad and a couple of my other sisters, so we made that trip often. Whatever he needed or wanted, we took care of it—even if it meant traveling back and forth to pick him up on Friday nights and taking him back on Sundays. One night, his mom (my older sister) and my three other sisters decided that we would ride together to take him back to college. I still don't know how we all fit in that car, but we did. Granted we weren't as heavy as we are now, but still! After dropping him off at school and heading back to Fort Worth, I missed my turn. That particular exit was easy to miss, but deep down I think I was a little fearful of making that mistake anyway, so I might have somewhat 'willed' that to happen. "What you think about you bring about." Right? I would always mention missing that exit any time my husband and I would travel that way for baseball trips or business with my nephew. You know how we tend to think other people are dealing with the same thing we're dealing with? He didn't have the problem of missing the exit – I did; but I figured I'd always warn him anyway.

I also could have missed the exit because we were probably laughing and talking and not paying attention. When I noticed we were headed the wrong way, I panicked. There was a gas station on the side of the freeway just beyond the exit, so I stopped there for directions. One of my sisters got out of the car with me so that the two of us could hear the directions. One of the other sisters got out to get something to drink. We walked up to the counter where there was a young lady probably in her early to mid-thirties. Another young lady who looked like she was in her early twenties was in the doorway of what resembled an office. She was holding a broom in a resting manner while she listened to what we were talking about with the woman at the counter. I am very observant whenever I go places, so she immediately got my attention with her facial expressions and body language. I don't know if the line of work that I have been involved in for more than twenty years made me observant or the fact that I don't trust unfamiliar small towns. Maybe it's all of the above coupled with the fact that my sister was kidnapped when she was in college. I like to see who I am dealing with, and I watch their body language and gestures.

I asked the woman at the counter how to get to Fort Worth. I don't know why we didn't just keep driving and find a turn around. It was so odd that night of how we went against everything we would normally do. She began telling me how to get back on the freeway where I had veered off. I didn't think it sounded right but at that time I was one who was lost. I repeated the directions back to her while pointing in the direction she had just given. The first turn was easy because it was right there in front of the store, and it was the only way to turn across the overpass. I looked at my sister and said, "You got that?" She said, "Yes. I got it." Hindsight is 20/20, but I should have listened to my gut. If my gut wasn't enough confirmation that something was wrong, it should have been the face of the young lady who was standing in the doorway. She had a look of concern and her countenance had dropped severely. She looked at me and I looked at her. She looked as if she wanted to intervene, but she knew better. The older of the two looked back at her as if she was daring her to say something. My sister and I both noticed it, but we had no idea what it was all about. We didn't know what we were about to encounter.

We took every turn the store clerk had directed us to take, in hopes of getting back to the freeway – which was supposed to be just down the way. The last turn that we were to take to get to the freeway took us down a long and narrow, pitch black dirt road. We couldn't even see our hands in front of us. Heck, we couldn't see each other in the car! My high beam lights were not bright enough to see more than a few feet in front of my car. We were scared *at this point. We knew we had been set up by the clerk at the store. While traveling down that long and narrow dirt road, we passed a police car parked in front of what looked to be a small house, but it was a police department that was probably manned by one police and a dispatcher. I don't know, this is strictly speculation of what I know about small towns. At that point, we weren't wanting to ask for any more directions, we just wanted to get to some lights again. We passed a city limit sign that read, ICE City Limits. (City name changed). We all said, "ICE? Where are we?" It was a small town buried in between surrounding towns near Fort Worth. The town was only about an hour and a half away from home, but it seemed like we were forever away from home. We drove trying to find a place to turn around, but ended up at the end of nowhere.*

To this day, it is hard to talk about that night because of the traumatic emotional experience we had. Imagine feeling like your mother and father will have to raise all of their grandkids because their daughters were murdered. I understand if you feel that this is total conjecture, and it is, but the bottom line is that is how we felt; and it has happened to many others in this world. In our guts we felt that we were going to be cornered by the police and probably some klan members at the end of the road, or after we ran into a ditch on that narrow road. We had that feeling, but we were some praying sisters! That dark, scary, 'run for your life' scene was all too familiar to my once kidnapped oldest sister. She already had a plan for the rest of us. That was just her way of doing things—taking care of us first. We have always watched out for her too so that she wouldn't have trigger moments of remembering being kidnapped by a Satanic cult when she was in college. Those are memories that we as a family would never forget. This time, we were all in. We weren't going to let her stay behind while we got away. We were all going to die or survive together. Although we were prepared to die, we vowed to fight until the end. We held hands and talked about what our children would do without us, but at least they would know we were all together. We knew no one would know what had happened to us, because either we would be disposed of or a story would be made up that five sisters ran off the road in Ice, Texas. The absolute worst case scenario had filled our minds. We reviewed the actions of the two clerks in the store and how we had not taken the signs the young lady had tried to give. We should have never turned to go across the bridge, but instead we should have gone up further and caught the next exit, but we believed the store clerk could get us back on track more quickly. Should haves and would haves mean nothing afterwards.

Finally, I had driven in one direction as far as I could and this time I dared not to ignore any more gut feelings and discernment. The street was so narrow that I could not turn around. It was nothing but the grace of God that I came to a ragged old ranch entry. I backed into the driveway that was barely big enough for my car to fit. I was afraid that one tire would miss and we would fall into the ditch, but we knew at that time our faith had to kick in. We might have planned our death a few moments ago, but then we decided that we would live at any cost. We knew if we had fallen into that ditch it would have been over for us. When I got that vehicle turned back around, I told my sisters to hold on because I was about to get us out of there. I floored it! I had made up in my mind that if anything or anyone came out in front of my car to block us, 'it' or they were going to be run over. That's how bad it was. We just knew that they were waiting on us to get to the end of the road that ended in what looked like heavy trees, brush and a body of water. Once turned around and on our way back, the police car was no longer there. I can't say for sure, but I felt and still feel that he was going to be waiting on our arrival at the end of the road where they expected us to end. We made it back to the freeway which was literally right on the other side of the station we stopped for directions. Funny how she couldn't tell us that. She sent us the wrong way on purpose, and I know that. I wonder how many people have been redirected to their death.

Sometime later we were at my mom's talking to my brother who is a truck driver. We were discussing what happened that night, and my brother stopped everything and said, "Y'all went to Ice? What in the world were y'all doing there?" We said, "Not on purpose!" We told him we were sent there by a store clerk at the station. We trusted stopping there because it was a big named station that wasn't a mom and pop type place. "Oh my God! They will hang you there! That town is very racist," he said. He went on to tell us how the store clerks in that town and other small towns around Texas would tell him to go to the back door for deliveries. I know; I was surprised too that they were still sending Blacks to the back door like back in the days of slavery and the Jim Crow era. My brother was bothered deeply by what happened because he knows that town and is very familiar with all that happens in 'those parts.'

How ridiculous is it for us to be afraid of being Black in a town more than being lost!

You're not welcomed here!

Back in 1986 when I was playing high school basketball, we had a game that was scheduled at one of the high schools that are less than fifteen minutes down the freeway from where I stay now. Our entire team was Black, but we had a White female coach. Our bus pulled up to a totally empty parking lot. How many times would a visiting school beat the home school team to their own gymnasium? Not often. We asked Coach if they had canceled on us. Since the parking lot was empty we could see everything out there. Near the entrance of the parking lot, a black Ford Mustang was strategically parked so that we could get a clear look at it. On the windshield of the *mustang these words were written in shoe polish, NO BLACKS ALLOWED. We were like, 'what the...' I had never experienced anything that blatant. I had heard about things like that, but I hadn't experienced it for myself. I had seen it in movies where those words would be written above water fountains, doors and other places. I've seen young Black school-aged teens have malts and drinks dashed in their faces by White boys and girls in diners. I've seen that on movies and old film reels, but never had I seen it for myself. Our coach was furious. We immediately said, "Coach Smith (name changed), we're not playing here. They don't want us here, so we don't want to be here." We didn't know which coward(s) wrote on the car but what we did know is that someone who knew we would be arriving and we were all Black wanted us to see what they felt about us.*

The same year of the black Mustang incident, we had another tournament at a different small suburb outside of Fort Worth. We had a similar experience to the one with the black Mustang. Before we went in, our coaches gave us the run down...stay together, don't go to the bathroom alone, and get on the bus together. Thinking back on those times, I am reminded of movies such as Glory Days, Pride, Remember the Titans, and some others that detailed racial tensions in towns back in the day.

This day and time, we tell our children to stay together, don't go anywhere alone because of human and sex trafficking; but we had fears of being kidnapped but most of all being Black.

Not here!

Fast forward to 2019, my husband already knows whenever we are thinking of places to eat, don't even mention that town to me. I know the incident was in high school, but it's just my feelings about it to this day. I tell him not to mention that 'No Blacks Allowed' town to me. I don't trust them. If you have ever experienced something of that magnitude as a youngster it's a possibility that you might have some reservations too. I was a child in the tenth grade. I was scared. It wasn't funny if it was meant to be a joke, we didn't laugh. I was scarred from that experience. I don't hate anyone, and I am smart enough to know that incident was in the late eighties, but I can't soon forget it. The whole town was that way back then. Some of us were terrified as to what could or would happen to us if we went inside of the gym. That might have been stretching it a bit, but again, we were kids. Keep in mind if you will, we were a generation of kids who weren't far removed from segregation. When I moved to Fort Worth, Texas in 1981, I was the first group of students that were bused across town to a school that was predominantly if not all White before we arrived.

When my husband was a boy, he experienced some things as well, but there was one incident that stood out the most that he often talked about. He repeats this story as if it's rooted in his head and heart. I think it was a pivotal moment in his young life that could very well still be affecting him in ways that he hasn't even thought about anymore.

He was born a year and a day before Dr. King was killed. Trust me, he says it every year, so I can't forget that. Whenever he shares his story of racism, he opens up about this particular story of when he was bused over to a school across town when he was in the third grade. The school had a football team, and when the Black boys got there, they were immediately part of the football team. I mean, they weren't chosen to be quarterbacks, but they could play in all of the positions that required running or catching. Of course changing the roster didn't sit well with the existing parents, and as a mom it probably wouldn't have set well with me either. The change made the team win games, but it was a tough transition for others. These kids were having fun playing football, but they were in a place where they didn't feel wanted, and had been uprooted from where they were comfortable and accepted.

Transportation to the games were a bit tough for some of the parents of the bused kids which made it harder for the boys to get to and from football practices and games, so my husband's mother along with maybe one other mother would load up their vehicles and take the boys to the games. He said that none of the White mothers would allow the Black boys to get into their cars. We are talking about elementary school kids. That happened more than forty years ago, but he still tells that story every single time we are over by the school that is located in the TCU area. When things so disheartening and traumatic happen to a person at an early age, those are seeds that are planted, and we know what happens to seeds.

No Shoes No Shirt No Service

When I was growing up and into my early adulthood it wasn't unusual to see signs in the windows of stores and establishments that read, No Shoes, No Shirt, No Service. It is crazy to say, but there are places that should read, No Service If You're Black. It happens, more times than some know, and more than some would like to know.

She Can Be Served, but Not You

Imagine how hard it is for a mom to tell her son to be careful constantly, just because he is in an interracial relationship living in a city notorious for racial inequality. I don't have to wonder, I am that mom.

Many stories have been shared with me about the unkind treatment they have received in places. My son doesn't share these things because he doesn't want me to worry. I learned of an incident that happened recently in a restaurant they had gone to eat at. I won't pinpoint the city since it's relevant, but not really since it's happening almost everywhere all the time. My daughter-in-law was sharing with me the hurt and anger that she felt when a server chose not to serve her and my son. At first she overlooked the treatment, but when the server flat out refused to serve them, she had had it. The most awful part of it all is that they are justified for their actions in places of business. Most people would say, "Just don't go back, or talk to a manager." I would say those things as well, but I also know that sometimes it doesn't do any good, because the manager oftentimes condone their employees' behavior and them feeling that way. Out of respect for their position, the manager will say they will talk to the employee about their behavior and never do. If a person presses the issue, and only if they do, or take it to the media then something more will [possibly] be done. I'm grateful for video on cell phones now that allow people to capture bad behavior and share it with the world of social media users. If it's bad enough, then the news will oftentimes acquire the video and air it. I like that they are doing that now because for too long things were going unnoticed and unheard of because of the ways things could be hidden.

Too bad she didn't think to record the unfair treatment they received from the waiter.

Although not all Black people are supportive of interracial relationships, it is more accepting in the Black race than in the White race. I rarely hear Black people talk negatively about interracial relationships. I know that I am only one person and I haven't been around everybody everywhere, but I can say what I have noticed. Most Black people accept interracial relationships and they move on. Even if they don't accept it, they don't try to make the individuals miserable or threaten their lives.

It's Still Happening...

February 13, 2020, my daughter and a couple of her college roommates went to a local Wendy's restaurant in Wichita Falls, Texas. My daughter called me at 10:46 p.m. My phone is automatically set to 'do not disturb mode' after 9:00 p.m., but I have a list that my children and my mom are on that will allow calls to show up. I found it strange that she would call me so late, so immediately I went into momma mode of thinking something was wrong. I answered the phone and my daughter immediately started with, "Mom, guess what happened to me?" Since I was facetiming with her I knew it wasn't something life threatening, so that was a relief. I said, "What happened, Punkin?" She went on to tell me about an incident that occurred at Wendy's. The worker (manager) decided to tell her that the store was closed. A guy was sitting inside, which I understood because establishments don't make a habit of kicking customers out just because they're closed. Well, that's what I thought had happened.

My daughter let me know that she understood that if that was the case, but it wasn't. She was visibly upset and couldn't believe that she would be treated unfairly and have a person justify their actions. The manager told her and her friends that they were closed – period, and she didn't have any cooks, although there were two employees there cooking. Finally the manager told them to go to McDonald's or somewhere else to get their food. One of the friends asked her what was the problem and then asked if she was afraid of them. She replied, "Yes!" My daughter and the friends left and went to get something to eat at Subway. They came back through going back to campus and saw multiple cars in the drive-through. They went through the drive-through and when she saw it was them she picked up the phone as if she was calling the police. Needless to say I was very angry, and even angrier that my daughter and her friends had to experience someone treating them that way and outright saying they are to be feared because they are Black. The girls are all barely 100 pounds or a little over and only 19 years old. Why is this still happening in 2020?

The version of the story that I got from the manager was that she only told them the lobby was closed. She never said she told them to go to the drive-through but said she told them she didn't have anyone to work the register (*really?*), but never told them she didn't have any cooks. It didn't make sense to me either. She apologized for saying that she was afraid of them.

Regretfully, I told my daughter I wasn't a bit surprised, and welcome to our world.

No One Will Know What Happened to Your Son

Several years ago my husband and I were debating about sending our eldest son to a nearby college in the same town one of the incidents happened nearly twenty-five years ago. A close friend of mine who I've known since my son was a little boy, warned me about the college we were considering. He didn't warn me about the school as much as he did about the town it was located in, and the surrounding towns that my son would have to drive through to get there. By the way, my friend is White.

My friend told me that not only would he be in danger driving through the towns, but the police would probably stop him every time they see him driving through. He himself had been a victim of racial profiling because of the car he drives. Since he drove a distance from work, he drove an older model car with tinted windows and rims in order to keep the mileage off of his nice vehicles. His car wasn't what the average White guy would drive around that town. His car would be the type of car one would expect a Black or Hispanic guy to drive. I know I am being stereotypical here, but it's for a reason. It's the truth, and if I can own up to that, then I know that others would think the same.

Time after time my friend would tell me how he had been pulled over by White police officers, but when they would stop him they'd make up a reason for the stop. They'd say something like he didn't make a complete stop at the stop sign. He always worked the late shift, so he would encounter the police near midnight. I'm not making an excuse for the police, but we all know many of them in small towns are looking for something to do around that time.

I'm aware of White boys being pulled over by police in the past and present. In my hometown some boys were picked on and stopped more than others. The White boys who were pulled over were the ones that did petty things or those that hung with the Black boys. I am also aware of White boys who have been pulled over and given tickets or just harassed, but that's about all they'd have to worry about. Our young Black men of today aren't getting tickets—many of them are getting beat or killed.

Speaking of Small Town and Police

A few days ago we were taking our daughter to a small town in another part of Oklahoma for a college visit. It was late, raining hard and very cold. Our visits tend to get us into towns late because we normally leave after she gets out of school, and we have long drives.

One of the coaches of the school we were visiting had warned us about the small towns we have to go through and the police that would be lurking waiting to stop travelers. My husband kept that in mind, watched the speed limit very closely, and I was there to point out anything that got close to the limit. The last stretch was a dark, two-lane road that was about seventy-five minutes long according to Siri. We were about midway through when it happened… Each car we'd face my husband would dim his bright lights, and this time he didn't dim them soon enough. Yes, you got it. The police passed us and immediately flipped his overheads on. My husband started using a quick process of elimination to figure out why we were being stopped. We knew everything on the car was working, which is one main reason we rent vehicles for the trips, and to keep miles off of my car. We couldn't figure out what happened, so we waited for the police to come to the window and tell us. I was half asleep by that time, but I woke all the way up when I saw that we were being pulled over.

My daughter was in the backseat asleep, but when we came to a stop coupled with the blinding lights of the police cruiser she woke up. She asked what was going on. I told her everything would be okay. She all of a sudden said in a high-pitched tone, "Dad! Do like they did in 'The Hate You Give' movie. Put your hands on the dash! Hurry! Put'em on there Dad!" I had to reassure her that it was okay and everything would be okay. I didn't know that *it would be okay, but my job was to make her feel that it would. At first I thought about her being frightened and felt it was my fault that she saw the movie. Then I realized it wasn't the movie – it was real life that made her fear being pulled over by police, and she didn't want her Black father to be killed. That bothers me to my core. It makes me angry and it hurts that my daughter was so afraid of what should have been a routine traffic stop. Thank God the officer was nice. He told my husband that he stopped him because he didn't dim his bright lights while driving towards him. Petty? Maybe. I'm okay with it though. Maybe I'm saying that because my family was unharmed and my husband didn't go to jail and he is still alive. My husband had dimmed his lights at every passing car, but not (quick enough) this time. There were no streetlights, and if he hadn't used his high beam lights we might have hit something along the way, or even worse—ran off the road. Every few miles we saw signs that indicated 'watch for deer.' I'm not saying that we were pulled over for being Black, because honestly, I don't think the officer could even see in the car that quickly, but I don't know. Well, I guess it was obvious that we weren't White—now that I think about it, but that's not the main issue. The problem we had was being fearful we wouldn't make it past the stop.*

For the record, the officer did exactly what he should have done during the stop. He walked up to the car and asked where we were headed. We told him. He knew about the school we were going to visit. He asked for my husband's license and registration. Since my husband is a licensed handgun carrier, the officer asked where the gun was located and he went back to the vehicle to run the license. That was how a stop was supposed to go. We made sure to use that moment as a teaching time for our daughter. We talked to her about the importance of not having unpaid tickets that are in warrant status, and how to comply. If an officer is making the stop correctly, give him or her no ammunition for trouble. We advised her of how a routine stop could have turned out totally different. Thank God we made it out safely.

Chapter Three
Black this and Black that.
What is that all about?

Black people might have flaunted the Black power symbols in the past, but have you ever wondered why? The black fist could have very well been raised to say, 'No more. You can't make us feel weak and disgraced. Many Black people won't allow others to treat them like garbage or any other way that we had been encouraged to think about ourselves.'

Please don't ever think that this White supremacy crap just started. The ones that are on fire right now have been tucking their sheets away since their ancestors passed them down. Many were just waiting for the right time to get them out, wash them up and cut fresh eyelets in them. These bad actors are taught very early in life how to hate, and the others who join allow a seed of hate to be planted and watered in their hearts.

I believe the only reason they kept their sheets under wraps is because they were afraid. They were afraid because they knew that Black people were no longer totally under their thumbs and outwardly controlled by their power. Notice I said totally and outwardly. I strategically chose those words as a way of pointing out that there are still some ways that White people are in control and hold power. That is what the skinheads, racists and nationalists are afraid of losing. They can no longer have every company controlled by White people who only hire White people. They can no longer openly beat and hang Black people as a sport and easily get away with it. They might be doing the hangings and beatings still today, but it's not in their sheets—they are using other legal attire. Is that the power they are marching to keep? Do they want to be able to throw Black people off of buses and burn down their houses while they watch the Black families run out? I'm just trying to figure out what they really want.

These people have come out of the backwoods now because they feel empowered again because of the unleashing of the beast allowing this ugliness to happen. What do I mean by allowing it to happen? If a person doesn't stand against something then they stand for it—especially when they have the power to halt the hate crimes, talk and activity. I understand that no one but God can remove the hate from their hearts, but even God needs a willing heart. Some people have said they are glad that they are coming out in the opening with their hatred. Yes and no. Whenever beasts openly walk down the streets like Nazi murderers and it is condoned, the killing will increase. When they had to hide and kill Black people they had a harder time doing so. Now all they have to say is that they fear for their life or throw an amendment out there and call it a 'right.' All rights aren't right.

Chapter
Education in America

I honestly believe the little things in life sometimes have a huge effect on how we do things and how we feel about important issues. It is easy to comment or make snide remarks about issues when the issues have nothing to do with you or your loved ones. I like to say, "You don't have a dog in that hunt." If I don't trade places with the person or persons going through a situation, I could easily make comments like, "They shouldn't be acting like that" or "Why are they marching all the time?" I have found myself needing to be educated on some things regarding issues I had not been exposed to in my life. For example, I never in my life knew about what some people in the urban areas and inner cities go through in their school systems. It wasn't until I got into the education field and started education courses that caused me to have to research topics that I never thought of before then. I was in my small bubble of beliefs, and that's all that I knew. I had never seen schools with chain-link fencing around them like a prison. I had only seen that on television. Sad thing is that the fence is there to keep the kids safe inside – not to lock them up like prisoners. Over the course of a couple of semesters, I had to write about certain issues that urged me to research stories and watch films about problems that I knew nothing about. I started learning about things that I never knew existed. I read books that explained and explored grueling stories that made me so sad. I have always had an underlying belief in my heart that people were making excuses to live a certain way, and had settled. My God. I'm so sorry that I felt that way. I had become biased and prejudiced in my own right, but when I learn the truth, I take it to heart.

I remember looking at a video of a school in Detroit that looked like it had been condemned or should have been condemned, but the children were attending that school each day. The gym had places on the floor that looked like speed bumps on steroids. There was visible mold on the walls. Ceiling was damaged. If I recall correctly, part of it was due to a leak in the roof. I shouldn't say that was the cause, because the cause was the roof had never been addressed. That kind of damage doesn't happen overnight, and it definitely wasn't one rain storm that caused that problem. You and I who have never seen such a thing would not be able to understand why a child might drop out of school at an early age, while attending schools in such conditions. We might not understand why their academic performance might be low. We might not understand the constant complaints of the parents. We haven't been there and experienced it for ourselves so talk is easy. As they said when I was younger, *talk is cheap.* Who wants to attend a school like that? I saw all of this on a short video clip that only showed one classroom and a gymnasium. It would be really hard for me (as a student there) to believe that the school district cares about me. It would be hard for a child to believe their principal cares for them since they are the highest office on the premises. I know it's not the principal's fault, but a kid won't know that. What about you? Would you want to go to that school or one similar? What if you didn't have a choice because you lived in the district and had no transportation elsewhere or even worse...all of the school choices were like that? It's hard to feel loved or cared for when love isn't shown through actions. I could go on and on about stories like this one, but it would take the rest of the book to tell them all.

About twenty years or so ago (I can't believe it has been that long), I was going to see my niece play basketball at a school in the Poly area of Fort Worth. She was in middle school at an 'away' school.

When I first walked in the door there were steps to go up to another level. I was holding on to the rail looking around with the climbing of each step. I was thinking to myself that they were playing in a condemned school, and I wanted to know why. The tiles on the floor and ceiling were filthy and uneven. Chunks were missing from the tiles, there were water stains on the tile, and the bathroom was a mess. I didn't go in, but I could see it from an open door. It was dim and dingy in the school. I kept walking toward the gym door and that's when I noticed the hall lockers were hanging off the wall with the content exposed. I finally said, "Why are we playing in this condemned school? What did I say that for? Oh my word! One of the moms from that school read me my rights. She told me off so badly that I even had to laugh. She told me how she didn't appreciate me saying that about their kids' school and if I was too good to be over there I should leave. I told her that she should think her kids were too good to be at the school too. After I apologized for what I said, I went inside the gym to watch the game. As I sat in the bleachers I couldn't help but notice the young girls and boys that attended that school. Tears rolled down my cheeks involuntarily. My husband looked at me and said, "I already know." I thought to myself, "These poor kids don't even know what it's like to be treated like they are special around here. What will happen to the esteem of these children? What will these little girls do to fit in? How will they react to the first boy that comes and tell them something good?" My mind was going crazy. My mind was racing at a high rate of speed. It was then when I realized why I went to barber school and became a barber stylist. I realized I had to be the one who would help those that are underprivileged and had no one able to help them, or care enough to help. I realized at that time that my calling wasn't always going to be pretty or accepted, but necessary. I had come from an area that I know would not allow students to play there. My husband and his assistant coach have gone to baseball fields that they wouldn't allow the boys to play due to the dangers of getting hurt. A bad field can cause injuries. Why are those children treated differently? They are all part of the Fort Worth ISD, and only minutes from other schools that didn't look like that. Why them? One disheartening fact is that I reached out to a couple of administrators about giving free services to some of the students who would be willing to accept the services. Just like so many other times I've offered my services, I met with negative results. Either the schools are afraid of liability or they don't care.

When we sit back in our nice school districts with multiple gymnasiums, and new ones are being built before the current ones can get old, it's easy to not 'get it.' Baseball fields are re-turfed and batting cages are being built while other schools can't get a decent classroom. Right now my daughter's high school gym has been torn down in order to make it into a stadium. It's going to be state of the art, but nothing was wrong with that gym they had.

I have friends who live in areas where they are completely disconnected from the reality of what I just shared. It would shock them if they were exposed to other school districts. I'm not knocking them because it's easy to become that way. I don't live in the poverty-stricken areas but I'm not completely disconnected and ignorant of their reality and neither am I disconnected from their pain.

It is the job of people like me to expose and share the truth so that we can bring about change. Not everyone will care since after all, they 'worked' for what they have and to be where they are now. I get that, but some people don't have choices. I don't have to live in poverty to empathize with it. I won't say that I understand because I don't understand completely. I haven't had to find meals for my children to eat at home. My kids didn't have to look forward to going to school to get their only meal for the day. (Thank God)! I didn't grow up worrying about what I would eat or where I would sleep. I have never walked to school through gang territory or being shot at (or around) just to get to school. I haven't had to attend a school that won't heat or cool in the winter and summer months. My kids haven't attended schools that have books that are several editions behind. Yes it happens all the time. In some school districts the students are given books that other school districts have donated. These books are earlier editions that might have much of the same content, but the updates are not included. Donated books? You donate things you no longer want or have been used up!

I took a Human Sexuality class one semester and I wanted to purchase the book since the one I had during the semester was rented. It was an informative and relevant textbook for what I was doing in my non-profit as well as my life coaching. My book that I had for class was the fourth edition and it included information regarding the latest STIs and LGBTQ information. I wanted a book that had today's topics in it and not things that were taught years ago. That's what is happening with the kids in the ISDs getting hand-me-down textbooks. The students are getting the books from students that are ahead because they have been privileged to learn first. Can you see the gap? Can you see the importance of having updated information? Knowledge is power; therefore, outdated information is irrelevant and it keeps the space between the haves and the have nots. One subtle way of doing so is to continue to have staggered learning in the classrooms and school districts.

Money Can't Buy Me Love, but It Can Buy Me A Seat In Prestigious Colleges and Universities!

Kelly Williams-Bolar was sent to jail for using her father's address so that her two daughters could attend a better school. This mother did what many mothers did when I was in high school. Many of the schools weren't safe and oftentimes the curriculum were below average; therefore, parents used the addresses of relatives in order to send their children to better schools. Williams-Bolar didn't pay someone to take a test for her daughters to get into school. She didn't pay a coach or coaches to lie and say that her daughter would be playing a sport or would be on some other extracurricular activity team. None of that. She simply used an address of someone she knew – her father. On the other hand, you have Felicity Huffman and Lori Loughlin only to name two of several (and still counting) parents who paid thousands and even millions of dollars for people to take entry tests for their princesses to enter prestigious universities. They paid individuals who would lie and say their students would be athletes for the colleges of choice – even though most of them never even played the sport they were 'signed' up to play. How do you explain that unequal treatment? Money talks, but race screams. One after another is coming forward or being exposed for their part in the college scandal. Even if they are fined, it won't hurt them. It won't hurt their pockets nor will they lose anything. Let us see what will happen to them.

There are coaches in predominantly White upper to high dollar areas who seek out athletes in other areas and offer the students in-district addresses or places to stay so that they can better their sports program. It's nothing new. We all know that it has gone on and it still happens today!

Sat And Act

Let's talk about two major tests that have helped determine the fate of so many students. Much like those state mandated tests that students spend their entire school year prepping for, I would like to know are they really necessary. Many of the students aren't being taught the necessary subjects in school that cross over into real life after graduation, because the teachers are focused on making sure their students perform high on the tests. The teachers need the students to pass because they are graded according to how many pass or fail. The schools are graded as well, so more emphasis is on the tests than actual school subjects. Those tests (in my opinion) don't show what a student knows or doesn't know. Those tests are biased and they are not created with every student in mind. It's another separation tool that we have in America. If you made this grade - go here. If you made this grade - go there.

It is so unfortunate that colleges rely heavily upon SAT and ACT scores. Many students are shaking in their boots in their high school years and not able to fully enjoy their years because they are wondering if they will be able to go to college or not. It's not just money that will keep them out, but now the possibility of low test scores will eliminate their ability of choice when it comes to schools. I believe they are subtle ways of keeping certain students out of colleges. It won't keep out all they would like to keep out, but it will keep enough out. College administrators will have a hard time saying they don't want Blacks in their schools, so they now have a way to weed out students with their test scores. Scoring low on a test does not prove that a child can't do the work in college. Think about it. If they can't do the work, then why are some college requirements lower than other colleges? Apparently they know the work can be done, but it's a way that predominate schools can keep the bar up high and integration low. It hasn't been proven or maybe the theory hasn't been visited, but I believe to my heart that it is a tool that many are using because they can get away with it. It has a name now, and that name is Test Scores.

Let's get this straight right quick… Before Blacks and Whites alike get upset at what I just said, I'll remind you of what I said earlier in the book. I'm not talking about everybody. I have a child who graduated from college, one almost finished and one going into college this fall. I also have many cousins who graduated high school and received scholarships and went on to graduate from college, so I don't make blanket statements that will say all people are any one way. Many had SAT scores that would get them into almost any college of choice. I mentioned the tests because many average students cannot score high enough on the test because of the questions they ask and how they are posed. Those test scores will determine the choices they have for colleges. The lower the score, the shorter their list will be – if they can even have a list. If a child has never been exposed to some of the events and subjects that are posed as questions on the test, the child has a slim chance of knowing the right answers. I was looking at example questions and I had to scratch my head on some of the questions myself. All I'm saying is that the playing field is uneven and they (those in charge) know it. I don't believe in giving passes because people are on another level by choice, and I don't believe in pulling the race cards, but I do believe in revealing the truth. I am not saying that all kids can't learn the same things, but I am saying that not all kids have been taught the same things or exposed to the same information.

Learning Differently

Let me tell you about my son. I believe his story would enlighten more than anything else, because it's not hearsay for me, but lived-out experiences. State mandated tests do not show what a child knows or doesn't know (all the time). My middle son had taken tests year after year in elementary school, and he always failed the tests. He made A's and B's during the school year, but he was not successful in the testing. Fast forwarding the story... I believe it was his third grade year when one of his teachers that I think of as his guardian angel on earth asked me if I would allow him to be tested. I didn't take offense to her asking. I was glad that someone would take the time and interest in finding out why his grades weren't matching his test results. I was desperate for answers. I noticed that we would spell small words around the house so that his baby sister couldn't figure out what we were saying, but he would turn the words around completely! I thought, "How did he get that word out of that word?" Then I'd think, "Oh wow! He spelled it backwards!" His teacher recognized him having some of the same traits that her older son had at my son's age, but she had missed out on having him tested in his younger days. She told me that her son ended up being tested in high school, after he had struggled through elementary, middle and the first year or so of high school. That's a long time! She told me that my frustrations and behavior were much like her son's, and come to find out her son was dyslexic. It took a long time for the district to administer the test, but I was persistent. I was about to have my son's pediatrician refer us to a professional, but finally the school came through. The time I had waited was worth it.

My son's test results revealed that he was severely dyslexic. Due to the testing, we learned that my son wasn't even close to being in special education, because there wasn't anything wrong with him other than he was dyslexic. The timing of his testing was unfortunate – since he had to take the spring mandated test the day before he was tested a final time. No, he didn't pass it because at the time no accommodations had been put in place. This time when he failed he knew why. It didn't make it easier that he would be going to summer school again to pass a stupid test, but at least he knew it wasn't about what he didn't know. It's very difficult to explain mandatory summer school to a child who was making good grades and being on the honor roll most six weeks.

The final results of the test allowed us to learn how to deal with my son. Persistence and being consistent about his education and being relentless regarding him becoming a statistic made all of the difference. I had seen kids placed in special education because no one knew what to do with them. That wasn't happening to my child on my watch. I researched what it meant to be dyslexic, and I found many brilliant actors and performers who soared with dyslexia. Cher, Tom Cruise, Les Brown, just to name a few. Even Albert Einstein was said to be dyslexic. I explained to my son what that meant, which included his limitations are the ones that he places on himself. It wasn't easy. I had spent his first few years of school crying right along with him because he couldn't understand his school work. While children his age were enjoying the fun part of projects and fun things, he was spending too much time working on the core subjects that he ran out of time for the subjects that he would have liked to enjoy. I felt so sorry for him, and as a parent it hurts!

Throughout the school years (after testing), I met with counselors, therapists and teachers in what they call 504 meetings. The meetings were about his progress and making sure everybody was still onboard and following the plans that were in place. Part of the planning was to make sure he was able to have extra time to finish his assignments, testing was split into two days instead of one, and he was encouraged to use a yellow overlay for his work or wear yellow lensed glasses. Another accommodation was for him to participate in small groups for reading. He didn't like the small grouping, but he knew it was necessary at the time. Those were small things that made a difference in his life. He wasn't dumb, he had a different way of processing things in his brain.

His last year of middle school the teachers and administrators became lazy. I'll refrain from saying that they stopped caring, so I'll say they backed off somewhat because my son was doing better and didn't want to be singled out by leaving the class going to another class for small groups which caused him to be behind on what they were doing in class while he was gone. His eighth grade year he had taken an extra math class that was supposed to be geared towards him passing his mandated test that year. He made the honor roll again, but lo and behold, I get a call from the school that was left on my answering machine that my son was set up for summer school which started the next day. Are you kidding me? This has got to be a bad joke or a nightmare! As hard as we both had worked, and he had worked in school to bring up all of his grades and excel I was supposed to tell him to get ready for summer school the next morning? I came unglued! His report cards were the best that I had ever seen him bring home. I was teaching kids about healthy self-esteems and self-worth, but I had no idea how I would handle keeping his esteem up at this time. I didn't know how to tell him that his best wasn't good enough, once again. I went to that school before the administrators left for the summer. Thank God I happened to have been at home that day to get the call before the school day was over. I went to the school and called an emergency meeting. I wanted to talk to any and everybody who was involved in my son's school year and advancing to the ninth grade. My husband and I met with all of the teachers and counselors, and the principal. After it was all said and done, my son was promoted to high school. We didn't go to the school to intimidate anyone. We went to support our son and make sure he was being treated fairly by the administration. Too many times if a parent isn't consistent with their communication and persistent with what they expect from a school, nothing happens. My husband suggested that maybe we should send our son to school on test days only since it didn't matter what kind of grades he was bringing home each six weeks on his report card. No one knew how to respond to him no matter how sarcastic it sounded, it made sense. Had we let that slide by and made him go to summer school once again and hope that he passes to go to high school after that, there's no telling what the outcome would have been. He probably would have been a statistic.

At the time the district didn't have anyone in place to work directly with dyslexic students. His modifications were supposed to be still documented for high school. At first I was told that he wouldn't be able to have accommodations in high school, but I asked if they expect him to grow out of dyslexia just because he was going to high school. Again, they looked like I had cussed them out.

I started wondering how many more children had gone through what my son had gone through. How many of them have been written off as bad actors because no one understood them? I ask those questions because my son's dyslexia was so severe that the testing counselor said that he could have easily been looked at as problematic with behavior issues. That was not the case at all. He was a great student, and a good kid who had problems. Recently, through studies and reading documentaries, I have learned that the prison system is filled with young men just like my son—ones with struggles that didn't have anyone to push them or look into their problems. They were not problem kids or dumb, they just needed someone to get to the root. The

Black race of young men and women are notorious for being called stupid or labeled as not wanting to learn or listen to anyone. Maybe they are struggling with something that they need to be medically and professionally diagnosed. Maybe they need someone who cares enough to say that, or parents that can and will take the time to identify issues at hand.

When I worked at a predominately White populated school, almost a third (guesstimating) of the children were on some kind of medication. If it wasn't Ritalin it was Thorazine or Prozac. I don't agree with those heavy medications, but it tells me they had been checked out and diagnosed by a professional.

No Pass No Play (House Bill 72)

Businessman Ross Perot was appointed by Governor Rick White (1984) to lead a study on education reform in Texas. No Pass No Play was created. When the Texas state law of No Pass No Play rule was put into place, I had a problem with it. Why? Sometimes it is the sport or the extracurricular activity that keeps kids interested in school. I'm sorry, but it's true. Like almost any law, bill or rule, you can find good in it or reasons for the rule, so I understand having guidelines in place, but I don't think enough of the right people are involved in the decision making and rule setting. The No Pass No Play caused many kids in my day and the days of my kids to be sidelined. Some of them have quit sports altogether – either for the difficulty of passing or losing the interest and have found something else to do with their time. Unfortunately their choices of how they spend their time isn't always in the best interest of the child or their parents. Sports and extracurricular activities have been said that they keep kids off the streets and out of trouble. I wonder if anyone thought about this when the rule was put into place. Maybe they did think about it and that's why it was done.

There is no inheritance in housekeeping!

My dad worked as a truck driver for more than four decades. In our hometown, he owned his own trucking business and had other drivers working for him as long as I can remember. In the seventies, I remember my dad would get paid every Friday, and he would give my mother a check to cash, and it would be sometimes $800-$1,000 for a week. That was in the seventies. My daddy would say, "Here honey. Cash the small one." I remember thinking to myself, "The small one? This is small?" Now that I am an adult, I am still saying, "That was small?" Some of you can't imagine making that amount of money in a week because of the opportunities that are afforded to some of us this day and time, but some people are probably thinking like I thought, *that's small?* I never knew anything other than my dad calling the shots and making his own schedule. I briefly remember him working at the wheat gin and the cotton gin, but those memories are somewhat vague. I know he taught history at school because he told me, and I have heard conversations between him and his older friends tell stories that line up with his confessions of teaching.

Daddy was reluctant to move to the city—especially at the age he moved. He was in his late forties, and when we get to a certain age, it's not as easy to get a job as it is when you are younger. Since I am older now than he was when he moved here, it's not easy to face that truth about being hard for people in their mid-forties to find employment. Daddy wasn't used to working for anyone – it had been a long time since he had had an employer. I grew up with my daddy owning businesses, traveling from town to town with bank accounts in several surrounding towns. We had anything we wanted, but then he moved to the city and everything changed. We had already moved to Fort Worth, Texas, prior to Dad's arrival, while he stayed behind to work. It was hard for him to give up the money he was making and the status he had in town, but he did to be with his family. He moved to the city and had to find a job. He found a trucking job again, and worked for some great people, but there was only one problem…they didn't pay my daddy fairly. My adult siblings and I didn't know that until he passed away or shortly before his passing. Daddy had been working for the company for the same amount of money for years. His pride wouldn't allow him to let anyone know. Daddy's pride wasn't an unhealthy one, so I would be better saying that being the man that he was wouldn't allow him to speak to us about it. He was an older man with a family and knew that he couldn't just go out and get another job at his age and lacked the skills that were relevant at the time. He didn't have computer skills or office skills because he had never done that kind of work. He was a man that paved a way as an entrepreneur when Black men weren't making those moves regularly around our area. Daddy didn't have the education that he needed to start over in the city, and the truth is, it probably wouldn't have mattered anyway since most of the good jobs were taken by ex-military men.

Daddy started working for a trucking company located right outside of the city, in a somewhat rural area. His supervisors were nice to him and treated him with respect, but they used him. Maybe that's not respect after all. They respected him as in knowing he was a good man – I should say. My daddy was making minimum wage for experience that had been more than thirty or more years. We found out he didn't even have a decent insurance policy with the company. The owners of the company took advantage of my father and doing so, it left my mother with nothing to fall back on after my dad's death other than social security. Daddy had other friends that he had assisted in gaining employment with the company, and they made far more than he did. I wondered how such nice people could do something so wrong to my father. They couldn't have thought anything was wrong with what they were doing, because they continued to do it for far too long. I try not to think about it because it angers me when I do. The question remains... How could the jobs that many of our fathers and grandfathers held pass anything down to their families? My mom was left with nothing after my daddy passed, and it was not because he didn't want to leave anything. It took all that he had to make ends meet when he was living. When it rained, he couldn't drive because he was hauling. Whenever it rained extensively, he would have to fill out paperwork at the unemployment office so that he could get paid for hours that were less than forty hours for the week. He did it anyway. He'd take those papers down the unemployment office to get them processed and wait for his small weekly check to come in until he could go back to work. Any money my dad would get he made sure to report it to the unemployment office, because that's who he was as a man.

I have had several conversations with friends of mine about retirement and inheritances. It is very interesting how different the conversations flow depending on who I talk to and most of the times the race of the individual plays a huge role.

One conversation I had with a very good friend of mine that I will never forget. We talked about the passing of his father. We shared how hard it was to lose a parent, and even harder to see our parents struggle not only with the loss, but the responsibility of paying bills. He started telling me that his father had left his mom 'fixed up.' I told him, that's great that he could say that, because I couldn't. I told him, "Housekeeping doesn't leave an inheritance." Although he knew I wasn't talking about housekeeping literally, but it was included in the professions that Blacks had that didn't allow an inheritance to be left to their children. They didn't even have insurance. Their children couldn't get braces on their teeth if needed, or have corrections done medically necessary. He wasn't the first person to make a statement as such, and there have been many other making claims to me like that. I am not upset at anyone for being able to do well towards their family. What is upsetting is the fact that not everyone had the same or similar opportunities. A simple opportunity would have been a game changer for more people than we could probably put a number to.

My husband's mother cleaned houses for many years. In fact, cleaning house is the only job that I have ever heard him talk about her having. What could she possibly leave to her children when she passed on? No one wants to lose their parents, but any good parent wants to leave money and security for their children. I know I do.

I have Black friends who have had military parents or fathers who happened to work on jobs that are popular around the area that had great benefits; therefore, I am not talking about all Black people leaving their families without anything, some have been able to utilize their 401k's and other means of saving. They are still way behind—about 400 years to be close.

The reason I am on this subject is that it is more likely to happen to my generation of fathers who didn't have an opportunity to work jobs that had benefits to leave behind. My friend's mom had money to do whatever she wanted to do whenever she wanted to do it. I'm not exaggerating here.

When I was ignorant (lacked knowledge) to what the truth was, I was upset to think that Black men would leave their wife and children without a 'cushion' when they were gone. It hurt me to know that many of them had nothing to leave. I apologize at the core of my heart for thinking so negatively for so long. I am forty-eight years old. Friends my age and older probably had parents that either had housekeeping jobs—especially if they were from the country. Sometime later factory jobs became available, but some of our parents were almost out of the working years. My dad hauled hay before he started his own business. He was an entrepreneur at heart, and was a very smart man. It was not his inability to learn to do something else, it was because he couldn't attain a job that would pay enough to put money back. He saved thousands upon thousands of dollars with his trucking business, but if you've ever had to dip into your savings to relocate and keep bills paid, you'd know that it doesn't take long to deplete your savings—especially when you're unable to put money back in. You see, when my daddy was growing up as a boy, he was working in fields while other kids his age were in school. When he was out of school, it wasn't easy for men of color to attend college—at least not for my dad.

As I grew older and had gotten to know my grandfather as an adult granddaughter instead of a little girl, I found out where my dad's entrepreneurial spirit came from; but I also found out why my dad didn't go to college. It was hard for him to get anything as a Black man, and his father had already moved on with another family (son). Several years after my dad's death we learned that my grandfather was thinking about my dad. He did do what was right and left wealth to my father. It is extremely unfortunate that my family and I are just now learning of the wealth and taking measures to seize what is rightfully my mother's and ours. That's another story for a different book that would be called, *Cheated*.

My dad wasn't the type of man who did not know how to save. He had created wealth before we moved, but money was depleted after several years of living in the city, working on a cheating job, and taking care of a family. Dad made sure that he paid their house off so that my mom could have a place to live. That, he did!

I'm going to be just like my dad and grandfather when I grow up!

In my profession, oftentimes men talk about a lineage of police officers that exist in their families. The dad, the grandfather and maybe great-grandfathers. I'm talking about some of the officers' descents dating back to the early 1900's. Many of them have their father's duty shoes or their badges that are all polished and on display for all to see. I'm sure it feels real good to feel that you're walking in your father's footsteps. They are able to see pictures of their fathers and grandfathers with prestigious positions. It would be easy to feel superior or privileged. Wouldn't you say? What am I going to have on display? My daddy's truck keys? You know what? I'm good with those truck keys because that's what he had that represented the living that he made for me. I want you to stop and think about what I am saying. I can't help but wonder what my father and grandfather would have been if they were not 'colored' growing up. They couldn't be police officers! They weren't hired as police officers! How can the ruled become rulers? Allowing a Black man back in the day to be a police officer would be like giving a lion the gun. For years Black men weren't even allowed to be in the military in the United States! If they won't let them fight, they sure weren't going to allow them to patrol the streets. They didn't see Black men or Black people as human beings. That angers the hell out of me. It really does.

Leaving an inheritance is our duty, so I'm not saying it's a bad thing because I think it's awesome. I think it's cool! I just wish that all of us could have had or have that privilege before now. It's still an uneven field, but at least we can stand at the fence and watch the game. The Black family has $5.04 to a White family's $100. The reason I am talking about it is so that we can stop and think of how something that simple can be so devastating to several generations' economy.

Think these got better? Well, let's see...

Let's talk about how Black people thought things were getting better, but systemic racism was still on the rise in a different form.

It's Hard to get over it, when you're Underneath It

One of the most frustrating things someone can say to me is, "move on." I don't care what the person is referring to, but if it's something that hurt or caused problems, it's not that easy to just get over. I am careful when I say things to someone regarding serious issues; so when someone says get over it when referring to slavery and racism, I don't have much respect for that statement.

Getting over something is so much easier when the hurt ceases. If someone steps on my toe in a pair of stilettos, it can stop hurting once they get off of my foot. If they continue to stand there or add someone else to stand with them, it would be hard to stop hurting. If the pain gets too intense, the foot would probably go numb. You see, I have had things done to me physically, emotionally and verbally. I can't even name all of the incidents that hurt me but I have been able to forgive and move on. Please don't expect a person to forget about something that continues to be done over and over. If a person cheats on someone and says they are sorry, but they can continue to do it over and over, they are not sorry. They are sorry that the other person knows, but not sorry enough to quit

It's easy to be righteous and forgiving when someone else is experiencing the turmoil. We can put on our Sunday best and say what God says to do when someone hurts us, and it's easy to say let bye-gone be bye-gone. Wounds heal quickly on others – so we think. Indirect pain doesn't send you to the emergency room or to the grave, but it can if not dealt with on an emotional level.

I have shared a lot of information in this book, and I have poured out my heart at times. I have said it before and this won't be the last time you will hear me say that I am a very private person. I don't give much insight into my life, but I have learned throughout this writing that it is healing to share.

While writing I learned of things in my own life that might have blocked my happiness and freedom from time to time. I heard sermons that made me take one more stroke on the computer to finish this work that I started. I've had times that I thought what I was saying was becoming irrelevant because I would see a change or two in the country, but then I would be reminded that things hadn't changed after all. There were times that I wanted to quit, and I would hear my pastor, Patrick E. Winfield or my bishop, T.D. Jakes said something that urged me to keep doing what I was called to do—which is tell my story. There were times that the news prompted me to pick up the laptop again; but my children that I looked at every day was what really reminded me that I couldn't quit. This project was started years ago—something like ten or eleven years by now, but it actually started long before then in my heart. I couldn't quit.

During the course of reading this book, many of you might have experienced feelings that you have never tapped into before, while some of you might be still trying to wrap your head around what you have taken in. If you don't get it right now, it's okay. Seeds that we plant oftentimes grow at different rates, so it's okay.

I have shared many truths that were hard for me to talk about at times, but they were harder for me to keep to myself. There are too many people that I feel personally responsible for knowing my truth, and my truth is the truth of millions of others in different places, walks of life and different ages. It is unfortunate that many people have probably already said, "Me too" while reading certain passages in this book. Some have said, "I thought it was just me." Others might have said, "I needed this." You might be one of the individuals who said, "Finally someone gets it." Whatever the case may be, I am sure that something resonated with you. The best thing about all of what I have shared is that we are victorious. I owe it to myself, my mother and my deceased father as well as those who feel they have no voice in this world. Most of all, I owe it to my heavenly Father, to use the gifts that he has given me. Far too many people have gone to their grave with pain and stories still inside. I will share my stories for them. I will share their stories for them. It might not be the exact story, but stories of their oppression will not go unnoticed. They will not be called stupid, dumb, lazy or unambitious. They were limited and I had to share that reality. When I was in New Orleans, Louisiana I wanted to go to the Plantation cemetery, just to hear the souls speak. I honestly felt that I would have been able to say, "I'll do it for you, but thank you."

We are so much stronger than we sometimes give ourselves credit for, and given credit. We carry a crucial responsibility to use that strength in a positive manner. Our growth and our kids and grandkids and the future generations' growth depends on what we do with what you have right now.

I am grateful to say that we have had many changes in the world thus far, but we have had numerous setbacks when it comes to open bigotry, hate and racism. Even integration is being challenged in some areas.

As I close this book, I am still being inundated with new stories that I can only 'shake my head to' and ask, "Really?" Government officials exposed for their racism and biases. Mass murders are taking place at synagogues, churches and mosques. Ignorance and hate is breeding across the county. Most recent, an engineering student was killed in Maryland in his apartment building who allegedly asked for a restraining order against the self-proclaimed White supremacist that murdered him.

While many Black lives have been taken by police, the family of a young woman from Australia will be paid $20 million dollars for her death by a police officer. I will leave it right there for now. Story after story, life after life taken. I can't possibly tell it all in one book. We have hundreds of years of stories told and untold.

It's not that we are just tired, we are down-right sick to our stomachs about things that are going on around the country and the world that flood our inboxes, our social media feeds, newspapers and the daily news reports. Some people say they don't watch the news anymore because it's all bad news and there's nothing good in the news. I agree that we get the reports of bad things, but I am glad that they are exposing what is going on, that we otherwise would never hear about. If it weren't for modern technology and cell phones that capture bad behavior as well as good behavior, we wouldn't see the murders of unarmed men sitting in their cars or running with their hands up while being gunned down. I wonder how many innocent people were killed and nothing was ever said or done before cell phones.

As far as this news being fake, the videos are there. We all know that videos can be edited and they oftentimes are for television, but it's hard to edit a Facebook live video while in progress. That is not fake, and too bad it can't be pulled off as fake news. It's not fake when we see a young man walking his sobbing little sister out of a Christian school after being expelled for having braids. That's not fake.

I believe in order to understand why issues are still talked about on a regular basis, we would have to allow ourselves to understand that unhealed wounds don't heal when the scab is pulled off each time before actually healing at the core. Seems that each time we hope things are getting better and we attempt to heal from the last incident something new arises.

Understand that we don't want explanations and excuses, we want the hate to cease. We do not live in a perfect world free of hate (thanks to sin – the fall of man), but we are tired of the choices that people make to be hateful towards Black people for no reason.

It's Very Personal

When I tell you I have been through hell as a Black woman, believe me! Let's see, I've been done like many others. I've been criticized, ostracized, fired, and denied...all blatantly because of the color of my skin – my race.

Early on while reading and writing my work, I would get upset and have moments of feeling embarrassed and angry at other times. The more I'd read and tweak, I felt myself accepting that it happened and feeling it's no big deal and I made it through. That's how we end up carrying buried down pain inside and it becomes who we are. We become numb to the treatment either to deal with it or to try to let it go.

I know some people are probably thinking I'm about to start talking about the poor, insignificant, 'woe is me' Black woman. I'm not, and I don't feel that we are insignificant at all. I wouldn't waste my energy or time writing anything that does not have a positive purpose. So, no worries. It's not that kind of book. I'm just telling you the truth of what I have seen, experienced and also have been told by trustworthy individuals who have experienced things as well.

Sharing is only the beginning of how we will break the myths and stereotypical thinking and judging of a group of women that is unknown to most. Bring it out! Highlight the issues! See our side! Hear how we feel and how we have felt! When you've been told all of your life who you are, who you are not, and who you can't be, then it becomes a journey to find the truth.

The cycle must be broken to heal the future generations. We have sat back and watched people mock and make fun of us for far too long. Some of us laughed right along with them.

A Change Is Going to Come

Not only was *A Change is Going to Come* change into a good song, but I stand on that hope. It might not come in our season, but it will come. Dr. Martin Luther King Jr. predicted that a change would come when we would see little Black girls and White girls and Black boys and White boys holding hands playing. Not only are they playing, but they are growing up and marrying one another.

I am not a racist person, and I won't lie and say that no one has a right or a reason to feel a certain kind of way about people that have caused them great pain and harm; but I know better. I know that anytime I justify any feelings of hate or deep rooted anger I am allowing my flesh to speak and win. I would just like to say this, if my parents, grandparents and ancestors who experienced murders and witnessed hangings of their loved ones for reasons as small as looking at a White woman can still love persons of other races...then by all means the ancestors of those who did it should be able to do the same.

With all of the wrong that is going on around the world, there is still a lot that is right. We've seen a Black president. We've seen Black people buy houses in areas that they are not wanted in and once could not even visit, but now they can call home. We've come a long way, but we have a long way to go.

God has kept us. He kept us in the days of slavery, and He is keeping us now. Our only hope is in Him and Him alone.

In the thoughts of Dr. Martin Luther King Jr., we shall overcome. We are already overcoming.

The End!